Beyond Suppression

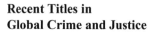

**Recent Titles in
Global Crime and Justice**

Outsmarting the Terrorists
Ronald V. Clarke and Graeme R. Newman

Human Trafficking, Human Misery: The Global Trade in Human Beings
Alexis A. Aronowitz

Police Use of Force: A Global Perspective
Joseph B. Kuhns and Johannes Knutsson

BEYOND SUPPRESSION

Global Perspectives on Youth Violence

JOAN SERRA HOFFMAN, LYNDEE KNOX, AND ROBERT COHEN, EDITORS

Global Crime and Justice

Graeme R. Newman, Series Editor

 PRAEGER

AN IMPRINT OF ABC-CLIO, LLC
Santa Barbara, California • Denver, Colorado • Oxford, England

Library of Congress Cataloging-in-Publication Data

Beyond suppression : global perspectives on youth violence / Joan Serra
Hoffman, Lyndee Knox, and Robert Cohen, editors.
    p. cm.—(Global crime and justice)
  Includes bibliographical references and index.
  ISBN 978-0-313-38345-8 (hbk. : alk. paper)—ISBN 978-0-313-
38346-5 (ebook) 1. Violence and youth. 2. Violence in adolescence.
I. Hoffman, Joan Serra, 1960- II. Knox, Lyndee M. III. Cohen,
Robert, 1941-
  HQ799.2.V56B49   2011
  303.60835—dc22

ISBN: 978-0-313-38345-8
EISBN: 978-0-313-38346-5

15 14 13 12 11   1 2 3 4 5

This book is also available on the World Wide Web as an eBook.
Visit www.abc-clio.com for details.

Praeger
An Imprint of ABC-CLIO, LLC

ABC-CLIO, LLC
130 Cremona Drive, P.O. Box 1911
Santa Barbara, California 93116-1911

This book is printed on acid-free paper ∞

Manufactured in the United States of America

Contents

Series Foreword

IN MY SERIES foreword to *Police Use of Force*, the title that precedes this book in the Global Crime and Justice Series, I noted that in some countries of the world it is difficult to distinguish between the police and the military. Some of the chapters in the present book show that, in communities torn by political strife, in which regular police are ineffective or not trusted, parallel policing organizations often emerge, using violence to see that "justice" is done. See, for example, the chapter on Northern Ireland (chapter 9). Or, perhaps more pervasive in the urban ghettoes of big cities in developing and developed countries alike, youth gangs use violence to maintain a semblance of "social control" in their communities, and to protect themselves from other gangs. The chapters on urban gangs in Los Angeles (chapter 11), Harlem, Iraq (chapter 6), and many Latin American (chapter 16 and chapter 18) countries, including Haiti, provide moving accounts of these violent, foreign worlds. This volume addresses the flip side of the force that underwrites regular police activity: the violence of youth that irresistibly entices police to respond in kind to suppress it. In fact, myriad ways to prevent youth violence are practiced in many different parts of the world, depending on how violence is perceived.

The authors of this book effectively demonstrate that youth violence occurs in many different forms. It is a problem of public health, criminal justice, culture, economics, religion, politics, and even the military. Violence is a male, youthful phenomenon found in every corner of the world. And it has always been so. Its reach is so vast that one is tempted to conclude that it is wired into the human condition. Why try to prevent violence if it is inevitable? This book is a testimony to the fact that enough community workers and social scientists in many parts of the world think it is worthwhile to mitigate or reduce the levels of youth violence, and many chapters show that reductions in youth violence can and have been achieved.

The skeptics charge: "Show us the evidence." This book does just that, at the same time calling for the adoption of evidence-based policy for reducing and preventing violence. This impressive volume has brought together from many parts of the world case studies, individual stories, descriptions of government and nongovernmental programs, and a number of scientific evaluations of violence prevention projects. All of these chapters provide the evidence needed to move forward, and many of these clear facts could be acted upon. For example, several chapters report that wherever weapons are easily available, violence will escalate. This is not rocket science. The obvious solution is to work toward making weapons less available. Unfortunately, the political will to do so is lacking. Clear evidence does not easily or automatically lead to policy.

No matter how strong and clear, however, evidence is not enough. These actions also require faith on the part of those who are prepared to devote their lives to implementing such programs—faith in their own efforts and in the support of the communities they are trying to repair. Another requirement is the political will on the part of governments to sustain these efforts in the face of inevitable criticism. Science is by definition skeptical and critical. We need science to evaluate "what works" in intervention programs, but even the best scientific study will not, of itself, be enough to generate the faith and will that the violence mitigation programs described in this volume demand if they are to have any chance of success. That is up to law enforcement agencies, policy makers, and the communities in which they serve. What is needed now is the political will, both internationally and nationally, to move forward with the violence reduction policies that are the product of this outstanding book.

Graeme R. Newman
University at Albany, United States

Preface

THE PROBLEM OF violence among youth has reached epidemic proportions. Globally, approximately 200,000 young people between the ages of 10 and 29 years die each year as a result of interpersonal violence. Although there is universal concern about the toll that violence is taking on our youth, the ways in which we understand this aggression and attempt to prevent and control violence vary considerably among cultures.

This book was written to raise awareness of the problems of youth violence throughout the world and to foster a greater understanding of what triggers violence and how communities can prevent violence while also responding constructively to victims as well as perpetrators. By providing a conceptual framework for understanding the various approaches to preventing violence, we hope to give the reader a sense of the complexity of the issues surrounding violence, and of the variations and differences that may be found in approaches used to combat this problem. We have selected examples of strategies used to address youth violence from many parts of the world. These case studies illustrate how communities and governments have translated these concepts into action and highlight how contextual influences, such as cultural, political, social, and economic factors, shape the responses of specific communities and countries.

Although we attempted to provide the reader with a comprehensive view of violence prevention, the 14 case examples we selected represent many areas of the world but not all. In addition, the material in this book addresses many aspects of interpersonal violence but does not provide a specific focus on some aspects of violent behavior, such as domestic violence or suicide, and largely focuses on violence prevention among adolescents and young adults.

Acknowledgments

IN PREPARING THIS book, we received valuable assistance from many individuals. In addition to the contributors of case examples that are listed in a later section, we are indebted to the following individuals. We are grateful to Graeme Newman, the series editor, for giving us the opportunity to write this book. We appreciate our editor, Michael Wilt, for his guidance throughout the project.

We thank Jorge Lamas for reviewing the book. We are grateful to Tara Emrani for her compassionate spirit and excellent assistance in pulling the book together and helping us identify authors for some of the case studies; Maryam Komaie for her ongoing assistance and support, and ability to remain unruffled even in the most stressful circumstances; and Madelene Harris for her timely help with literature reviews and editing. We appreciate all of the assistance and support provided by Nancy Guerra.

We thank Dana Schultz for providing excellent clerical support and Raquel Halfond who helped us identify relevant literature. We also are grateful for the wisdom and support provided by our colleagues who are engaged in the struggle to prevent youth violence. These include the people who work at the Virginia Commonwealth University (VCU) Clark-Hill Institute for Positive Youth Development, the National Coordinating Center on Youth Violence Prevention, The VCU Bridging the Gap Program, the Southern California Center of Academic Excellence on Youth Violence Prevention, the National Academic Centers of Excellence on Youth Violence, and the Division of Violence Prevention at the Centers for Disease Control and Prevention.

We also thank international colleagues and contributors who assisted us in the development of the book, and from whom we have much to learn. These include individuals at Brandeis University's Heller School, CeaseFire Chicago and Iraq, Education Development Center, the Institute for Public Research, Inter-American Development Bank, University of Ottawa, Viva Rio, the World Bank, and YouthBuild International.

PART I

Background

An Introduction to Youth Violence

IN THE 21ST century, 1.5 billion people are between the ages of 12 and 24 world-wide, 1.3 billion of them are in developing countries, the most ever in history. This number will continue to rise (World Bank 2007). Because of the achievements in health and social infrastructure development over the past decades, the world's youth are the healthiest and best educated in history. Together, their experience will determine the quality of the next generation of workers, parents, and leaders. Most policy makers know that young people will greatly influence the future of their nations. Taking full advantage of this "demographic boon" will require specific and careful attention to ensure the successful transition of these youths from childhood to adulthood. With the right policies in place, many believe this demographic phenomenon presents significant opportunities for national and global development.

Successfully surviving the scourges of childhood, young people are enter-ing an age laden with opportunities, not just for themselves but also for their families, communities, societies, and economies. These opportunities, however, are fraught with risks. Young people around the globe are confronting new health threats at a vulnerable time, as they enter the age of identity-seeking and risk-taking. Violence is among the principal threats. In all regions of the world, with the exception of Sub-Saharan Africa where HIV/AIDS is the leading cause of death among young people ages 15 to 29, noncommunicable diseases are now the leading cause of death for young women, and injuries caused by accidents and youth violence are the leading causes for young men (WHO 2002; World Bank 2007).

There are striking variations in the incidence across regions and continents, among countries, and within countries. Latin America has the highest murder rates in the world for people between the ages of 15 and 24. Figures from a 2002–2005 study of youth homicides in 83 countries estimate the murder rate for young people was 36.6 for every 100,000 people in Latin America, with the Caribbean ranking a close second at 31.6 per 100,000. The murder rate in Africa was 16.1, Asia 2.4, Oceania 1.6, and Europe 1.2. The corresponding figure for Canada was 2.5 (Waiselfisz 2008). Apart from the United States, where the

Defined as violence committed by or against individuals between the ages of 10 and 29, youth violence claims the lives of many young people around the globe. Violence is understood differently in different countries and among different cultures. Although there is no universally accepted definition of violence, this manual follows the definition of violence put forth in the *World Report on Violence and Health:* "intentional use of physical force or power, threatened or actual, against oneself, another person, or against a group or community that either results in or has a high likelihood of resulting in injury, death, psychological harm, maldevelopment or deprivation" (Krug et al. 2002). Youth violence covers a broad range of outcomes, going beyond physical acts, which can result in injury or death and imposes a substantial burden on individuals, families, communities, and countries worldwide. In 2000, an estimated 199,000 youth homicides were committed globally—that is, 9.2 deaths per 100,000 people. In other words, an average of 565 children, adolescents, and young adults between the ages of 10 and 29 years die each day as a result of interpersonal violence. Based on studies of nonfatal violence, it was further estimated that for every youth homicide there are 20 to 40 victims of nonfatal youth violence receiving hospital treatment (Krug et al. 2002). Between 1980 and 1994, the incidence of youth homicide among males increased steadily and among females increased slightly (WHO 2007). Additionally, the involvement of firearms in violence involving youths, over less lethal means, also increased steadily (WHO 2007). Furthermore, studies estimate that as many as 300,000 youths under the age of 18 are now or recently have been involved in armed conflict, and another 500,000 have been recruited into military or paramilitary forces (World Bank 2007).

rate stands at 12.9 per 100,000, most of the countries with youth homicide rates above 10 per 100,000 are either developing countries or those experiencing rapid social and economic changes. According to the World Health Organization, any country with a rate of more than 10 homicides per 100,000 is experiencing an epidemic of youth homicide (see table 1.1 and figure 1.1).

The countries with lowest rates of youth homicide tend to be in Western Europe—for example, France (0.7 per 100,000) and Germany (0.7 per 100,000)—or in Asia, such as Japan (0.3 per 100,000). Several countries (such as Singapore and Bermuda) have fewer than 20 youth homicides a year (Waiselfisz 2008). Almost everywhere, youth homicide rates are substantially lower among females than among males, suggesting that being a male is a strong demographic risk factor. A disproportionate number of deaths because of violence occur in low- and middle-income countries where many of the world's youth reside. An estimated 91 percent of the global burden of homicide is disproportionately shouldered by low- and middle-income countries, compared with 9 percent by developed countries (IOM 2008).

Table 1.1   Youth, Non-youth and Overall Homicide Rates by Region/Continent

Region/Continent	Youth	Non-youth	Total
Africa	16.1	8.5	10.1
North America	12.0	4.6	5.6
Latin America	36.6	16.1	19.9
Asia	2.4	2.1	2.1
Caribbean	31.6	13.2	16.3
Europe	1.2	1.3	1.2
Oceania	1.6	1.2	1.3

Figure 1.1   Homicide Rates for Youth and Non-youth (Children and Adults) by Regions

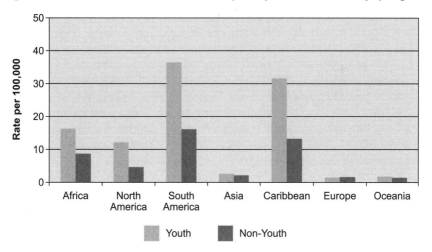

Source: Waiselfisz, 2008

Regardless of the scale of the problem across nations and regions, children and youth around the globe are suffering the effects of violence at the hands of their peers and adults. The 2006 "World Report on Violence against Children," carried out at the behest of the U.N. General Assembly by the secretary-general, found that in every region of the world, much violence against children remains legal, state-authorized, and socially approved (UN 2006). Many children are routinely exposed to physical, sexual, and psychological violence in their homes and schools, in care and justice systems, in places of work, and in their communities. This physical violence and psychological abuse have devastating consequences for the health and well-being of these young persons, both in the short and long term.

The effects of youth violence can be enormous. The most visible physical consequences of youth violence are death and injuries. But a variety of other, less obvious consequences can affect an individual throughout his or her life. The damaging effects of violence have been linked with varied harmful health and developmental outcomes. The full effect is often felt only in adulthood. There is an increasingly recognized and documented intersection of violence with other health conditions, such as links to long-term health conditions and disability, including chronic diseases such as cancer, ischemic heart disease, and chronic lung disease, in part the result of unhealthy behaviors like smoking, use of alcohol and drugs, and physical inactivity, as well as increased HIV/AIDS exposure and infection, especially for women. Child maltreatment has been shown to contribute to high-risk behaviors in adulthood, such as alcohol and substance use (Edwards et al. 2005; Felitti et al. 1998). For many young people, involvement in violence will lead to involvement in the criminal justice system.

Violence not only profoundly harms the youth who is involved, but also his or her family, the surrounding community, and the broader society. Youth violence has collateral effects on education and schooling, commerce and business, criminal justice and law enforcement, the environment, leadership and capacity for governance, and societal productivity and cohesion in general. Meeting the direct costs of health, criminal justice, and social welfare responses to violence diverts critical and sizeable resources from more constructive societal spending. It has direct costs (for example, health care, judicial costs) and indirect or non-monetary, intangible costs (for example, morbidity, mortality, stigma, reductions in social capital, pain). The much larger indirect costs of violence resulting from lost productivity and lost investment in education work together to slow economic development, increase socioeconomic inequality, and erode human and social capital. Direct and indirect costs of youth violence (for example, medical, lost productivity, quality of life) in the United States alone exceed $158 billion each year (Children's Safety Network Economics & Data Analysis Resource Center 2000). Cascading social and economic consequences of violence can include reductions in social capital and heightened fears of violence, preventing people from participating fully in society, inhibiting movement in some parts of a city, keeping youth and children from parks or from using public transportation. Similarly, youth's labor assets are severely affected when violence limits their access to jobs because of the risk of violence in the street, or because a community lacks jobs due to its bad reputation. Fear can result in changes to the physical environment; the fear of violence may result in wealthier communities erecting physical barriers to separate them from poorer communities, which in turn can exacerbate social distance and exclusion. Lastly, heightened fear of violence and real and perceived lack of security can result in political responses emphasizing "law and order" measures that may not be based on evidence-based approaches, often targeted at youth.

Ensuring a healthy and productive transition to adulthood for many of the world's youth hinges on the development of sound youth violence prevention and reduction policies. In turn, heightened interest and investment in youth violence prevention policies can confer beneficial returns not only to the places and young people most affected by violence, but also to local economies and development—by saving lives, improving health outcomes, and facilitating economic growth and social development (Butchart, 2008). Investing in evidence-based early prevention interventions that work with at-risk youth and recidivism reduction for young offenders yields big dividends, freeing up funds from state and local budgets that can be used for other development purposes (Drake, Aos, and Miller 2009). In the United States, a Nurse Family Partnership program that provides maternal and early childhood health programs for families most in need returns $5 in net benefits associated with crime reduction and child abuse and neglect prevention and increased education test scores for each dollar spent. Functional Family Therapy (FFT) yields a high net benefit of $31,821, at a program cost of $2,325 per juvenile participant. The 15.9 percent reduction in the recidivism rate achieved by this program generates $34,146 in benefits to taxpayers and crime victims per youth served (Aos 2009).

A few efforts have been made to estimate the potential benefits of violence prevention to national economies. According to a study by the United Nations Office on Drugs and Crime and the World Bank (2007), a comparison of data from Costa Rica (homicide rate 8.1 per 100,000) with four nearby countries (Haiti with 33.9; Jamaica 33.8; Dominican Republic 16.5; Guyana 16.1) suggests significant gains by the latter could be made if violence could be reduced to Costa Rican levels. Haiti and Jamaica both could increase annual economic growth per capita by an estimated 5.4 percent, while the Dominican Republic and Guyana also would benefit from growth rate increases of 1.8 and 1.7 percent, respectively. Increased growth and development, in turn, may contribute to political, civil, and economic stability in many low- and middle-income countries, promoting greater social and economic inclusion.

Where many once thought that violence was an unavoidable element of life, and even a "rite of passage" for youth, years of development and prevention science indicate the opposite. Experience and variation on youth violence rates across countries suggests that youth violence is not only predictable but also preventable. The science base for developing effective violence prevention strategies and therapeutic interventions is expanding. The capacity to learn is much greater for the young than for older people, so opportunities to acquire skills, good health habits, and the desire to engage in the community and society can yield tremendous dividends. Indeed, solutions to this problem are being crafted around the globe and are showing great promise for preventing the conditions that lead to youth violence and occurrences of this violence, for mitigating damage in youths who already have been exposed, and for promoting rehabilitation and healing. Informed violence prevention policies can do much to help young people manage these risks and to help youth attain a safe and healthy transition to adulthood.

Youth violence prevention efforts take many forms and reflect the histories and the varying socioeconomic and cultural contexts of the communities and countries in which they are developed and implemented. Multiple factors can account for violence in a single place and context, and a range of approaches or combinations of strategies to reduce this violence are being employed in different countries and contexts. This book showcases efforts around the globe that are attempting to address the problem of youth violence. High rates of offending and victimization nevertheless often extend to the 30- to 35-year-old age-group, and this group of older, young adults is also taken into account, because they also are included in some of the efforts to understand and prevent youth violence presented. The book lays out a typology or framework for youth violence prevention in the international community and provides case examples of each. It discusses cultural and societal contexts that give rise to the various approaches, the goodness of fit of the approaches with their particular host communities, and their potential relevance to the international community. Case studies have been selected that have shown evidence of or promise for reducing youth violence and its consequences. These range from small-scale individual, sectoral, and community efforts to municipal, country-level, and multinational efforts throughout different regions of the world that are working toward the reduction of youth violence. Although the majority of such interventions that have been documented and formally evaluated are to be found in wealthier parts of the world, many innovative interventions exist in developing countries, and this book presents some of this work as well. The concluding chapter includes a discussion of next steps in youth violence prevention globally and a call to action for lay readers as well as policy makers.

The goal of the book is to inform the lay public as well as practitioners and policy makers, highlighting promising approaches and evidence-based approaches that engaged readers will find interesting and compelling, and perhaps stimulate not only reflection but also thoughtful action as participants in civic processes. The case studies in this book focus on efforts to reduce or prevent youth interpersonal violence, violence related to criminal activities, gang violence, and politically motivated violence, and also include examples of youth violence prevention and reduction efforts in conflict and armed violence contexts around the world. For example, experience in Northern Ireland and Colombia with disarmament, demobilization, and rehabilitation programs shows that it is possible for young combatants to reconstruct their lives in peacetime. Efforts to intervene with gang members in Los Angeles, in the United States, suggest that it is never too late to reorient youth who have joined violent street groups. A public health approach to violence reduction has led to significant decreases in homicides in Iraq, the deadliest armed conflict globally between 2004 and 2007. In Israel, a national data collection system assists schools in developing support and intervention services tailored to the specific needs of their students. In Japan, as rates of youth violence climb in response to social and economic forces, efforts are under way to enhance child welfare and mental health services to address the increasing needs in this area. In Medellin, Colombia, multileveled municipal, state, and national violence prevention and reduction efforts starting in the mid-1990s contributed to a dramatic reduction in the level of youth and urban criminality (from 381 per 100,000 inhabitants in 1991 to 32 per 100,000 in 2008).

There is much that we can learn from each other in our efforts to build better futures for our youth and communities and much we can learn from the work going on not only in our own communities and countries, but also abroad. With the increasing globalization of the world economy as well as social systems, the effects of social issues such as youth violence—and their potential solutions—no longer are isolated to their particular region. These social issues affect the well-being of all nations through their impact on human capital both current and future.

We are well poised to make a greater global commitment to youth violence prevention and reduction. The case studies in this book can strengthen the case for greater international investment in youth violence prevention, illustrating how schools, communities, countries, and regions are working to promote the peaceful, healthy development of youth. Despite the enormous diversity that exists across the world in culture, wealth, and perspective, global citizens are connected through a common interest in youth, peace, and development. It is because of this common interest that we are compelled to work across borders with greater purpose and commitment to prevent violence.

REFERENCES

Aos, S. 2009. "Return on (Taxpayer) Investment: Evidence-Based Prevention and Intervention—Initial Report to the Legislature on Study Design." Public Policy Approaches to Youth Violence Prevention. Olympia, WA: Washington State Institute for Public Policy.

Butchart, A. 2008. *Preventing Violence and Reducing Its Impact: How Development Agencies Can Help.* Geneva. Switzerland: World Health Organization.

Children's Safety Network Economics & Data Analysis Resource Center. 2000. "State Costs of Violence Perpetrated by Youth." www.edarc.org/pubs/tables/youth-viol .htm (accessed July 31, 2006).

Drake, E., S. Aos, and M. Miller. 2009. *Evidence-Based Public Policy Options to Reduce Crime and Criminal Justice Costs: Implications in Washington State.* Olympia: Washington State Institute for Public Policy.

Edwards, V. J., R. F. Anda, S. R. Dube, M. Dong, D. F. Chapman, and V. J. Felitti. 2005. "The Wide-Ranging Health Consequences of Adverse Childhood Experiences." In *Victimization of Children and Youth: Patterns of Abuse, Response Strategies*, ed. Kathleen Kendall-Tackett and Sarah Giacomoni. Kingston, NJ: Civic Research Institute.

Felitti, V. J., R. F. Anda, D. Nordenberg, D. F. Williamson, A. M. Spitz, V. Edwards, M. P. Koss, and J. S. Marks. 1998. "Relationship of Childhood Abuse and Household Dysfunction to Many of the Leading Causes of Death in Adults: The Adverse Childhood Experiences (ACE) Study." *American Journal of Preventive Medicine* 14: 245–258.

OM (Institute of Medicine). 2008. *Violence Prevention in Low- and Middle-Income Countries: Finding a Place on the Global Agenda*. Board on Global Health. Institute of Medicine of the National Academies. Washington, DC: IOM.

Krug, E. G., L. L. Dahlberg, J. A. Mercy, A. B. Zwi, and R. Lozano. 2002. *World Report on Violence and Health*. Geneva, Switzerland: World Health Organization.

United Nations Office on Drugs and Crime and the World Bank. 2007. *Crime, Violence, and Development: Trends, Costs, and Policy Options in the Caribbean*. Washington, D.C., and Vienna, Austria: United Nations Office on Drugs and Crime and the Latin America and the Caribbean Region of the World Bank.

United Nations Secretary-General. 2006. *Study on Violence against Children*. New York: United Nations.

Waiselfisz, J. J. 2008. *Mapa de la violencia: los jóvenes de América Latina 2008*. Brasília DF, Brazil: RILTLA.

WHO (World Health Organization). 2007. *Third Milestones of a Global Campaign for Violence Prevention Report 2007: Scaling-up*. Geneva, Switzerland: WHO.

World Bank. 2007. *World Development Report 2007: Development and the Next Generation*. Washington, DC: World Bank.

2

What We Know about the Nature and Causes of Youth Violence

YOUTH VIOLENCE AND crime has been a subject of serious study for more six decades, and a large body of literature covers factors and processes that decrease the likelihood that young people exposed to risk factors for violence will engage in violence and that help young persons who already are involved in violent activities to recover. Over the past 20 years, research using longitudinal data has exploded. Longitudinal data are collected on the same group of individuals over long periods of time, sometimes a decade or more, and allow researchers to the look at the interaction of risk and protective factors over time, as well as the developmental course of violence. The majority of this research has been carried out in high-income countries like the United States, Canada, and Western Europe and thus is most relevant to young people from these countries. It has yielded important insights into the development of violent offending in individuals over the life course (Farrington 2002; Office of the Surgeon General 2001).

Two prominent developmental trajectories for the emergence of youth violence have been identified, one characterized by an early onset of violence and one by a late onset, with strikingly different implications for prevention. Children who commit their first serious violent act before puberty are in the early onset group, whereas youths who do not become violent until adolescence are in the late-onset group. Some children exhibit problem behavior in early childhood that gradually escalates to more severe forms of aggression before and during adolescence and then dissipates during the early adulthood years. A few of these young people will continue their violent behavior into adulthood and are responsible for committing the most serious acts of violence. These lifetime offenders, however, represent only a small proportion of those committing violence. The vast majority of aggressive children and children with behavioral disorders do not become serious violent offenders.

The most common pathway for violent behavior, however, is the second, or late-onset group. Most youth violence begins in adolescence and ends with the transition into adulthood, with these young people engaging in violent behavior over a short period of time. Termed "adolescence-limited offenders," these youth show little or no evidence of high levels of aggression or other problem behaviors during their childhood. About 30 to 40 percent of male youths and 15 to 30 percent of female youths report having committed a serious violent offense by age 17. Young people involved in serious violence often commit many other types of crimes and exhibit other problem behaviors; violence is part of a lifestyle that includes drugs, guns, drinking, truancy, precocious sex, and other risky behaviors presenting a serious challenge to intervention efforts. Successful interventions must confront not only the violent behavior of these young people, but also their lifestyles (Office of the Surgeon General 2001).

Another characteristic of youth violence that varies according to the age of the participant includes motive. Reasons given for violent offending up to late teenage years include utilitarian, excitement, and anger, but for youths age 20 and upwards, rational or utilitarian motives are the dominant motive for all crimes involving prior planning, psychological intimidation, and the use of weapons. Most offenses up to late teenage years are committed with others, whereas most offenses from age 20 onward are committed alone. Generally, young violent offenders are versatile rather than specialized in the types of crimes they commit; and they typically commit more nonviolent offences than violent offences over-all. Furthermore, the onset of different types of "offending" tends to occur at distinctly different ages, moving from shoplifting to burglary to robbery, with the addition of new types of offending until age 20. After this, youths may specialize in a particular type of violence or criminal activity (Farrington 2002).

The need for specialized prevention programs to address both early and late-onset violence and criminal behavior often is not recognized. In particular, few programs target late-onset violence, and the types of interventions that are most effective in preventing it still are not well understood. Indeed, while early prevention with younger children is vitally important, targeting preven-tion programs solely to younger children with problem behaviors misses more than half of the children who eventually will become serious violent offenders. Some evidence indicates that universal prevention programs in childhood may be effective in preventing late-onset violence (Office of the Surgeon General 2001). Both types of violence also have unique characteristics that require specially targeted interventions. A comprehensive community prevention strategy should address both early and late-onset patterns and ferret out the underlying causes and risk factors. Risk factors associated with both early and late-onset violence include aggression, attitudes supportive of violence, antisocial parents, low socio-economic status, harsh, lax, or inconsistent discipline, family conflict, abusive parents, poor relationship with parents, poor attitude and performance in school, and weak social ties and antisocial peers, and for late-onset violence, neighbor-hood crime and disorganization. But some studies show that some youths with late-onset violence did not experience the childhood risk factors responsible for early onset violence. For these youths, risk factors for violence emerged only in adolescence (Office of the Surgeon General 2001).

Understanding how patterns of serious violence develop over time and change as a young person transitions to adulthood, is essential to designing effective policies and programs for violence prevention across a young person's life span. Grasping when and under what circumstances violent behavior typically occurs, and what risk factors predict violence among youths, helps those developing responses to violence target these critical periods in a young person's development. Because much of the research literature is based on data from developed countries, and largely from the United States, these findings do not necessarily translate to other countries and especially to developing countries. It is critical to understand how youth violence varies based on the complex interaction of individual, relationship, community, and societal factors—from birth through adolescence—and how these vary by country, particularly developing nations, and in countries with markedly different cultures—to develop effective interventions in each. Culture and nation-specific research is under way and studies of youth violence in Latin America and the Caribbean region is beginning to yield valuable information on the nature and developmental course of violence in these countries (Gallardo and Gomez 2008).

WHAT CAUSES YOUTH VIOLENCE?

Extensive research in recent decades has sought to identify personal characteristics and environmental conditions that place either children or adolescents at risk of violent behavior or that seem to protect them from the effects of risk. Risk and protective factors can be found in every area of life. Exerting different effects at different stages of development, they tend to appear in clusters, and they appear to gain strength in numbers. One study, for example, has found that a 10-year-old exposed to six or more risk factors is 10 times more likely to be violent by age 18 than a 10-year-old exposed to only one factor (Herrenkohl et al. 2000). These risk probabilities apply to groups, not to individuals. Although risk factors are not necessarily causes of violence in and of themselves, identifying these predictors and determining when in the life course they typically come into play can help the design of well-timed, effective preventive programs. Similarly, protective factors or assets have been identified that can decrease the likelihood of a young person engaging in violence. Protective factors are scientifically established as decreasing the likelihood of violence, thus "protecting" children and youth from risk or adversity. In settings or situations in which violence is more likely, youth who manage to do well in spite of exposure to risk factors have been labeled resilient. Resiliency emphasizes the ability to overcome obstacles, bounce back from frustration, and become a healthy and productive individual in the context of considerable risk. Drawing on this approach, interventions can be designed to decrease risk factors, enhance protective factors, and create conditions necessary to support development of resilience.

The traditional approach to studying risk factors for violence emphasizes identifying what is "wrong" with children, families, or communities. More recently, identifying and focusing on assets in children, youth and families has been embraced as an alternate paradigm, and one that builds on what is "right" or what should be made right in schools and communities. "Protective factors are those factors that mediate or moderate the effect of exposures to risk factors, resulting in reduced incidence of problem behavior" (Pollard, Hawkins, and Arthur 1999, 146). Other theorists suggest that protective factors have their effect by reducing risk, reducing negative chain reactions, establishing self-esteem and self-efficacy, and opening up opportunities (Rutter 1999). Protective factors have been viewed as both the absence of risk and as something entirely different from it (Office of the Surgeon General 2001). In truth, many protective factors reflect the opposite end of the risk spectrum. For instance, just as child abuse or neglect is a risk factor, parental warmth and caring is a protective factor or asset. In fact, just like risk factors, protective factors (or assets) exist within the individual, family, peer group, school, and community. Thus, risk factors often can be recast as protective factors or assets to guide interventions by encouraging positive development.

A shifting focus to assets and protection over risk has led to a new paradigm of positive youth development and positive psychology that emphasizes building personal assets, providing opportunities for young people to participate in challenging and engaging activities that build their skills and competencies. Within a positive youth development framework, adolescents are viewed as able to contribute to their school and community, empowered to participate in decision making and encouraged to assume meaningful roles in their community and in society (National Research Council and Institute of Medicine 2002). One of the challenges to understanding youth violence is the complex, multilayered nature of the phenomenon. Ecological models that attempt to outline the environmental context of development such as those first used by Bronfenbrenner (1979) and Garbarino (1985) are useful in this regard. Such models can help us to understand the multifaceted nature of violence and the holistic processes that shape youth development, assisting in the examination of factors that influence behavior—or which increase or diminish the risk of committing or being a victim of violence—and how they interact with and reinforce one another. The ecological model of human development outlined by Bronfenbrenner was first used as a tool for understanding factors leading to child abuse and subsequently was adopted for use in other fields of violence research (WHO 2002). The original ecological model proposed by Bronfenbrenner is complex, examining relationships within and among different levels of the ecology. A greatly simplified version of this framework has been popularized that identifies four levels of the human ecology. The first level consists of the individual and his or her unique biological, cognitive, and behavioral history and how these factors may or may not constitute risk factors for early or late-onset violence. The second level contains relationships with family, friends, intimate partners, and close peers, and explores how these relationships increase the risk of being a victim. The third level contains the community contexts in which social relationships occur, such as schools, workplaces, and neighborhoods, and relationships between the young person and these settings, and among these settings and how each contribute to or mitigate

Figure 2.1

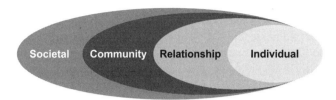

the risk for violence. The fourth level looks at the broad societal factors that create a climate in which violence is encouraged. Figure 2.1 displays the simplified ecological model. Potential risk and protective factors for youth violence (both perpetration and victimization) can be found at all levels, so that if we are to effectively end violence, we must address the factors at each level that can or do contribute to the perpetuation of violence in our society: individual, relationship, community, and societal. Lastly, although not included in the model, the concept of the *chronosystem* has been portrayed as a further level that includes the passage of *time* from both individual and historical perspectives.

An important contribution since the 1990s has been the development of integrative theories and related studies that emphasize multiple influences on development, mechanisms that explain the risk-behavior relation and highlight the mechanisms or process by which aggression develops, and how risk is linked across multiple contexts. A further advance has been an increased understanding of the adaptive functions of aggression and violence in some settings and under some conditions.

INDIVIDUAL RISK FACTORS ASSOCIATED WITH VIOLENCE

Many aspects of an individual's attitudes and behaviors, as well as experiences can influence the risk of using violence. These include gender, age, biological, and physiological characteristics, and the family environment. These can increase an individual's predisposition to violence. Brain abnormalities, neurological dysfunctions, learning disabilities, early exposures to neurotoxicants (such as lead exposure), prenatal and perinatal complications, and head injuries can affect a young person's ability to regulate mood and impulses and contribute to violence. Factors such as alcohol and drug use by an individual are identified as inciters or "facilitators" to violence (Jewkes 2002; Parker and Auerhahn 1998).

RELATIONSHIP RISK FACTORS ASSOCIATED WITH VIOLENCE

People in an individual's closest social circle—peers, partners, and family members—all have the potential to shape that person's behavior and experience.

The influence of families usually is the greatest in this respect during childhood, while during adolescence, friends and peers have an increasingly important effect. Poor monitoring and supervision of children by parents, poor attachment between parents and children and the use of harsh, physical punishment to discipline children are strong predictors of violence during adolescence and adulthood. Other factors include household size and density, a large number of children in the family, a mother who had her first child at an early age, possibly as a teenager, history of family violence, beliefs supporting the use of violence in relationships, low levels of family cohesion, unemployment, and poor socio-economic background. Following global trends, survey data from Mexico City indicate that child victims of domestic abuse have a greater disposition for acting violent in their adult lives, suggesting an intergenerational transfer of violence (Knaul and Ramírez 2002). Although many individuals who become abusers were victims of abuse and violence as children, the vast majority of the individuals who are abused as children do not go on to be violent or abusive (Office of the Surgeon General 2001). In fact, much of the research in this area suggests a "cycle" of violence in which the young people who perpetrate violence, for example, as a member of a gang, are also victims of violence, having witnessed it in their communities or experienced it in their homes. Given these factors, youth violence would be expected to increase in family structures that have disintegrated because of wars, epidemics, migration, or rapid social change. For older children and youth, family factors lose predictive value relative to peer-oriented risk factors, such as weak social ties to conventional peers, antisocial or delinquent friends, and membership in a gang.

COMMUNITY RISK FACTORS FOR VIOLENCE

Community environments such as schools, workplaces, and neighborhoods shape an individual's behavior and beliefs. Generally speaking, boys and young men living in urban areas are more likely to be involved in violent behavior than those living in rural areas, as are those young people living in neighborhoods with higher levels of violence and crime. Factors that increase risk in these areas include gangs, the presence of guns, illicit markets, and low levels of community integration. The presence of gangs, guns, and drugs in a locality is a volatile mixture, increasing the likelihood of violence.

The issue of firearm access and youth violence is important. The fact is that the vast majority of youth homicides are gun related (Fingerhut and Christoffel 2002). Countries with strict gun control laws often have the lowest levels of youth homicide (Fingerhut and Christoffel 2002; Hepburn and Hemenway 2004). A study of children in organized armed violence in Brazil, Colombia, the Philippines, and Northern Ireland found in all cases young males between the ages of 15 and 24 years are more affected by firearms mortality than any other age-group (Dowdney 2005). Furthermore, women of all age-groups are considerably less affected by gun deaths in comparison with males in all age-groups. The availability of firearms means that juvenile feuds quickly become lethal. Although not at war, currently more people (and specifically youth and children) are dying from small arms fire in Rio de Janeiro than in many low-level armed conflicts in other cities around the world (ISER and Viva Rio 2002). Across the Americas, the communities from which at-risk persons originate and in which the acts of gun-related criminality tend to be concentrated bear many similarities. Called "ghettos" in North America, *barrios marginales*, *villas miseria*, *barrios callampa*, *pueblos jovenes*, or *favelas* in Latin America (depending on the country) and "garrison communities" in the Caribbean, they tend to be urban, densely populated, and underserved, with lower-than-national levels of most social indicators and standards of living, and increasing levels of gun density. Across the region, certain characteristics are common to both perpetrators and victims in gun violence. Research conducted in Latin America and the Caribbean shows that the majority of victims and perpetrators of violence are young men of low socioeconomic status, with a low level of education and poor prospects for income generation, who have witnessed violence at close range (World Bank 2007).

The *2006 Small Arms Survey* of the Graduate Institute of International Studies in Geneva, Switzerland, has analyzed the devastating impact that the traffic in small arms has had in terms of increasing the level of lethal violence among young men in countries in various regions, from Sub-Saharan Africa to Latin America, from the Caribbean to Polynesia (Bevan and Florquin 2006).

> We were 14 years old then. That was the time when we threw stones. I saw that wasn't going to work, because we threw stones at them and they shot at us. So I decided to get a gun too and shoot back as well. You shoot at me and therefore I will shoot back at you.
>
> —Junior HL gang member, South Africa

A study of crime and violence in the Caribbean found the strongest explanation for the relatively high rates of crime and violence rates in the region—and their apparent rise in recent years—is narcotics trafficking. The drug trade drives crime in a number of ways: through violence tied to trafficking, by normalizing illegal behavior, by diverting criminal justice resources from other activities, by provoking property crime related to addiction, by contributing to the widespread availability of firearms, and by undermining and corrupting societal institutions (World Bank 2007).

The degree of social integration within a community also affects rates of youth violence. Social capital is a concept that attempts to measure such community integration, and encompasses the rules, norms, obligations, reciprocity, and trust that exist in social relations and institutions, and a study on the relation between social capital and crime rates in a wide range of countries during the period 1980– 1994, found that the level of trust among community members had a strong effect on the incidence of violent crimes (Lederman, Loayza, and Menendez 1999).

Young people living in places that lack social capital tend to perform poorly in school and have a greater probability of dropping out altogether. Moser and Holland (1997) studied five poor urban communities in Jamaica. They found a cyclical relationship between violence and the destruction of social capital. When community violence occurred, physical mobility in the particular locality was restricted, employment and education opportunities were reduced, businesses were reluctant to invest in the area, and local people were less likely to build new houses or repair or improve existing property. This reduction in social capital—the increased mistrust resulting from the destruction of infrastructure, amenities and opportunities—increased the likelihood of violent behavior, especially among young people.

SOCIETAL RISK FACTORS FOR VIOLENCE

Personal relationships and community interactions are influenced heavily by broader societal forces, such as economic interests, social norms, cultural beliefs, laws and policies, institutional practices, and political ideologies. Weak police and legal systems and widespread impunity affect levels of crime and violence. Media violence often is cited as an important influence on violent behavior not only among children (youth violence, gangs) but also among adults (domestic violence, rape) (WHO 2002). Economic and social policies that create or sustain gaps and tensions between and among groups of people, weak laws and policies related to violence, war and militarism, and all forms of exploitation are established risk factors. Although poverty alone does not appear to be consistently associated with violence, the juxtaposition of extreme poverty with extreme wealth appears to be associated with interpersonal and collective violence. The inverse relationship between family income and juvenile crime is well documented globally (World Bank 2006). During the deep economic and financial crisis of 2003–2004, extreme poverty doubled from 7 percent to 14 percent (World Bank and IDB 2006). Violent crimes also rose dramatically; from 2002 to 2005, the rate of violent death nearly doubled from 14.5 to 26.4 per 100,000 residents (Aleph 2006). In addition to poverty, the income inequality demonstrated by drug dons, foreign tourists, and the media in the Caribbean encourages engagement in easy money activities, including drugs and prostitution (Cunningham and Correia 2003).

In their study of Jamaica, Moser and Rodgers (2005) argue that a link exits between violence and unequal access to employment, education, health, and basic physical infrastructure, and that situations of widespread, severe inequality heighten the potential for alienated, frustrated, and excluded populations (particularly younger men) to engage in different forms of violence, including economic-related gang violence, politically motivated identity conflict, and domestic violence. Equally, the work of Richards (1996) on Sierra Leone suggests that youth exclusion in a context of state decay and in which patrons use state resources to secure the loyalty of clients in the general population, contributed to youth involvement in violence. The study also suggests, however, that while social exclusion and horizontal inequalities provide fertile ground for grievances to grow, they alone are not enough to cause conflict and other proximate or trigger factors also are required. Programs or policies that reduce or minimize the impact of income inequality therefore may be highly relevant to violence prevention, although the evidence base for such interventions has not yet been established.

Governance can have an impact on violence, particularly as it affects young people. Noronha et al. (1999) in their study on violence affecting various ethnic groups in Salvador, Bahia, Brazil, concluded that dissatisfaction with the police, the justice system, and prisons increased the use of unofficial modes of justice. In Rio de Janeiro, Brazil, Minayo and Souza (1999) found that the police were among the principal perpetrators of violence against young people. Police actions—particularly against young men from lower socioeconomic classes—involved physical violence, sexual abuse, rape, and bribery. The majority of respondents in youth focus groups in the Dominican Republic noted that even if they were caught committing a crime, the possibility of buying one's way out through bribes to police was always a feasible option, as well as that of using *padrinos* (godfathers) who could intervene on their behalf and have court decisions suspended, or even have prison inmates freed (Aleph 2006). The national police report an average of 36 shooting deaths per month by the members of its force (Aleph 2006). In 2005, 18 percent of all violent deaths and homicides were a result of police shootings. Although the ages of the victims are not known, anecdotal evidence suggests that a large number of these deaths are youth: one study cited 23 unprovoked killings of street children by *los cirujanos* ("the surgeons," a police unit that conducts night sweeps) in three neighborhoods of Santo Domingo over an eight-month period (World Bank 2007).

Cultural norms and gender socialization are critical risk factors. As Barker and Ricardo's (2005) work in Africa and the Caribbean shows, the nature of gender socialization is critical. Based on an extensive literature review and interviews with young men and those working with young men in Uganda, South Africa, Botswana, and Nigeria, Barker and Ricardo found that male socialization and constructions of manhood and masculinity in Africa often are key factors in violence and conflict. Young men's participation in conflict and the use of violence become ways to obtain empowerment and status, particularly among those who do not achieve a sense of socially respected manhood. These young men may be more likely to engage in violence. Young men also may find camaraderie with male peers in some armed groups and, in some cases, male role models, surrogate fathers, or substitute families. Furthermore, in some contexts, notions of manhood and masculinity may be implicitly tied to showing aggression, including against women. Using violence to resolve conflicts often is valued and glorified, with more conciliatory attitudes being seen as weak and warranting the accusation of not being a "real man" (UNDP 2007). Similarly, salient notions of manhood sometimes are linked to the possession of small arms, and guns may symbolize empowerment, status, and recognition (Dowdney 2005).

A brief case study on youth violence in a context of political transition in South Africa illustrates this model (Higson-Smith 2006):

> A young man who has become involved in a civil conflict as a member of a paramilitary group becomes involved in local peace initiatives. When things do not work out as he intended, he is accused of "selling-out" to the enemy. Since other youths have been murdered for this "crime" in his community, such accusations are extremely frightening and traumatic (individual effects). However, such victimization is seldom restricted to the individual and very often family and friends are similarly threatened. In some cases families are forced to protect themselves by turning against the individual or fleeing the community (small group effects). Such suspicion and threat within communities makes individuals very reluctant to be seen with people and agencies from beyond the community. This isolates the community from important developmental opportunities (community effects). Where this situation exists in numerous communities, social services, including health, welfare, education and security, become compromised (societal effects).
>
> At the level of the individual we are concerned with the personal histories, beliefs, values, and psychologies of people. At the relationship level, family dynamics, friendships, work colleagues and the other most significant human relationships of our lives are of great importance. At the level of community we are concerned with neighbourhood dynamics, schooling, religious practices, sporting and other social structures and so forth. Finally, the level of society involves the issues of international relations, economic differences, wars, and other macro level dynamics.

YOUTH GROUPS, GANGS, AND ORGANIZED ARMED VIOLENCE

Youth violence committed by youth groups and gangs is a growing concern in many countries. Worldwide, those youth most likely to participate in delinquent or violent activities usually are part of a group, although this association tends to be higher for theft, robbery, and rape, and lower for premeditated murder and assault with the intent to inflict grievous bodily harm (United Nations 2003).

Although general consensus is lacking on what is a youth gang, there is some agreement that many different types of youth groups and gangs exists, with varying characteristics in terms of their formation, roles, levels of crime involvement, stability, and longevity. These gangs all seem to answer a basic need to belong to a group and create a self-identity. Gangs once were thought to be primarily a male phenomenon, but in countries such as the United States, one in every four gang members is a female. Gang members can range in age from 7 to 35 years, but typically they are in their teens or early 20s. They tend to come from economically deprived areas, and from low-income and working-class urban and suburban environments. Often, gang members may have dropped out of school and hold low-skilled or low-paying jobs. Many gangs consist of people from ethnic or racial minorities who may be socially marginalized.

A complex interaction of factors leads young people to opt for gang life. A study of youth gangs in the Dominican Republic concluded that gangs are satisfying the needs of young Dominicans at various levels: at the individual level (through respect, power, authority, recognition, and financial gain), the relationship level (support, caring, friendship, and health services and medical attention), and the community level (rules, training, protection, financial benefits) (Aleph 2006; World Bank 2007).

Gangs seem to proliferate in places where the established social order has broken down and where alternative forms of shared cultural behavior are lacking. Other socioeconomic, community, and interpersonal factors that encourage young people to join gangs include the following:

- a lack of opportunity for social or economic mobility, within a society that aggressively promotes consumption;
- a decline locally in the enforcement of law and order;
- interrupted schooling, combined with low rates of pay for unskilled labor;
- a lack of guidance, supervision, and support from parents and other family members;
- harsh physical punishment or victimization in the home; and
- having peers who are already involved in a gang.

Youth groups and gangs vary widely in their composition, life span, and characteristics, including loose groups of young people; groups and "wanna-bes" often associated with a neighborhood or territory; more formalized and identified street gangs with a hierarchy and some criminal involvement; gangs with some links to organized crime; and institutionalized gangs using organized armed violence (Dowdney 2005; Klein et al. 2001). There is also some agreement that the risk factors for involvement of youth in urban crime and violence include not only personal characteristics or family circumstances and a lack of schooling or education opportunities, but also exacerbating factors such as marginalization, poverty and relative deprivation, racism, unemployment, drug and small arms trafficking, deportation policies, government and police corruption, and connections to transnational organized crime.

Although the risk and exacerbating factors for involvement in serious youth gang violence may be similar, the scale of the problems as well as the complexity of the links with local communities and histories can be quite different. As Shaw (2007) notes in her review of comparative global approaches to youth violence and crime prevention, "while the youth gangs of the United States have long held a fascination for Northern academics, in theory and in practice they are not necessarily the most appropriate model on which to base policies and interventions in other regions or countries." Citing the Children in Organized Armed Violence comparative case studies (Dowdney 2005), she notes the emergence of children and youth employed or otherwise participating in organized armed violence that features elements of a command structure and power over territory, local population, or resources. Examples have been identified in Colombia, Ecuador, El Salvador, Jamaica, Nigeria, Northern Ireland, the Philippines, South Africa, and parts of the United States. These range from groups that do not openly carry arms but use them in fights with other groups or the police, to groups that are openly armed and patrol their communities. The latter tend to be found in areas without strong state police or security forces and, sometimes, work with local government forces. Research by Viva Rio (Dowdney 2005) found that young people tend to get involved in armed groups through a gradual process of socialization: in many cases, dominant armed groups become part of a child's social experience, making the groups appear to be legitimate social institutions. The complexity of such groups requires tailored preventive policies.

REFERENCES

Aleph. 2006. *Estudio sobre la violencia juvenil.* Dominican Republic: Santo Domingo.

Barker, G., and C. Ricardo. 2005. "Young Men and the Construction of Masculinity in Sub-Saharan Africa: Implications for HIV/AIDS, Conflict, and Violence." Social Development Papers, Conflict Prevention and Reconstruction, Working Paper No. 26, World Bank, Washington, DC.

Bevan, J., and N. Florquin. 2006. *Few Options but the Gun: Angry Young Men. Small Arms Survey 2006: Unfinished Business.* Geneva: Small Arms Survey. Oxford: Oxford University Press.

Bronfenbrenner, U. 1979. *The Ecology of Human Development: Experiments by Nature and Design.* Cambridge, MA: Harvard University Press.

Cunningham, W., and M. Correia. 2003. *Caribbean Youth Development: Issues and Policy Directions.* Washington, DC: World Bank.

Dowdney, L. 2005. *International Comparisons of Children and Youth in Organized Armed Violence: Neither Peace nor War.* Rio de Janeiro: Children in Organized Armed Violence (COAV).

Farrington, D. P. 2002. *Understanding and Preventing Youth Crime.* New York: Sage.

Fingerhut, L. A., and K. K. Christoffel Firearm-related death and injury among children and adolescents. The Future of Children 2002; 12: 24–37.

Gallardo, J. M. A., and J.A. Gomez. 2008. ¡*Preparados, Listos, Ya! Una síntesis de intervenciones efectivas para la prevenciónde violencia que afecta a adolescentes y jóvenes.* Washington, DC: Organización Panamericana de Salud, GTZ.

Garbarino, J. 1985. "An Ecological Approach to Child Maltreatment." In *The social context of child abuse and neglect,* ed. L. H. Pelton, 228–267. New York: Human Sciences.

Hepburn, L. M., and D. Hemenway. 2004. "Firearm Availability and Homicide: A Review of the Literature." *Aggression and Violent Behavior* 9 (4): 417–440.

Herrenkohl, T. I., E. Maguin, K. G. Hill, J. D. Hawkins, R. D. Abbott, and R. F. Catalano. 2000. "Developmental Risk Factors for Risk Violence." *Journal of Adolescent Health* 26 (3): 176–186.

Higson-Smith, C. 2006. "Youth Violence in South Africa: The Impact of Political Transition." In *International perspectives on youth conflict and development*, ed. C. Daiute, Z. F. Kykont, and L. Nucci, 177–193. New York: Oxford University Press.

ISER (Instituto de Estudos da Religião) and Viva Rio. 2002. *Children of the Drug Trade: A Case Study of Children in Organized Armed Violence in Rio de Janeiro.* Seminar on Children Affected by Organized Armed Violence in Rio de Janeiro, Brazil. September 2002

Jewkes, R. 2002. "Intimate Partner Violence: Causes and Prevention." *The Lancet* 359 (9315): 1423–1429.

Klein, M. W., H. J. Kerner, C. L. Maxson, and E. G. Weitekamp, eds. 2001. *The Eurogang Paradox: Street Gangs and Youth Groups in the U.S. and Europe.* Norwell, MA: Kluwer Academic Publishers.

Knaul, F. M., and M. A. Ramírez. 2002. *Family Violence and Child Abuse in Latin America and the Caribbean: The cases of Colombia and Mexico.* Sustainable Development Department, Technical Papers Series. Washington, DC: Inter-American Development Bank.

Lederman, D., N. Loayza, and A. M. Menendez. 1999. *Violent Crime: Does Social Capital Matter?* Washington, DC: World Bank.

Minayo, M. C. S., and E. R. Souza. 1999. "Épossível prevenir a violência? Reflexões a partir do campo da Saúde Pública." *Revista Ciência & Saúde Coletiva* 4 (1): 7–32.

Moser, C., and J. Holland. 1997. *Urban Poverty and Violence in Jamaica.* Washington, DC: World Bank.

Moser, C., and D. Rodgers. 2005. "Change, Violence and Insecurity in Non-conflict Situations." ODI Working Paper No 245. London, Overseas Development Institute.

National Research Council and Institute of Medicine. 2002. *Community Programs to Promote Youth Development.* Washington, DC: National Academy Press.

Noronha, C. V., et al. 1999. "Violencia, etnia e cor: um estudo dos diferenciais na regiaõ metropolitana de Salvador, Bahia, Brasil." [Violence, ethnic groups and skin color: A study on differences in the metropolitan region of Salvador, Bahia, Brazil.] *Revista Panamericana de Salud Publica.* 1999;5: 268–277.

Office of the Surgeon General (US). 2001. *Youth Violence: A Report of the Surgeon General.*

Rockville, MD: United States Department of Health and Human Services, United States Public Health Service.

Parker, R. N., and K. Auerhahn. 1998. "Alcohol, Drugs, and Violence." *Annual Review of Sociology* 24:1, 291–311.

Pollard, J. A., J. D. Hawkins, and M. W. Arthur. 1999. "Risk and Protection: Are Both Necessary to Understand Diverse Behavioral Outcomes in Adolescence?" *Social Work Research* 23 (8): 145–58.

Richards, P. 1996. *Fighting for the Rain Forest. War, Youth & Resources in Sierra Leone.* Oxford: James Currey.

Rutter, M. 1979. "Protective Factors in Children's Responses to Stress and Disadvantage." In *Primary Prevention of Psychopathology: Vol. 3. SOCIAL Competence in Children*, ed. M. W. Kent and J. E. Rolf, 49–74. Hanover, NH: University Press of New England.

Shaw, Margaret. 2007. *Comparative Approaches to Urban Crime Prevention Focusing on Youth.* Montreal: International Center for the Prevention of Crime.

UNDP (United Nations Development Program). 2007. *United National Development Programme Annual Report: Making Globalization Work for Everyone.* New York: UNDP. www.undp.org/publications/annualreport2007/IAR07-ENG.pdf. Accessed August 28, 2010.

United Nations. 2003. *World Youth Report: The Global Situation of Young People.* United Nations Publication No. E.03.IV.7. New York: United Nations.

WHO (World Health Organization). 2002. *World Report on Violence and Health: Summary.* Geneva: World Health Organization.

World Bank. 2006. "Preventing Youth Risky Behavior through Early Child Development." *Youth Development Notes Series* 1 (3). Human Development Network. Washington, DC: World Bank.

World Bank. 2007. *Crime, Violence, and Development: Trends, Costs, and Policy Options in the Caribbean.* Washington, DC: United Nations Office on Drugs and Crime and the Latin America and the Caribbean Region of the World Bank.

World Bank and IDB (International Development Bank). 2006. *Dominican Republic Poverty Assessment: Achieving More Pro-Poor Growth.* Report No. 32422-DO. Washington, DC: World Bank.

3

What We Know about Preventing Violence

THE MOST IMPORTANT thing we have learned after decades of research on violence is that violence, and more specifically, youth violence, can be prevented. It is not inevitable. Rigorously evaluated youth violence prevention efforts have yielded many examples of policies, programs, and approaches that improve the well-being and opportunities for young persons, increase the likelihood they will transition successfully into adult roles in their respective societies, and decrease the likelihood they will become involved in, or if already involved, continue with violent behaviors.

It is *never too early, or too late, to prevent and redirect violent* conduct among children and youths. A growing body of evidence shows that opportunities exist for intervening to prevent a young person's involvement in violence beginning the day he or she is born, and in fact, even beginning during his or her mother's pregnancy. Aggressive and violent behavior, even at very young ages, as well as early academic problems, are predictive of violent behavior and other social problems later in life and a range of early violence prevention programs for parents, schools, and communities have been developed and evaluated, and found to be effective in countries throughout the world.

The wealth of research on the long-term impacts of early childhood interventions (at ages one to five) indicates that investing in early child development may be one of the most effective means to reduce and prevent children from engaging in violence and other risky behaviors. In countries as diverse as Jamaica, the Philippines, Turkey, and the United States, enriched child care and preschool programs that improve the foundations before children reach adolescence (through early investments in nutrition, health, and psychosocial development) have led to higher achievement test scores, higher graduation rates from high school, and lower crime rates for participants well into their 20s (World Bank 2006).

Focusing on children as young as age eight to help them prepare for their upcoming transition into adolescence is another important window for preventing youth involvement in violence. Most violence begins in the second decade of life, with the peak age of onset of offending occurring when a young person is between 8 and 14, arrests increasing in aggregate data as a whole around 13 or 14, and the prevalence of offending peaking in the late teenage years (15 to 19). Programs for preteens such as mentoring can prevent children from engaging in delinquency, keeping them engaged in prosocial activities as they enter their teen years.

Well-designed comprehensive interventions can successfully divert older children and young adolescents away from violent activities and peers. Finally, interventions can expedite the rate of exit from high-risk behaviors and circumstances among adolescents and young adults by providing proper support and monitoring. Most research in criminology suggests that violence and crime careers are short: for instance, arrest rates for most crimes tend to peak during late adolescence or early adulthood (early 20s). The majority of youth who become involved with crime and violence during the highest risk part of their lives are not destined for a life of crime. Most eventually will desist naturally from these activities. Opportunities exist to intervene and help young people transition out of their criminal careers throughout the high-risk ages—even up through their 20s (Farrington 2002; Office of the Surgeon General 2001).

INDIVIDUAL-LEVEL INTERVENTION PROGRAMS

Intervention programs at the individual level focus on development of social skills, conflict resolution skills, cognitive and problem-solving skills, peer relations, exposure to violent media, and changing individual beliefs about violence. Two approaches that have considerable research support for its effectiveness are cognitive-behavioral skills training programs and social development programs. These programs aim to increase empathy, and reduce impulsive, antisocial, and aggressive behavior in children and youth. They typically are offered through schools and can be delivered universally to all youth in a particular age-group or area regardless of their level of risk or current behaviors, or to a targeted group of children who are selected because of their exposure to a particular risk factor for violence (such as poverty or domestic violence) or behavior (fighting with peers, early interest in gangs, and so on). These types of programs also appear to be most effective with younger children, from preschool and primary school environments, rather than with older students (WHO 2002).

Related programs for older youth focus on strengthening academic performance and enhancing vocational opportunities through academic enrichment programs, providing incentives for youths at high risk for violence to complete secondary schooling and to pursue courses of higher education, as well as vocational training for underprivileged youths and young adults. These programs show promise in reducing violence, but they need further research to confirm these effects and determine which youth are likely to derive the greatest benefits from these approaches.

Programs that provide multiple services to an individual often across multiple sectors such as school, mental health, social services, and job training are referred to as "wraparound" programs and are another example of individual level services.

FAMILY-LEVEL INTERVENTION PROGRAMS

At the family level, interventions seek to affect factors within the family that contribute to violence, such as domestic violence and child abuse, negative parent-child interactions, ineffective or dysfunctional parenting, parental mental illness, depression, and isolation. These interventions most often seek to replace coercive communication and interaction patterns occurring between a parent and child with more positive, supportive interactions; and to reduce harsh discipline strategies associated with aggressive outcomes with more effective discipline approaches. Interventions can focus on restructuring the parent-child interaction, improving the spousal relationship, or affecting the entire family system. They also may focus on addressing specific pathology within family members, such as substance abuse or depression. These interventions may extend beyond relationships to addressing basic needs, such as safe housing and adequate food, assisting parents in finding employment and learning to manage family finances.

COMMUNITY-LEVEL AND MUNICIPAL INTERVENTION PROGRAMS

Community-level and municipal strategies seek to affect community-level factors, such as inadequate living conditions, including poor housing and the lack of safe or supervised places for youths and their families. Although far more evaluation research is required at this level, a number of community-based interventions have been identified that show promise in reducing the levels of serious youth violence and other forms of violence. These include interventions to reduce the availability of alcohol (for example, through restrictions on marketing approaches) and efforts to mitigate the effects of rapid social change. Also included are municipal reforms designed to reduce access to alcohol and guns as well as efforts that seek to strengthen local capacity to prevent violence. They frequently involve partnerships across service sectors and build connections among individuals and families within the communities. Other kinds of community-level strategies involve community outreach programs; these can include police-youth mentoring programs, peer support programs, and programs in which community elders teach their values and traditions. Programs that provide adult-supervised, socially, and culturally appropriate opportunities for recreation and cultural expression, as well as programs that build pro-social skills among at-risk youth are other examples. These programs hold promise as ways to restore the types of social connection and community cohesion needed to provide critical social support and modeling to young persons, and to inhibit, through collective action, negative behaviors.

NATIONAL- AND STATE-LEVEL INTERVENTION PROGRAMS

National- and state-level strategies usually involve policy decisions and larger scale initiatives to address such issues as racism, discrimination, and poverty.

Access to firearms, lack of economic and education opportunity, and lack of access to support services are targeted. These efforts may strengthen a community's capacity to prevent violence by providing affordable and accessible high-quality infant and child care and quality afterschool programs; by implementing policies supporting good parenting, such as paid maternity and paternity leave and flex time, or universal health care; or by restructuring and realigning service and funding structures to encourage multisector collaboration on these issues.

Table 3.1 presents widely accepted examples of youth violence prevention strategies that have proven effective—and ineffective—in a range of contexts, and others that are widely used but that have not yet been evaluated, so their potential contribution has yet to be assessed. The framework addresses two important considerations: (1) the developmental stages of an individual (from early childhood to early adulthood); and (2) the ecological levels (individual, relationship, community, and society) through which risks can be addressed. The strategies presented here are not exhaustive, but rather are meant to emphasize the spectrum of possible solutions. Although this book is focused on adolescence and early adulthood, early violence prevention is a key component of a balanced youth violence prevention effort. A comprehensive youth prevention program typically will incorporate programs and services at each or most of these levels. The most effective programs combine components that address individual, relationship, and environmental conditions. They build individual skills and competencies, provide training for parents for greater effectiveness, increase access to good education and employment, and improve the social climate and safety of school. They also provide "second chances" to those who have dropped out of the formal schooling system, including school equivalency programs, job and life-skills training, and apprenticeships.

Although there have been important advances, there are also significant gaps in our understanding of what works to prevent violence. A large proportion of the programs and policies that have the strongest evidence, that is, programs with statistically rigorous evaluations of effectiveness, are developmentally oriented, and focus on early aggression. They tackle the root causes of the development of deviant behavior and thus are aimed largely at early onset youth offenders, the group that is found to commit the largest proportion of offenses. Success with "adolescence-limited" offenders is less evident, and systematic reviews of the effectiveness of these types of programs are lacking—even in industrial nations with greater resources and long-standing prevention efforts with these populations. A particularly large gap exists in programs dealing with gang violence. Systematic reviews have found that there are no randomized controlled trials for gang-prevention through opportunity provision (Fisher, Montgomery, and Gardner 2008a) or through cognitive behavioral treatment (Fisher, Montgomery, and Gardner 2008b) in industrial country settings. Learning more about what works and does not work in these areas must be a priority in the coming years.

In contrast, in developing countries, very little evidence demonstrates the effectiveness of interpersonal violence prevention programs, and much of the

Table 3.1 Violence Prevention Strategies by Developmental Stage and Ecological Context

	Early Childhood (0–5 years)	Middle Childhood (6–11 years)	Adolescence (12–19 years)	Early Adulthood (20–29 years)
Individual	• Early child development and preschool enrichment programs for at-risk children (a)	• Parenting training (a) • Programs providing information about drug abuse (b)	• Providing incentives for youth at high risk for violence to complete secondary schooling (a) • Academic enrichment programs for those at risk of dropping out • Individual counseling (b) • Probation or parole programs that include meetings with prison inmates describing the brutality of prison life (b) • Residential programs in psychiatric or correctional institutions (b) • Programs providing information about drug abuse (b) • Training in the safe use of guns (b) • Programs modeled on basic military training (b) • Trying young offenders in adult courts (b)	• Providing incentives to pursue courses in higher education • Parenting training • Job training combined with life skills and internships • Residential programs for offenders (b) • Psychotherapy for high-risk youth and offenders (b)

(Continued)

Table 3.1 Continued

Relationship (e.g., family, peers)	• Preventing unintended pregnancies • Parenting training • Increasing access to prenatal and postnatal care • Home visitation (a) • Training in parenting (a) • Marital and family therapy	• Mentoring programs (a) • Targeted incentives to mother to keep child in school (a) • Home-school partnership programs to promote parental involvement	• Mentoring programs (a) • Family therapy (a) • Temporary foster care programs for serious and chronic delinquents • Peer mediation or peer counseling (b) • Gang membership prevention/intervention programs (b)	• Programs to strengthen ties to family and jobs, and reduce involvement in violent behavior
Community	• Monitoring lead levels and removing toxins from homes • Increasing the availability and quality of early child development and child-care facilities	• Creating safe routes for children on their way to and from school or other community activities • Improving school settings, including teacher practices, school policies, and security	• Creating safe routes for youths on their way to and from school or other community activities • Improving school settings, including teacher practices, school policies, and security • Extracurricular activities/supervised afterschool programs • Positive youth development programs	• Establishing adult recreational programs • Community policing • Proactive arrests • Directed patrols • Reducing availability of alcohol • Improving emergency response, trauma care and access to health services

- Providing after school programs to extend adult supervision
- Extracurricular activities

- Supporting classroom management techniques
- Behavior modification via "thinking" skills
- Providing "second chance" education programs (equivalency)
- Life skills training
- Training health care workers to identify and refer youths at high risk for violence
- Community policing
- Reducing the availability of alcohol
- Improving emergency response, trauma care, and access to health services
- National youth service programs
- Buying back guns (b)

- High-quality rehabilitation programs
- Imprisonment of high-rate career criminals
- Prison-based drug rehab programs
- National youth service programs
- Corporal punishment in schools (b)
- Citizen patrols (b)
- Social casework: counseling, close supervision and social services (b)
- Reactive arrests (b)
- Random patrols (b)
- Buying back guns (b)
- Trying young offenders in adult courts (b)

Societal

- Deconcentrating poverty
- Reducing income inequality
- Reducing media violence
- Public information campaigns

- Deconcentrating poverty
- Reducing inequality
- Reducing media violence
- Public information campaigns
- Reforming educational systems

- Deconcentrating poverty
- Reducing income inequality
- Public information campaigns
- Reducing media violence
- Enforcing laws prohibiting illegal transfers of guns to youth
- Strengthening and improving police and judicial systems
- Reforming educational systems

- Deconcentrating poverty
- Reducing income inequality
- Job creation programs for the chronically unemployed
- Public information campaigns
- Promoting safe and secure storage of firearms
- Strengthening and improving police and juvenile justice systems

Sources: Crime, Violence, and Development: Trends, Costs, and Policy Options in the Caribbean, the World Bank 2007, WHO 2002

(a) Demonstrated to be effective in reducing youth violence or risk factors for youth violence

(b) Least promising or shown to be ineffective in reducing youth violence or risk factors for youth violence

focus of efforts in these settings has been on community-based violence, such as gangs. As part of a multicountry study to document interpersonal violence prevention efforts, some 600 programs in seven countries (Brazil, India, Jamaica, Jordan, Mozambique, South Africa, and the Former Yugoslav Republic of Macedonia) were reviewed in 2005 by the World Health Organization. Very few of these programs had been designed systematically, that is, had been based on data that defined the nature of the violence problem, its causes, and the interventions most likely to work; and few attempted to measure the real effects of these intervention on known risk factors for violence and on the rates of the type of violence the program was intending to prevent (WHO 2007).

Although the international knowledge base on youth violence prevention is growing slowly, and is still dominated by studies from industrial and Western countries, the number and quality of evaluations from countries around the world are increasing. A recent report from the Pan American Health Organization reported on the effectiveness of violence prevention programs for adolescents and youth in Latin America. The report identified rigorously evaluated programs targeted to youth in developing countries aimed at vocational, life, and leadership building skills, engaging youth through education, sports, and most often vocational skills. The latter is a popular type of program and emerging evidence supports its effectiveness in building self-efficacy, social skills, and self-esteem, all of which are important protective factors for preventing youth violence (Gallardo and Gomez 2008).

Significant community-level violence prevention approaches with evidence have surfaced from developing country contexts, and they have made a global contribution to advancing knowledge and expanding the repertoire of potential prevention strategies, building the evidence base for more macro-level strategies for consideration in a youth violence prevention efforts. These efforts are effective in terms of the results of most of their research findings, but knowledge is insufficient of the causality and the conditions under which the interventions work, making it difficult to determine the minimum quality standards for a successful implementation. Also, the long-term prevention effects are unknown, or whether they hold up when applied in different contexts or with populations with varying levels of risk. They are interventions that are ready to be taken to scale, providing that the replication process is carefully monitored and evaluated. These include a study of the impact of a ban on carrying firearms on homicide rates in Cali and Bogota, Colombia, finding lower homicide during the time the policy was in effect. In the mid-1990s, Colombian officials in Bogota and Cali noted that homicide rates increased during weekends following paydays, on national holidays, and near elections. After carrying handguns during these times was banned, a 14 percent reduction in homicide rates occurred (Villaveces et al. 2000). Another study of pre- and postintervention data of an alcohol sales restriction policy in the City of Diadema, Brazil, was found to be associated with the reduction in homicides as well as violence against women (Duailibi et al. 2007). Interventions focused on handgun restrictions and drug and alcohol consumption among youth in neighborhoods with youth gangs and high homicide and crime rates in the *favelas* (informal settlements, or shantytowns) in Belo Horizonte, Brazil, were successful in reducing homicide.

Community or problem-oriented policing has become an important law enforcement strategy for addressing youth violence and other criminal problems in many parts of the world. Burdened with high crime rates and low public trust in the police, a number of industrial and developing countries have adopted this concept, in some cases with impressive results, including reductions in crime. It can take many forms, but its core ingredients are building community partnerships and solving community problems. A recent study examining community policing programs in São Paulo and Belo Horizonte (Brazil), Bogotá (Colombia), and Villa Nueva (Guatemala) concludes that the results were generally positive. Lower crime rates have not been the principal benefit of community policing programs in many successful cases, including those of Chicago and New York City in the United States. Instead, many advocates of these programs, both in Latin America and in other regions, claim that the most important benefit of these initiatives is to reduce abuses by the police. Frühling (2004) also cites public opinion polls that show much higher levels of approval toward the police in places where community policing has been introduced. The four initiatives, launched between 1998 and 2000, are now sustainable and enjoy widespread local support. Their impact on crime rates is harder to determine, because local authorities did not conduct the kind of follow-up research that would make it possible to determine changes in that regard. Such programs need to be more rigorously evaluated, but closer ties between the police and the community "revitalized existing police forces, increased the levels of social support, and encouraged far-reaching changes in their structures and operation" (Frühling 2004).

Community mobilization is another area in which some evidence of effectiveness is emerging. Community mobilization and participation strategies facilitate a broader, collective response to community-defined social and health needs and give communities an effective voice in program delivery, service, and policy. A critical determinant of success is the degree to which community members, groups, and organizations are mobilized to participate and collaborate in addressing community social and health issues (Kim-Ju et al. 2008).

Typically, community mobilization efforts encompass three strategies that can be carried out independently or jointly: (1) projects that aim to establish links and communication channels with the citizenry, the municipal authorities, and the police; (2) initiatives focused on youth and young adults, which seek to develop alternative spaces and activities for youth, such as rehabilitating spaces and facilities where young people can meet; and (3) projects with a focus on increasing informal social controls, carrying out activities that increase neighborhood cohesion, pride, and a sense of belonging. Community mobilization is a key component of a comprehensive strategy to prevent youth violence and in building safe, healthy, and peaceful communities. Although there is some evidence of impact on crime in the short term, long-term results findings are not conclusive.

INFORMING POLICY

"Supporting Youth at Risk: A Policy Toolkit for Middle Income Countries" developed by the World Bank (World Bank 2008) provides rigorous evidence of programs and policies that have been proven to prevent risky youth behavior and offers a typology for improved targeting for at-risk youth that has been extremely useful in crime and violence prevention efforts in less-resourced settings. It permits distinguishing the levels of risk that young people are exposed to at various stages of their development to formulate the most appropriate policies. Three types of at-risk youth, with particular programmatic approaches are identified:

Type I

Type I includes young people who face risk factors in their lives but who have not yet engaged in risky behavior (for example, those living in disadvantaged situations who are at risk of dropping out of school or being unemployed). These are the young people who would be reached in primary violence prevention efforts. Youth who *live in situations of urban poverty and are at risk* of dropping out of school or otherwise are compromising their safe and healthy development because of *environmental, familial, and social factors.* They are fundamentally attached to their families, communities, and social institutions, but they are at risk of losing these connections and suffering from situations that could compromise their integration into society and transition to adulthood.

Type II

Type II includes young people who engage in risky behavior but who have not yet suffered severe negative consequences (for example, youth who often are absent from school but have not yet dropped out, youth who are involved in delinquency but have not yet been arrested, or youth at risk for abuse or other forms of violence and who face specific stress factors that put them at direct risk for an identifiable and harmful situation). These young people who have *moved from a general to a specific risk* are typically targeted in secondary prevention efforts. They continue to live at home and have some (often weakening) connections with their community and social institutions.

Type III

Type III includes young people experiencing severe negative consequences as a result of risky behavior (for example, youth who have dropped out of school, youth who are in violent street groups or gangs, young people who are being released from correctional institutions back into their communities, or youth victims of gun and other forms of violence). These young people are targeted in tertiary prevention approaches. These young people *have moved from being "at risk" of a situation to suffering the impact of a particular situation*, and include youth whose connections with their families, communities, and social institutions have been severely weakened or severed—that is, youth living in the streets, youth involved in drug trafficking or youth gangs, or adolescent mothers. Assistance would require intensive social services and interventions, which can involve out-of-home care or alternative living situations.

The World Bank toolkit proposes strategies for implementation of a youth portfolio in a budget-constrained environment, presenting a menu of evidence-based policy options (core polices, promising approaches and general policies with a disproportionately positive effect on youth at risk).

Core Policies

The core policies consist of rigorously evaluated interventions with a proven track record in reducing crime and violence and related risk factors: (1) expanding integrated early child development for children from poor households; (2) increasing the number of young people who complete secondary school, particularly those from poor families; (3) using the fact that students are a captive audience while in school to provide them with key risk prevention messages and to identify at-risk youth who are in need of remedial support; (4) developing youth-friendly health services; (5) using the media to describe the costs of risky behavior and present alternatives (combined with improved services); and (6) promoting effective parenting of and by young people.

Promising Approaches

Promising approaches focus on helping those affected by risky behavior to recover and return to a safe, productive path to adulthood. Young people in this category range from school dropouts to the incarcerated and are more difficult to reach than others in their age-group. Although not as many of the interventions in this category have yet been evaluated, there is sufficient evidence to enable us to make some recommendations in the areas of (1) education equivalency, (2) job training, (3) financial incentives for completing secondary school, (4) afterschool programs, (5) formal youth service programs, (6) mentoring, (7) employment services, (8) life-skills training in all interventions aimed at youth at risk, and (9) self-employment and entrepreneur programs.

General Policies with a Positive Effect on Youth at Risk

The following seven policies address critical risk factors at the community and macro levels (see figure 3.1). These policies also have been shown to be particularly effective at reducing risky behavior by young people and therefore should form an essential part of an overall strategy to reduce the number of youth at risk: (1) safe neighborhood investments that support community policing and improved services for high-violence communities, (2) reducing the availability of firearms,

Figure 3.1 Prevention of Negative Youth Outcomes

		Early Childhood (in utero-5)	Youth (12-24) Type I-II Type III	
Individual	Target high-risk households and individuals	Focus intensively on early child development (ECD)	Keep kids in school through secondary completion, and keep them "connected" Provide remedial services to those exhibiting risk behaviors	Provide second chances (such as education equivalency, job training with life skills training)
Micro Level Interpersonal (family, peers) Community (schools, neighborhood, police, health centers)		Provide support to parents and other caregivers in effective parenting Expand ECD services targeted to poor communities	Provide effective parenting support to parents and other caregivers of at-risk youth Improve services for disadvantaged youth and their communities (such as "safe neighborhood" interventions, sex education in all schools, supervised after-school programs)	Provide caring adults (such as mentoring, family therapy) Focus on treatment rather than "mano dura" for high-risk youth (such as multidemsional treatment foster care, drug rehabilitation)
Macro Level (poverty, media, law, cultural norms)		• Improve economic growth and employment conditions • Enforce laws reducing access to firearms, alcohol, and tobacco (for example, increase prices)	• Ease labor market regulations biased against youth • Provide birth registration to the undocumented	

(3) restricting the sale of alcohol, (4) increasing access to contraception, (5) promoting antiviolence messages in all media, (6) strengthening the justice system to focus on treating and rehabilitating rather than incarcerating young people, and (7) registering the undocumented.

The case studies in this book cover some of the efforts to expand this knowledge base, particularly for late onset youth violence.

The common denominator for all of these approaches is that successful interventions are evidence based, starting with a clear diagnosis of the types of violence, risk factors, and assets, and ending with a careful evaluation of the intervention's impact, which will inform future actions. Their utility hinges on context-specific information that allows us to design an appropriate mix of violence prevention programs. Such information permits an assessment of the mix of persistent and occasional offending, and provides an outline of the risk and protective factors that are most relevant. This information can be collected through a mix of quantitative and qualitative methods, and it can take the form of separate, stand-alone studies, or formative research underlying the design of an intervention.

FOCUSING EFFORTS

One the main obstacles to youth violence prevention continues to be the lack of institutional capacity to address these issues to accurately determine the scope and characteristics of violence; set priorities; guide the development of interventions, programs, and policies; and monitor progress. To understand the specific factors underlying the engagement of particular youth in violence, there is no substitute for an in-depth contextual analysis of the overall structural situation of youth and the proximate factors that make the difference between those who do and those who do not engage in violence. It is only in this way that we escape from stigmatizing and assigning guilt to youth, particularly young males, simply on the basis that they are young, unemployed, out-of-school, poor, and male (Barker and Ricardo 2005). Likewise, it is only through such contextual analysis, that one can determine how best to support vulnerable youth and prevent their engagement in and victimization by violence.

Data become a critical element of prevention planning. For communities, cities, or governments to engage effectively in comprehensive violence prevention planning, one must be able to identify where the greatest problems are, and the nature of those problems, to then be able to design interventions to address them and evaluate their impact. Developing data systems for routine monitoring of trends in violent behavior, in injuries, and in deaths should form the basis of prevention efforts. Such data will provide valuable information to formulate and evaluate public policies and programs to prevent youth violence. Simple approaches to the surveillance of youth violence are needed that can be applied in a wide range of resource and cultural settings.

All countries and regions should be encouraged to establish centers where routine information available from the health services (including emergency departments), the police, and other authorities, relevant to violence, can be collated and compared. This information will greatly help in formulating and implementing prevention programs. An important innovation of relevance to other national and subnational regions has been the development and multicountry implementation of low-cost and highly efficient georeferenced information systems. These systems and crime observatories in Latin America and the Caribbean have been used in middle-income countries to routinely collect descriptive information on a small number of key indicators that can be measured accurately. These systems use information from health services (including emergency departments), the police, forensic medicine, and other authorities that are relevant to violence. Such systems are essential to monitor trends in violent victimization in response to direct violence prevention efforts as well as to the indirect impact on violence of traditional development activities in such sectors as employment, education, economic development, and urban development.

Another key data improvement initiative started by countries in Latin America and the Caribbean is oriented toward the development of a regional system of standardized indicators of citizen security. This set of standard regional indicators will allow for the measurement, monitoring, and intercountry comparison of events affecting youth violence and other dimensions of citizen security in the region. Drawing from the crime observatory data and national victimization surveys, these indicators will capture unreported violence. In addition, through the use of south-south cooperation initiatives (through which developing countries collaborate in the exchange of expertise), the participating countries share their experience in what works and does not work in violence prevention. A key outcome of this initiative is the network of collaboration that has been established among the countries. This initiative has been so useful that the process, which was started by four countries (Peru, Colombia, Ecuador, and Honduras), has been joined by another six countries (Argentina, Chile, Uruguay, Paraguay, Guyana, and Dominican Republic). The goal is to cover the entire region. The use and development of regional tools and methodologies, augmenting those developed in high-income countries and research centers, appears to have played a key role in increasing the acceptability and perceived relevance of these methodologies.

REFERENCES

Barker, G., and C. Ricardo. 2005. "Young Men and the Construction of Masculinity in Sub-Saharan Africa: Implications for HIV/AIDS, Conflict, and Violence." Social Development Papers, Conflict Prevention and Reconstruction, Working Paper No. 26, Washington, DC: World Bank.

Duailibi, S., W. Ponicki, J. Grube, I. Pinsky, R. Laranjeira, and M. Raw. 2007. "The Effect of Restricting Opening Hours on Alcohol-Related Violence. *American Journal of Public Health* 97 (12): 2276–2280.

Farrington, D. P. 2002. *Understanding and Preventing Youth Crime.* New York: Sage.

Fisher, H., P. Montgomery, and F. E. M. Gardner. 2008a. "Opportunities Provision for Preventing Youth Gang Involvement For Children and Young People." *Cochrane Database of Systematic Reviews* 2: 7–16. Art. No.: CD007002. doi: 10.1002/14651858. CD007002.pub2.

Fisher, H., P. Montgomery, and F. E. M. Gardner. 2008b. "Cognitive-Behavioural Interventions for Preventing Youth Gang Involvement for Children and Young People." *Cochrane Database of Systematic Reviews* no. 2: 7–16. Art. No.: CD007008. doi: 10.1002/14651858.CD007008.pub2.

Frühling, H., ed. 2004. *Calles Mas Seguras: Estudios de Policía Comunitaria en América Latina.* Washington, DC: Inter-American Development Bank.

Gallardo, J. M. Abad, and J. A. Gómez. 2008. *¡Preparados, Listos, Ya! Una Síntesis de Intervenciones Efectivas para la Prevención de Violencia Que Afecta a Adolescentes y Jóvenes.* Washington, DC: Pan American Health Organization and GTZ German Cooperation.

Kim-Ju, G.,G.Y. Mark., R. Cohen., O. Garcia-Santiago., and P. Nguyen. Community Mobilization and Its Application to Youth Violence Prevention. American Journal of Preventive Medicine–March 2008 (Vol. 34, Issue 3, Supplement, Pages S5–S12).

Office of the Surgeon General. 2001. *Youth Violence: A Report of the Surgeon General.* Washington, DC: Office of the Surgeon General.

Villaveces A., P. Cummings, V. E. Espitia, T. D. Koepsell, B. McKnight, and A. L. Kellermann. 2000. "Effect of a Ban on Carrying Firearms on Homicide Rates in 2 Colombian Cities." *Journal of the American Medical Association* 283 (9): 1205–1209.

WHO (World Health Organization). 2002. *World Report on Violence and Health: Summary.* Geneva: World Health Organization.

WHO (World Health Organization). 2007. *Third Milestones of a Global Campaign for Violence Prevention Report 2007: Scaling Up.* Geneva: World Health Organization.

World Bank. 2006. *World Development Report 2006: Equity and Development.* Washington, DC: World Bank. http://go.worldbank.org/UWYLBR43C0. Accessed August 25th, 2010.

The World Bank. 2008. Supporting Youth at risk: A Policy Toolkit for Middle Income Countries. Washington, DC.

4

Public Policy Approaches to Youth Violence Prevention

THERE ARE MULTIPLE possible entry points to engage in youth violence prevention. The entry point may be made through a school, in the private sector, through faith-based organizations, or through a grassroots organization of concerned parents or community residents. Other entry points are part of municipal safe neighborhood projects, reform efforts in criminal justice systems, public national health initiatives, or international advocacy efforts. In almost all developing as well as industrial countries, youth violence prevention efforts are fragmented and uncoordinated, characterized by weak national planning, and low political status. When they do rise to national or local attention, it often is due to a recent, disturbing event. Responses are mainly reactive and politically expedient, focused only on short-term solutions such as suppression (perhaps paralleling the local election cycle). Short prevention funding cycles give limited consideration to the long-term, sustained, and comprehensive planning and coordination that can lead to significant and sustained reductions in violence along with improved outcomes for young people.

The societal home for violence prevention services often reflects the national and cultural beliefs about the nature of violence among young people, its level of priority in the society, the amount of political will available to address the problem, the traditions of intersectoral collaborations among government agencies and civil society groups. In societies in which violence is seen primarily as a criminal behavior, intervention efforts may emanate predominantly from the criminal justice sector. In societies in which youth violence is seen as resulting from a mental or emotional weakness or aberration, services and programming may be located in the mental health sector. In yet other societies in which violence is understood as a complex event involving not just individual and family elements, but also as having economic and social contributors, efforts to intervene often involve collaboration across multiple sectors, and may involve municipal or national actors. These various approaches are complementary and increasingly are used in combination, particularly given the complexity of youth violence and its prevention. These approaches also include youth development as a cross-cutting methodology. The case studies in parts II and III of this book provide examples of how these factors vary by country and how they influence program and policy development around the issue.

A policy and prevention framework developed by Moser and Winton (2002) that is focused on all forms of violence, including youth violence, but extending beyond it to other forms and age-groups, is a useful tool for understanding the range and types of global violence prevention efforts described in this book. Developed as a typology for Latin America and the Caribbean, the framework (see table 4.1) categorizes all violence by motivation and divides it into the following four categories:

- Social violence that is motivated by the will to attain or keep social power and control and often is gender based, including violence toward an intimate partner inside the home as well as sexual abuse in the public arena. Social violence also includes ethnic violence, disputes among peers, and territorial or identity-based violence linked with gangs.
- Economic violence that is motivated by material gain manifested in street crime (mugging, robbery) and in crime linked with drugs and kidnapping, including crime committed to feed a habit.
- Institutional violence that is perpetrated by state institutions such as the police, the judiciary, ministries of health and education, and by nonstate institutions such as vigilante groups.
- Political violence that is driven by the will to win or to hold political power and includes guerrilla warfare, paramilitary conflict, and political assassination.

The Moser and Winton framework identifies six different types of policy interventions (see table 4.1) that respond to these violence motivators. The first of these, criminal justice, focuses on violence deterrence and control and accomplishes this through higher arrest and conviction rates and more severe punishments. Policies and interventions located and led by the public health sector focus primarily on the reduction of risk factors for youth violence. Conflict transformation and human rights approaches focus on the nonviolent resolution of conflict through negotiation and legal enforcement of human rights within a country. Crime prevention through environmental design or urban renewal seeks to reduce the opportunity for violence by focusing on the settings of violence, rather than on the individuals perpetrating the violence. Citizen security approaches typically involve multiple measures across multiple sectors that aim to prevent and reduce violence. These efforts most often take place at the national and municipal levels. Finally social capital approaches invest in rebuilding social cohesion and trust within and between communities and formal and informal social institution (Moser 2002). An additional policy approach, youth development, has been added to this typology. It advocates for the provision of positive adults, supports, opportunities and services to ensure a healthy, safe, and productive transition to adulthood, thereby contributing to the prevention of youth violence.

Table 4.1 Public Policy Approaches and Interventions to Address Youth Violence

Policy approach	Goal	Types of violence addressed	Typical interventions
Sector-specific			
Criminal justice (Restorative justice)	Eliminating re-offending	• Youth violence • Youth delinquency • Robbery • Gender-based violence	Judicial reform, accessible justice systems Police reform, community policing Mobile courts
Public health	Preventing violence by reducing individual risk factors	• Youth violence • Homicide • Gender-based violence	Preschool programs Home visitation programs School-based social development programs Restriction of alcohol sales Restrictions on gun ownership
Conflict transformation and human rights	Resolving conflict nonviolently through negotiation and legal enforcement of human rights by states and other social actors	• Youth involvement in political, collective violence • Institutional violence • Human rights • Arbitrary detention	Traditional systems of justice Government human rights advocates or ombudsman Civil society advocacy NGOs
Cross-sectoral			
Crime prevention through environmental design / urban renewal	Reducing violence by focusing on the settings of crime rather than the perpetrators	• Youth violence • Economic violence • Social violence	Local level programs Urban renewal programs Integrated slum upgrading programs
Youth development	Promoting a healthy, safe and productive transition to adulthood, through provision of positive adults, supports, opportunities and services.	• Youth gangs • Youth violence • Social violence • Economic violence	Local level programs National level programs Youth services Sectoral programs
Citizen security/ public safety	Using cross-sector measures to prevent or reduce violence	• Youth violence • Youth gangs • Social violence • Economic violence	National level programs Local level programs

(Continued)

Table 4.1   Continued

Community-driven development (CDD)/social capital	Rebuilding social capital, trust, and cohesion in informal and formal social institutions	• Youth gangs • Youth violence • Gender-based violence	Community-based solutions Crisis services for victims Ongoing support and prevention Communication campaigns Programs for perpetrators

Source: Adapted Moser and Winton (2002) and Moser, Winton and Moser (2005)

Although all typologies have limitations, they can help policy makers and the public develop a more comprehensive and detailed understanding of approaches to violence prevention that extends beyond short-term, narrow institutional approaches and reactionary solutions. They also can assist these audiences in seeing the links among the various types of violence involving youth from early exposure to violence in the home to interpersonal and community-level violence. They highlight the policy implications of different forms of violence. Lastly, they can distinguish the different dimensions of violence in cases in which multiple factors may be supporting violence. For example, in the Northern Ireland case study (see chapter 9), it becomes difficult to distinguish between politically motivated and nonpolitical, social violence. Or in the case of Colombia (see chapter 16), reducing youth violence in contexts dominated by guerrilla and paramilitary warfare requires not only a political solution to the conflict but also an economic solution to address the unemployment of young ex-combatants as well as concerted efforts to address social violence prevention. The case study from Haiti (see chapter 15) underscores how the difficulties of establishing capable and stable democratic governance have contributed to the escalation of youth violence. Furthermore, the categorization explains why interventions that focus on one type of violence may not reduce another.

The *criminal justice approach* involves work with police, prosecutors, the judiciary, and prisons—and is a favored by policy approach to generate rapid decreases in crime and violence. It tries to reduce crime and violence through higher arrest rates, higher conviction rates, and longer sentences. The criminal justice approach aims to reduce crime through both deterrence (dissuading potential criminals from committing crimes) and incapacitation (preventing criminals from committing crimes because they are imprisoned).

Although much police practice necessarily focuses on dealing with violence after it has happened, and improved rates of detection and prosecution undoubtedly have a deterrent effect on some forms of violent crime, increasingly sophisticated forms of policing emphasize the prevention of problems before they happen. Evidence-based approaches increasingly are used in this regard, using the disciplines of criminology and sociology.

Finally, penal institutions are important parts of criminal justice systems that are both (1) locations where violence can be highly prevalent and (2) venues where a range of violence prevention strategies have considerable potential. Police and judicial reform is urgent both to reduce impunity and address deeper issues involving justice, corruption, and human rights abuses; impunity plays a large role in promoting economically motivated youth violence in many regions of the world. Police reform was a key component in the Northern Ireland peace agreement and, in 2001, following an independent review and report on police reform, resulted in the new service being based on a greater implementation of human rights principles and a focus on effective policing through working closely with members of local communities.

Correctional strategies, which reduce the risk that a perpetrator will repeat acts of violence, are a potentially important part of addressing youth and young adult offending. Meta-analyses of recidivism reduction programs, particularly among delinquent and violent youth, suggest that effective programs can divert a significant proportion of violent youth from future violence, especially if these programs incorporate the following: (1) structured evidence-based *multimodal, behavioral, and skills-oriented interventions* (including self-regulation, anger management, conflict resolution, and decision making); (2) *family clinical interventions* (structured, multicomponent interventions that address the individual and family contexts underlying delinquent and violent behavior); and (3) *wraparound services* used by justice systems to intensively supervise and provide tailored services to delinquent youth and young adults, which includes vocational training in marketable skills, and activities and structures to decrease alienation, marginalization, and hopelessness.

A recent review of the cost-benefit review of evidence-based rehabilitation and prevention programs to reduce recidivism found that 19 of the 29 programs for juvenile offenders and 12 of the 18 for adult offenders produced reductions in crime and benefits that outweighed the costs. These programs offer especially attractive future economic returns and should be a part of a comprehensive response to youth violence, although they often involve significant frontend costs (Aos 2009). In the corrections area, widespread serious reforms, capacity building in evidence-based program principles, and additional investment are needed if prisons are to have any prospect of rehabilitating young inmates, instead of just preventing them from committing crimes during their stays in prison.

Initiatives such as *Fica VIVO* (Stay Alive) in Belo Horizonte, Brazil, emerged partly in response to a fiscal crisis in policing services and was a strategy that partially was financed by the community. New police with different backgrounds and skills were hired and patrolling areas were divided into smaller areas, with the goal of bringing police and citizens closer. Within five months, homicide rates dropped by 47 percent, and the model was adopted statewide.

PUBLIC HEALTH APPROACH

Another example of a sector-specific approach is the public health approach, often called the epidemiological approach, a branch of medical science that deals with the incidence, distribution, and control of disease in a population. Deriving from a tradition of collaboration among a broad spectrum of scientific disciplines, a public health approach brought emphasis and commitment to identifying policies and programs to prevent youth violence. The idea of primary prevention—reaching young people earlier, before violence occurs—plays a critical role in garnering greater acceptance that youth violence is preventable among public health and other youth-serving professionals and the general public.

In the public health approach, interventions are tailored to address risk factors that are most important in a given locale, and significant emphasis is placed on evaluating the impacts of the interventions. Many of its most important interventions—such as programs to reduce unintended pregnancies and to promote early childhood development and parental training—may have considerable payoffs, in terms of reduced youth violence, only after some time has passed, although the bulk of the knowledge and attention has been on early onset youth violence. Not all public health–inspired interventions have delayed effects, and some have much promise in addressing violence among older youth, such as the CeaseFire project, described in chapter 6. Other measures such as limiting the availability of alcohol, providing recreational and mentoring programs for youth, and providing incentives for youth to remain in school, for example, may all produce relatively quick impacts (World Bank 2007).

CONFLICT TRANSFORMATION AND HUMAN RIGHTS APPROACHES

Cross-sectoral approaches include conflict transformation and human rights approaches. These efforts promote nonviolent conflict resolution through mediation, negotiation, and enforcement of human rights. Often used in postconflict settings, this approach is employed by nongovernmental organizations (NGOs) working to promote enfranchisement of marginal communities and their citizens and to address interpersonal violence. Conflict transformation is not about making a situation of injustice more bearable, but about transforming the very systems, structures, and relationships that give rise to violence and injustice. Conflict is viewed as a catalyst for social change and places primary emphasis on the question of social justice (Bloomfield, Fischer, and Schmelzle 2006; Lederach 2005; Mitchell 2002). Another innovative option is community peace-building efforts that directly involve citizens, strengthening the moral authority of the state's control institutions, as well as improving their effectiveness. Human rights approaches focus on the state's role in ensuring citizens' rights to be free from victimization and the threat of violence, drawing on a range of international human rights conventions. Although this perspective initially targeted governments that violated human rights, more recently it has included all social actors that deny or abuse rights, including guerrilla and paramilitary groups. Various aspects of these approaches were adopted in Northern Ireland, as illustrated in the case study, in working with warring factions in communities to mediate, establish ceasefires and community codes of conduct, and teach conflict resolution skills. Nongovernmental and other civil society groups play a central role in advocating for rights, especially for those populations excluded from the public policy process (Moser 2006). In the United States, human and civil rights groups were instrumental in outlawing the death penalty in 2005 for offenders who were under the age of 18 when their crimes were committed, in accordance with international rights of children conventions.

ENVIRONMENTAL DESIGN AND URBAN RENEWAL APPROACH

Crime prevention through environmental design (CPTED) and urban renewal approach is based on the premise that characteristics of the physical environment influence the amount of violent crime that occurs and, thus, that these crimes can be reduced by modifying the physical environment to make it more difficult and risky (and less rewarding) for potential criminals to commit crime. Public areas that are well lighted and open to surveillance deter crime and violence. Streets and buildings that communicate disorder and lack of control through the presence of trash, vandalism, graffiti, and minor infractions of civil behavior encourage further disruptive behavior and violence.

Similarly, school buildings that are overcrowded and poorly designed contribute to violence by reducing the capacity of students to avoid confrontations and the capacity of staff to monitor. Living in poor quality housing can adversely affect the physical and mental health of children and youth and is a well-established risk factor for behavioral and educational problems, which, in turn, are linked clearly to the higher likelihood of criminality (Waller and Weiler 1984). CPTED strategies (known by various acronyms, labels, or names around the world, such as Designing Out Crime) rely on the ability to influence offender decisions that precede criminal acts by affecting the built, social, and administrative environment. CPTED involves multidisciplinary interventions in the planning, design, and management phases of urban development projects that engage architects, urban planners, landscape architects, engineers, crime prevention police officers, security officials, building and facility managers, and community members who are involved in building safer places to prevent youth violence. Importantly, this approach can address not only objective levels of violence and crime, but also residents' fear, and can yield quick results. It usually is used in the context of community-based, multisector, "urban renewal" programs that address the causes of crime through targeted social, economic, and situational crime prevention measures in specific "hot-spot" neighborhoods (Moser, Winton, and Moser 2005). Also, support for urban upgrading and basic service provision in violent hot-spots can be a means to bring the state presence back into undergoverned areas, helping to rebuild state legitimacy in violence-affected communities. The incapacity of the state to meet the basic services for its citizens undermines governance and creates opportunities for nonstate criminal groups to supplant the state.

In Jamaica, this method has been mainstreamed in the infrastructure works of the projects through the training of the architects, engineers, and other technical staff. It includes the planning and installation of social infrastructure such as community centers, playing fields, public lighting, and zinc fence removal and installation of safe alternatives. The experience of the Jamaica Social Investment Fund's (JSIF) Inner City Community Services Project for the Poor calls attention to the importance of upgrading the physical environment in partnership with community, and incorporating crime and violence prevention through social development efforts with built environment projects that provide increased access and improve the quality of water, sanitation, solid waste collection systems, electricity, roads, drainage, and related community infrastructure. The social interventions have played a key role in building community capacity to organize against community violence, providing the necessary safety conditions for the physical infrastructure projects.

JSIF has worked to remove zinc fencing, a major hazard to public safety, and reduce the stigma associated with the fences and these impoverished communities. The construction of new, appealing, but shorter fences, according to residents, will lead to "better visibility and less hassle" for the police when carrying out their duties in the community, and enhance natural surveillance because "man can't hide behind your fence again. People can get to see then when they are hiding."

The project involved residents with the goal of fostering active community engagement, supporting positive social interaction, enhancing social cohesion, and building a strong sense of community, which in turn could affect the motives that cause crime in the first place. Unused public spaces are now sports fields where unattached youth can engage in positive activities and be recruited for prevention efforts ("Jamaica Social Investment Fund, Inner City Basic Services Project," August 2009).

COMMUNITY-DRIVEN SOCIAL DEVELOPMENT APPROACH

The community-driven social development approach focuses on rebuilding social cohesion in informal and formal institutions using small, participatory, and demand-driven projects that aim to create trust by building on the strengths and assets of poor communities affected by violence. Building on research that shows relationships between high levels of social capital and good outcomes for youth, this approach has been used most frequently in gang violence and domestic violence prevention efforts. Community-driven social development approaches are useful in targeted violence prevention efforts. They can broaden the focus to address broader community change and community building efforts. Based on bottom-up, participatory processes, it aims to create trust by building on the community's own identification of its needs and associated institutions. This approach has been adopted by nongovernmental agencies and scaled up by government programs all over the world.

In the United States, the experiences of largely resident-led community coalitions employing a community-driven social development approach to violence prevention in their communities can be used to illustrate the breadth of this approach, depending on local contexts, assets, and needs (ICP 2005). In New Orleans, the coalition rejected the emphasis on violence prevention and instead became the Crescent City Peace Alliance, which prioritized the peaceful outcomes that they were seeking. In Spartanburg, South Carolina, the Stop the Violence collaborative focused on the violence in some of their poorest communities by working to improve housing conditions. In Santa Barbara, the Pro Youth Coalition worked directly on gang violence, and engaged the gang-involved youths as part of the solution, to create positive settings for other youth. The resulting citywide programs included successful efforts to mediate a gang truce, the development of programs for youth in and outside of schools, the involvement of former gang members in gang prevention programs, parenting support, and education in engaging democratic structures.

Flint, Michigan, was developing a national reputation for violence that its disconnected residents felt unable to address. Concerned about the state of their community, young people in Flint embarked upon a Photovoice Project in which they photographed aspects of their communities that they wanted to change, proposed policy changes to address them, and presented the document to the city council, which enacted several of the suggested policies. Flint's Neighborhood Violence Prevention Collaborative gave rise to a community gardening initiative that physically transformed many areas of the city; exposed residents to racial diversity training that helped to address hostilities that led to violence; spawned a number of citizen groups to organize and build community, and began the slow transformation of Flint. In the words of Flint Community Police Officer Twanda Plair who patrols the area "I just walked by with my mouth wide open . . . for so long this neighborhood has been known as a downfall area, a violent area. This park has put a breath of excitement, motivation [into the community]. I've never seen beautification like this."

YOUTH DEVELOPMENT APPROACHES

Youth development approaches focus on strengthening the ongoing growth process in which all youth are engaged in attempting to (1) meet their basic personal and social needs to be safe, feel cared for, be valued, be useful, and be spiritually grounded, and (2) to build skills and competencies that allow them to function and contribute in their daily lives (National Research Council and Institute of Medicine 2002). Providing social and emotional supports to meet children's developmental needs has been found to make a difference in neighborhood youth violence and crime. Youths who participate in recreation and constructively use their leisure time are more likely to do well in school and to have high self-esteem and good social skills. These personal qualities have in turn been associated with a lower likelihood of involvement in criminal activity (Waller and Weiler 1984). A set of personal and social assets increases the healthy development and well-being of adolescents and facilitates a successful transition from childhood, through adolescence, and into adulthood. These factors and assets fit into eight categories: support, empowerment, boundaries and expectations, constructive use of time, commitment to learning, positive values, social competencies, and positive identity (National Research Council and Institute of Medicine 2002).

Youth development approaches exist in a variety of different places and forms, and under all sorts of different names. One advantage of youth development is that it is a flexible, holistic approach and can be implemented in a variety of settings. The approach balances efforts to prevent the engagement of young people in violent activities by providing them with a positive and meaningful role to fill in their communities and the larger society; and advocates for policies and programs that work toward the inclusion and involvement of youth in civic actions, rather than their containment or appeasement. Within a youth development framework, adolescents are seen as able to contribute to their community and participate in decision making, not just as clients or recipients of services. A youth development approach emphasizes opportunities for children and young people to participate in challenging and engaging activities that build their skills and competencies. For instance, youth development principles and approaches can inform services in such areas as education, health, juvenile justice, youth livelihood development (employment preparation and entrepreneurship, as well as enterprise creation and development), and others that exhibit the following: (1) relevant instruction and information; (2) challenging opportunities to express oneself, contribute, take on new roles, and be part of a group; and (3) supportive adults and peers who provide respect, high standards and expectations, guidance, and affirmation to young people. Some examples of this approach include a city government that engages youth in the policy making process through youth councils and youth positions in government departments, youth leadership programs run by local community organizations, or part of conflict-transformation programs in postconflict settings.

The YouthBuild case study in this book (see chapter 12) illustrates how youth development, urban upgrading, and community development approaches, in partnership with private and public sectors, are making a contribution to the reduction of youth, criminal, and political violence. These programs rebuild communities while building leadership, positive youth development, and resilience in at-risk youth. In the words of a graduate, YouthBuild

introduced me to a life of positive transformation, self accountability, and leadership. They offered me resources with the only cost of bettering myself. I participated full-time and earned my GED, while I learned job skills by building affordable housing for homeless and low income people while they offered me personal counseling, positive role models, a safe environment, and leadership skills. I even earned an AmeriCorps education award. They offered me resources that jails and probation officers never did. They offered me a key to open a door to a new road. A road that would forever change my life. Because of that key they offered me, I became an activist. Because of that key, I have developed a passion for community work and helped numerous people in diverse and challenging communities. That opportunity that is rarely given to people was given to me and has enabled me to become an expert in the field of Youth Development, Leadership Development, and Community Organizing and has allowed me to train others across this nation. That opportunity and handing of resources has given me congressional recognition by Hilda Solis and recognition from the city of Los Angeles. That recognition has even given me the opportunity to fly to Israel and devote my time to try and build peace amongst Israeli and Palestinian Youth. Imagine that; an ex gang member, drug addict and ex criminal that now offers his life and time to serve for the cause of peace and the people. I want you to imagine for a minute that me, the person that stands in front of you today, was never given that key for transformation. What would have I become? A long term prisoner, a wanted felon or just another city and national statistic. (Stoneman 2009)

CITIZEN SECURITY INITIATIVES

Another example of cross-sectoral initiatives are citizen security initiatives as developed by several countries in the Caribbean and Latin America—often with the support of the Inter-American Development Bank (IADB). Citizen security initiatives are epidemiological in nature in the sense that different risk factors are assessed and factored into an integrated risk management approach that relies on contributions from many departments and many sectors—health, education, family welfare, urban infrastructure, law enforcement, justice sector reform, police reform, and the media. Increasingly, bottom-up community-driven social development approaches are being incorporated into the citizen security programs. Building citizenship, substantive democracy, and democratization calls for an engagement of the community and all stakeholders—that is, youth, civil society, neighborhoods, the business sector, opinion leaders, government at all levels, the media, police, and law enforcement. This approach rests on the belief that violence is often a learned behavior, thereby positioning domestic violence as a precursor of violent behavior in the street. In many cases, IADB projects address issues or aspects of youth violence as well as child maltreatment and domestic violence, which can condition young people for violent behavior.

In Bogota, Colombia, a combination of strategies was implemented involving multiple sectors. Improvements in the criminal justice system were accompanied by improvements and reforms of social welfare systems. The violence mitigation and prevention work included developing strong community-police partnerships at the neighborhood level, helping to rebuild trust, developing a culture of citizenship, implementing citizen campaigns on disarmament, restricting alcohol sales, establishing family police stations for family violence prevention, professionalizing the police, investing in social services and urban upgrades in homicide hot-spots, and allocating municipal resources to the most economically disadvantaged. Under the strong leadership of the municipality, homicide rates fell from 80 to 28 per 100,000 people in 1993–2002, accidents were reduced by half, and police arrest rates increased by 400 percent without an increase in the force.

In Trinidad and Tobago the focus of the Citizen Security Programme (CSP) is on five priority areas, including youth firearm-related violence, juvenile delinquency, child maltreatment, domestic violence, and crimes against visitors. It contributes to the reduction of crime and violence at a community level by addressing the most proximal and modifiable risk factors. In particular, the program has three components: (1) the reduction of crime and violence through community-led collaborative initiatives with a focus on "high-needs" youth within partner communities; (2) capacity building within the Trinidad and Tobago Police Service (TTPS), focusing on their Policing for People initiative; and (3) capacity building within the Ministry of National Security in the area of evidence-based policy development.

These CSP efforts initially were supported by the IADB, which was the first development bank in 1998 to systematically lend for programs explicitly designed to address the underlying causes of youth violence. The IADB justified the funding of these efforts based on the economic and social benefits of investments in reducing violence. Citizen security efforts are national or municipally led and combine the public health approach. Investments in criminal justice systems reform crime prevention through environmental design, state capacity-building, and community-driven development.

INTEGRATING POLICY APPROACHES

Although policy approaches have been discussed as separate "ideal types," in reality they overlap, often combining traditional with more innovative perspectives. In fact, a cross-sectoral or integrated intervention framework is increasingly recognized as essential. The success of violence prevention efforts depends substantially on identifying the mix of policy solutions that can address the complexity of youth violence in local contexts, with a focus on selecting short-, medium-, and long-term strategies, and encouraging cooperation and coordination across sectors, whether at the grassroots, state, national, or international level.

Since the approval of the United Nations technical guidelines on crime prevention in 1997 and the adoption of the Economic and Social Council (ECO-SOC) resolution in 2002, countries and cities have been able to refer to norms and standards for the development of crime prevention strategies and policies (United Nations 2006). The guidelines contained in the resolution set out the basic principles for such policies, including the importance of the following:

1. Government leadership at all levels is required to create and maintain an institutional framework for effective crime prevention;
2. Socioeconomic development and inclusion refer to the need to integrate crime prevention into relevant social and economic policies, and focus on the social integration of at risk communities, children, families and youth;

3. Cooperation and partnerships between government ministries and authorities, civil society organizations, business sector, and private citizens are required, given the wide-ranging nature of the causes of crime and the skills and responsibilities required to address them;
4. Sustainability and accountability can only be achieved if adequate resources to establish and sustain programs and evaluation are made available, and clear accountability for funding, implementation, evaluation, and achievement of planned results is established;
5. Use of knowledge-based strategies, policies, and programs need to be based on a broad multidisciplinary foundation of knowledge and evidence about crime problems, their causes, and proven practices;
6. Human rights and a culture of lawfulness, including the rule of law and those human rights that are recognized in international instruments to which member states are parties, must be respected in all aspects of crime prevention, and a culture of lawfulness actively promoted;
7. Interdependency refers to the need for national crime prevention diagnoses and strategies that take into account, where appropriate, the links between local criminal problems and international organized crime; and
8. Differentiation calls for prevention strategies to pay due regard to the different needs of men and women and consider the special needs of vulnerable members of society.

The United Nations guidelines contained in ECOSOC resolution 2002/13 also provide a basis for the development of effective strategies for responding to youth violence and at-risk youth, including the following:

- Inclusive approaches which reduce youth marginalization;
- Participatory approaches;
- Integrated multisectoral strategies;
- Balanced strategies that include early intervention, social and education programs, restorative approaches, and crime control;
- Targeted and tailored strategies and programs to meet the needs of specific at-risk groups; and
- Approaches that respect the rights of children and young people.

There is clear evidence that carefully balanced and well-planned youth violence prevention policies not only prevent crime and victimization, but also promote broader community safety and contribute to sustainable development of countries. Effective, responsible youth violence prevention enhances the quality of life of all citizens. It has long-term benefits in terms of reducing the costs associated with the formal criminal justice system, as well as other social costs that result from violence. The world has learned a lot about preventing violence by and against youth even as many gaps in our understanding still exist. As many of the examples cited in this book, and myriad others exemplify, we cannot afford to wait until we have a complete understanding of the problems or perfect solutions.

Despite increased understanding of the role of youth violence and growing knowledge about how to tackle it and greater focus on developing comprehensive approaches in almost all developing and industrial countries, youth violence prevention efforts typically are fragmented and characterized by weak national planning and low political status. In addition, because of the lack of coordinated national youth policy and the absence of an organized constituency on behalf of youth policy, many countries have not established a precedent for working across sectors to develop a coherent, holistic, and intersectoral strategy, with clear priorities and measures for concrete action on behalf of youth. Youth issues are subsumed under a child welfare, family, or women's national policy agenda, or under sectoral ministries (such as health, education, sports, and culture). Without a coordinated national youth policy, along with effective structures to ensure that young people fully participate in national and community life, their particular needs are likely to remain unmet.

To apply these emerging practices, we must work together as a community in which it is safe to share project failures and build off each other's experiences and acquired knowledge, thereby facilitating the identification and evolution of best practices. This requires integrating efforts across government agencies and ministries, which can be difficult, and actively engaging civil society, community members, and especially youth in this work. The increasingly borderless nature of the problems that give rise to youth violence around the world require us to expand the search for solutions and to look for inspiration and great ideas in places around the globe (Van Soest 1997). As global citizens and advocates for youth, we must put valuable knowledge accumulated to date about violence prevention and positive youth development to use, expand our global consciousness, advocate for youth, and act now to improve the life chances for youth everywhere.

REFERENCES

Aos, S. 2009. "Return on (Taxpayer) Investment: Evidence-Based Prevention and Intervention—Initial Report to the Legislature on Study Design." Washington State Institute on Public Policy.

Bloomfield, D., M. Fischer, and B. Schmelzle, eds. 2006. *Social Change and Conflict Transformation (Berghof Handbook Dialogue No. 5)*. Berlin: Berghof Research Center. www.berghof-handbook.net/uploads/download/dialogue5_sochange_complete.pdf.

ICP (Institute for Community Peace). 2005. *Ten Years of Community Peace*. Washington, DC.

"Jamaica Social Investment Fund, Inner City Basic Services Project." August 2009. *ICBSP Newsletter* 2 (1). http://www.jsif.org/docsAttach/Vol_2_Iss_%20ICBSP%20 Newsletter.pdf

Lederach, J. P. 2005. *The Moral Imagination. The Art and Soul of Building Peace*. Oxford, New York: Oxford University Press.

Mitchell, C. 2002. "Beyond Resolution: What Does Conflict Transformation Actually Transform?" *Peace and Conflict Studies* 9 (1). www.gmu.edu/academic/pcs/CM83PCS.htm.

Moser C. 2006. "Reducing Violence in Developing Countries." Brookings Policy Brief 2006–01. Washington, DC: Brookings Institution..

Moser, C., and A. Winton, A. 2002. "Violence in the Central American Region: Towards an Integrated Framework for Violence Reduction," Working Paper No. 171, Overseas Development Institute, London.

Moser, C., A. Winton, and A. Moser. 2005. "Violence, Fear, and Insecurity among the Urban Poor in Latin America." In *The Urban Poor in Latin America,* ed. M. Fay. Washington, DC: World Bank.

National Research Council and Institute of Medicine. 2002. *Community Programs to Promote Youth Development.* Washington, DC: National Academy Press.

Stoneman, Dorothy. 2009. "The YouthBuild Program as an Example of What Works for Out-of-School Unemployed Low Income Youth." Statement of Dorothy Stoneman, President and Founder of YouthBuild USA before the U.S. House of Representatives Education and Labor Committee Hearing on *Ensuring Economic Opportunity for Young Americans* October 1, 2009.

United Nations. 2006. *Compendium of United Nations Standards and Norms in Crime Prevention and Criminal Justice.* New York: United Nations.

Van Soest, D. 1997. *The Global Crisis of Violence: Common Problems, Universal Causes, Shared Solutions.* Washington, DC: NASW Press.

Waller, I., and D. Weiler. 1984. "Crime Prevention through Social Development." Canadian Council on Social Development, Ottawa.

World Bank. 2007. *World Development Report 2007.* Washington, DC: World Bank.

PART II

Single-Sector Interventions

5

Addressing Aggression in Singapore Youths: An Evidence-Based Case Example

Daniel Shuen-Sheng Fung, Yoon Phaik Ooi, and Rebecca P. Ang

INTRODUCTION

SINGAPORE IS SMALL with a land area of just 710.2 square kilometers. It was established as a British colony in 1819. In 1963, it separated from Malaysia and became an independent state two years later. Its nearly 5 million inhabitants are made up largely of descendents of immigrants from the Malay Peninsula, China, and the Indian subcontinent. Singapore was ranked 20th in the world in per capita gross domestic product (GDP) in 2008 and sixth in the world in the physical health of its citizens in 2000 (Tan et al. 2008). The leading causes of morbidity and mortality in the adult population are major noncommunicable diseases, such as cancer and ischemic heart disease (Ministry of Health 2009). Among its young people, accidents and suicides are the main causes of death (Singapore Department of Statistics 2008). Workers are required by law to set aside 6.5 to 9 percent of their income into their personal health savings (Medisave), part of which forms the basic health insurance for catastrophic illnesses (Medishield). The poor have access to basic health services paid for by the government (Medifund). Social challenges facing the country in the 21st century include the low fertility rate of its citizens, one of the lowest in the world, and an aging population (Asher and Nandy 2008), as well as a growing divorce rate (Singapore Department of Statistics 2008).

YOUTH VIOLENCE IN SINGAPORE

Singapore has one of the lowest rates of youth homicide in the world (Krug et al. 2002) Gun injury and violence is rare because of the country's strict gun control laws. Drug-related violence is also rare because of strict laws and harsh punishments related to the sale of illicit drugs. Gang violence is also uncommon due to the high degree of parental supervision and monitoring and the relative affluence of the population (Singapore Police Force 2010). Youth gang activity is focused mainly on shoplifting, school fights, and, more recently, loan shark's use of young persons to collect payment on loans (Ministry of Community Development, Youth, and Sports 2009).

Suicide is the most frequent and pressing form of youth violence. In 2006, 20 young people between the ages of 5 and 24 committed suicide (WHO 2006). Cultural norms in Asian countries and in Singapore dictate that anger be internalized, which can result in self-directed violent acts. Although suicide for the general population is not unusually high relative to other countries, Singapore had one of the highest suicide rates in the world among youths age 14 and younger at the start of the 21st century (WHO 2006).

Bullying is another but less frequent concern. Because a high percentage of youths from Singapore are Internet connected with a majority of high school adolescents spending up to 26 hours a week online, cyber bullying has been identified as a growing problem. Unlike other countries, dating violence is thought to be less of a concern in Singapore, because children do not begin dating relationships as early as they do in other cultures. Instead they tend to socialize in groups until college, and these relationships are closely monitored by families.

According to a survey of 2,400 youths conducted by the Ministry of Education (MOE), 5 percent of children in Singapore schools exhibit evidence of externalizing disorder (nonnormative aggression, hostility, antisocial behavior toward others) based on the Child Behavior Checklist (Woo et al. 2007). Disruptive disorders are the most common reason for referral to child mental health services and referrals continue to show a rising trend (Lee, Fung, Cai, and Teo 2003).

RESPONDING TO YOUTH VIOLENCE IN SINGAPORE

Responses to youth violence in Singapore primarily are located in a single sector. Violent behaviors among younger children are framed as mental health issues and referred to the mental health system. Older children involved in criminal activities are referred to a juvenile justice system.

The juvenile court system deals with issues, including juvenile delinquency and instances in which a parent has been unable to control a youth's behavior. Young people may be admitted to juvenile detention facilities, but recently the system has begun to emphasize community-based rehabilitation as an alternative to incarceration. Although Singapore has capital punishment and extremely harsh punishments for certain crimes, in apparent contradiction to this, the system also emphasizes rehabilitation. For youth, the focus is more on rehabilitation than punishment. The goal is to create a second opportunity in life. For example, in the high publicity case of the American youth Michael P. Fay sentenced in 1994 to caning for vandalism, the entire story was not told. The punishment would have been followed by rehabilitation and a process of restorative justice that teaches basic life skills to juveniles and reintegrates them back to their families and the community (The Subordinate Courts of Singapore 2009).

The nation's system of Child Guidance Centers (CGCs) provides inpatient and outpatient mental health services for children. Originally called child psychiatric clinics, the name was changed to reduce the stigma associated with seeking mental health services. The education sector also provides resources to address risk for violence, and schools provide prevention and early detection and referral services. The education system is centralized, with approximately 400 mainstream schools and 20 special schools. The Ministry of Education oversees all 420 elementary and secondary schools in the country and thus is able to implement interventions capable of affecting the entire country. For example, the MOE initiated a number of programs that reduced secondary school drop out from 3.2 percent in 2003 to 1.6 percent in 2007. Singapore implemented a National Mental Health Blueprint to implement a comprehensive mental health program for mental health disorders. The blueprint for children and adolescents emphasizes schools as the basis for preventative and interventive services. Every school is provided with a full-time school counselor. Responding to high rates of youth suicide in the country, the MOE implemented a program to systematically educate teachers across the country about suicide risk and provide a referral system for teachers to use when even a minor concern is raised about a child's potential for self-harm.

Recently, the government has recognized the need for multisectoral interventions that introduce collaboration across multiple sectors similar to what has taken place for child protection and family violence. Over the last few years, the Ministry of Community Development, Youth, and Sports has worked closely with schools, the voluntary welfare sector, the courts, and police to establish relevant programs and services to address issues of juvenile delinquency and dysfunctional families (Ministry of Community Development, Youth, and Sports 2010).

A particular challenge is the lack of intervention programs designed for Asian youth. Cavell and Hughes (2000) highlight the fact that most violence intervention programs have been developed for Western Hemisphere cultures, and have not been validated with children and families for Asian cultures. They suggest the effects found in mainly North American children may not generalize to Asian children. Likewise, researchers in Asia have identified a critical need to develop and specifically examine the effectiveness of such programs with populations for which these programs will be used (Oei 1998).

THE REACH PROGRAM: COLLABORATION BETWEEN THE CHILD GUIDANCE CLINIC AND THE MINISTRY OF EDUCATION

In 2007, the Child Guidance Clinic and the MOE collaborated to form a community mental health pilot program called "Response, Early Intervention and Assessment in Community Mental Health for Students" (REACH). The key aims were to train and support school counselors in the early identification and support of children with behavioral and emotional difficulties. The program will be expanded to all primary and secondary schools, and junior colleges and centralized institutes by 2011.

REACH was designed to reduce the stigma associated with seeking mental health services, and families consider it an acceptable way to seek help when needed because their children are seen by professionals in the school settings (that is, school counselors) rather than someone from the mental health centers (for example, psychologists or psychiatrists). Families are not so open to having their child see professionals from the mental health centers because of the stigma of seeing a psychologist or a psychiatrist and the fear of finding out the severity of their child's problems.

Therefore, to reduce the stigma associated with seeking mental health services, community health teams are established in each school. Using the school counselor as the nexus for transmitting expertise, school teachers and staff are taught skills in identifying and managing problems early. At the same time, a network of family doctors and social services agencies within the school's vicinity are engaged in similar fashion, forming a network of community support for students and their families.

The REACH team, working closely with each school, identifies youth at risk for behavioral and emotional disturbance, including violence, and works to get these young people and their families into services before the emerging problems become severe. REACH also works to reduce school dropout and forms partnerships with local nongovernmental organizations (NGOs) to identify and respond to indicators of behavioral and emotional problems. REACH provides training on mental health issues to NGOs on risk indicators and assists them in developing services for these youth.

REACH uses a variety of tools and resources that originally were designed for use in tertiary child psychiatric settings and then modified these tools for use in the community. One of these examples was a Social Problem-Solving Skills Training (SPSST) intervention program (Ang and Ooi 2003a, 2003b) developed for use with Asian aggressive children and youth. The language, analogies, and examples have been tailored specifically for use with Asian children and youth. The SPSST intervention program consists of nine lessons that aim to teach aggressive youth and children a variety of coping skills that are helpful in anger control, conflict management, and problem-solving. The SPSST intervention program was built on a cognitive-behavioral framework that aims to address the various cognitive-behavioral difficulties manifested by aggressive youth and children (Crick and Dodge 1994).

CASE STUDY: INTEGRATING CARE IN THE COMMUNITY

CM was a 15-year-old boy, the eldest of two siblings. His father, age 55, was unemployed and his mother, age 46, was working as a cook. At home, parents felt that CM was obedient and kept a good relationship with them. He also got along well with his nine-year-old brother. Father gave a history that CM was bullied in class. CM was frequently late for school in the mornings and he informed the school counselor that it was due to conflicts with his father in the mornings before leaving for school.

CM was referred to the REACH Community team by the school counselor for frequent anger outbursts and fights in school. These fights involved the use of knives, and CM also would destroy tables and chairs in his fits of rage. CM's family was from a low socioeconomic status. CM easily was provoked by others over trivial incidents, comments, or criticism and such disruptive behavior had started one year earlier. He broke school rules by defying dress and grooming requirements. It was reported that CM had joined a youth gang that primarily engaged in shoplifting. He often was moody and claimed that he was worried about his friend's problems with teen gangs. Figure 5.1 provides a formulation of CM's aggressive behaviors.

The school had provided counseling and administered consequences such as caning, public apology, and suspension. During counseling, CM argued and blamed others for his misconduct. CM indicated that he could listen to teachers he liked but he would deny responsibilities. He shared with the counselor, "Society is unfair; I will manage it." CM often stayed out at night despite prohibitions by his parents. His father felt helpless and sought assessment by REACH.

Once when scolded by his father, CM had stomped out of the room and smashed a water cooler because he felt he "lost face," which is an important cultural value in Singapore. Another time his teacher asked that he keep his cell

Figure 5.1   Explanation of CM's Behaviors

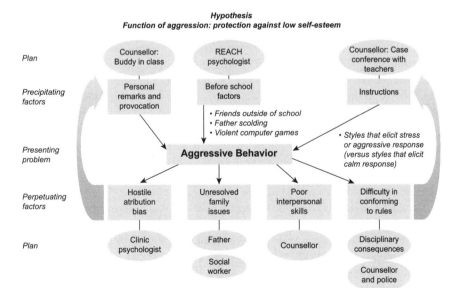

phone in his pocket. He did not comply because he did not have a pocket. The teacher called him a "stupid idiot," so he broke a mirror. He sometimes got into fights when others made insulting comments about his family, and he felt obligated to protect his family name.

With parental consent for accessing information, REACH noted that CM had been registered with CGC, although he had not attended previous appointments. Upon the doctor's review in the clinic, the team noted that CM exhibited traits of conduct and emotional disorders and would benefit from behavior management in school. The team shared its formulation of CM with the school counselor and conducted a behavior analysis to assist the latter in developing the school management plan, involving appropriate staff and students to help CM. REACH also provided individual therapy for the student and offered family counseling should the needs arise for CM. The school counselor remained the case manager for CM and collaborated with the various parties involved in the interventions.

At the six-month review of CM, the school counselor reported a moderate improvement over the referred problems and that CM was behaving much better in school.

EVALUATION OF EFFECTIVENESS

A preliminary study was conducted of the effectiveness of REACH for children with aggression. The review evaluated a total of 67 children ages 8 to 19 (mean = 11.27, Std. Dev. = 3.09) from an ambulatory child psychiatric clinic ($n = 25$) who did not participate in REACH and from a community sample ($n = 42$) who did participate in REACH.

Children in the community group showed improvements on aggressive behavior following treatment, whereas children from the clinic did not improve. Figure 5.2 shows the changes in aggression scores at pre- and post-treatment. The community-based program also showed improvements on social problems, attention problems, rule-breaking behavior, and externalizing problems, although not all were statistically significant (Figure 5.3). Limitations to this study include the fact that the community sample was older and had a mixture of different diagnoses, although the majority was suffering from attention deficit disorder and hyperactivity disorder (ADHD). The children from the clinic-based program were more likely to have severe aggression problems and may underestimate the effectiveness of the SPSST program in the clinic. The duration of treatment was also not comparable as the clinical sample was assessed immediately after treatment while the community sample was assessed over a six-month period.

Next steps will include expansion of REACH to all 400 primary and secondary schools in Singapore. A parallel program addressing the needs of young persons who have dropped out of school is under development. A forensic child mental health program to evaluate juvenile delinquents and divert those with mental health issues away from the juvenile justice system is in the planning stage.

Figure 5.2   Changes in Mean Scores for Aggressive Behavior

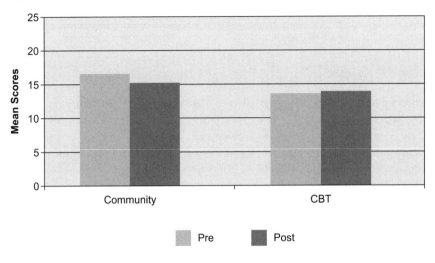

Figure 5.3   Changes in Mean Scores in the Community Sample

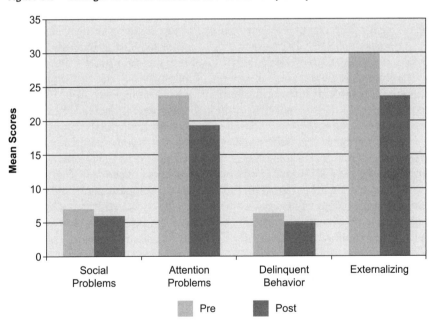

Finally, Singapore is supporting behavioral health and health services research to better understand the causal factors and evidence-based practices for managing violent children in high-density, high-stress societies such as Singapore.

LESSONS LEARNED

The implementation of the REACH program helped to dramatically reduce the stigma of seeking mental health services in addition to greater treatment adherence. Because youths with aggression problems are managed by trained counselors in the school or community setting, families are more open to having them be supported. These youths are able to make appointments to see the school counselor during school hours, which makes mental health services easily available and accessible and, therefore, helps to improve treatment adherence.

The multidisciplinary community team is a challenging one to maintain and one key issue is retention of staff and providing ongoing training. The work of the REACH team can be rather demanding as it involves providing support to school counselors and families beyond regular school hours and beyond the school setting (for example, conducting home visits). As a result, the risk of burnout and staff turnover rate is high. One approach to addressing burnout and retention of staff is to have a supportive working environment, and this has been achieved by having regular meetings to enable staff to share the difficulties encountered when managing a case. Staff are given regular supervision, and annual training retreats also have been implemented.

Because the REACH program is new in Singapore, it is important for the REACH team to receive the appropriate training to provide mental health services in the community. As such, collaboration with other countries and regions can be a useful source of training for the team. A multidisciplinary team currently is participating in a training fellowship in Canada to learn how teams function together while doing this challenging community work.

As the program begins to produce outcomes, it is important that such outcomes are shared in a whole-of-government approach. This will bring together the diverse expertise of both government and nongovernment agencies working with youth and their families. This process, though complex, may yield positive social results that go beyond reducing violence in the young. It is our hope that the national collaborative framework will strengthen family ties, increase social support, and improve the emotional well-being of youth in Singapore.

REFERENCES

Ang, R., and Y. P. Ooi. 2003a. *Activity Workbook. Helping Angry Children and Youth: Strategies That Work.* Singapore: Armour Publishing.

Ang, R., and Y. P. Ooi. 2003b. *Training Manual. Helping Angry Children and Youth: Strategies That Work.* Singapore: Armour Publishing.

Asher, M., and A. Nandy. 2008. *Managing Prolonged Low Fertility: The Case of Singapore*. Singapore: ADB Institute.

Cavell, T. A., and J. N. Hughes. 2000. "Secondary Prevention as Context for Assessing Change Processes in Aggressive Children." *Journal of School Psychology* 38: 199–235.

Crick, N. R., and Dodge, K. A. 1994. "A Review and Reformulation of Social Information Processing Mechanisms in Children's Social Adjustment." *Psychological Bulletin* 115: 74–101.

Krug, E. G., L. L. Dahlberg, J. A. Mercy, A. B. Zwi, and R. Lozano. 2002. *World Report on Violence and Health*. Geneva: World Health Organization.

Lee, N. B. C., D. S. S. Fung, Y. Cai, and J. Teo. 2003. "A Five-Year Review of Adolescent Mental Health Usage in Singapore." *Annals Academy of Medicine, Singapore* 32 (1): 7–11.

Ministry of Community Development, Youth, and Sports. 2009. "Singapore's Second and Third Periodic Report to the United Nations Committee on the Rights of the Child." http://app.mcys.gov.sg/web/indv_uncrc.asp (accessed January 15, 2010).

Ministry of Community Development, Youth, and Sports. 2010. "Press Releases." http://app.mcys.gov.sg/web/corp_press.asp (accessed April 18, 2010).

Ministry of Health. 2009. "Health Facts Singapore." http://www.moh.gov.sg/mohcorp/statistics.aspx?id=240 (accessed January 16, 2010).

Oei, T. P., ed. 1998. *Behaviour Therapy and Cognitive Behaviour Therapy in Asia*. New South Wales, Australia: Edumedia.

Phua, H. P., A. V. L. Chua, S. Ma, D. Heng, and S. K. Chew. 2009. "Singapore's Burden of Disease and Injury 2004." *Singapore Medical Journal* 50 (5): 468–478.

Singapore Department of Statistics. 2008. *Yearbook of Statistics Singapore*. Singapore: Ministry of Trade and Industry.

Singapore Police Force. 2010. "Crime Situation 2009." http://www.spf.gov.sg/stats/stats2009_intro.htm (accessed April 18, 2010).

The Subordinate Courts of Singapore. 2009. "Introduction to Restorative Programs." http://app.subcourts.gov.sg/juvenile/page.aspx?pageid=3860 (accessed April 18, 2010).

Tan S., D.S.S. Fung, S.F. Hung, and J. Rey. 2008. "Growing Wealth and Growing Pains: Child and Adolescent Psychiatry in Hong Kong, Malaysia and Singapore." *Australasian Psychiatry* 2008: 1 – 6

World Health Organization. 2006. "Suicide Rates (per 100,000), by Gender, Singapore, 1960–2006." http://www.who.int/mental_health/media/sing.pdf (accessed April 14, 2010).

Woo, B.C., T.P. Ng, D.S. Fung, Y.H. Chan, Y.P. Lee, J.B.K. Koh, et al. 2007. "Emotional and Behavioral Problems in Singaporean Children Based on Parent, Teacher and Child Reports." *Singapore Medical Journal* 48 (12): 1100–1106.

The CeaseFire Method Applied to Iraq: Changing Thinking and Reducing Violence

Gary Slutkin, Zainab al-Suwaij, Karen Volker, R. Brent Decker, and Josh Gryniewicz

Basrah, Iraq. It is a sweltering 118 degree day. Under normal circumstances, such scorching heat might be enough to fray even the steadiest of nerves—and the situation in war-torn Iraq is far from normal. Electricity is available two hours for every four, leaving a brief window in which to cool a home. Armed with a loaded shotgun a man furiously strides across a back alleyway to confront his neighbor. He is following a thick black cable running across the yards, proof that the neighbor is a "thief" who has been siphoning electricity from his family's generator.

WHEN VIOLENCE HAS been normalized to a great degree, small incidents like this can flare up in instant, costing lives, and sometimes escalating into large-scale family disputes. The Basrah Anti-Violence Campaign (BAVC) a collaboration between CeaseFire, a public health violence reduction model and the American Islamic Congress (AIC), intervenes in situations of community conflict (youth violence, car and motorbike accidents, bad business transactions, and tribal conflicts) before they result in bloodshed. Outreach staff in Basrah, like their Chicago-based counterparts, focus primarily on personal clashes intervening in issues between people before they deteriorate into larger group conflicts. These conflicts often incorporate tribal affiliations, which can start from a community problem, but grow out of longstanding rivalries between competing tribal groups, as well as family violence between in-laws in different tribes.

In the situation involving the generator, the mediator was able to get the neighbors talking, before the gun was used. The neighbor responsible for the theft complained that the generator was a loud, noisy machine and that the generator-owner had allowed other neighbors access to the electricity to compensate. He felt slighted that he had not been offered the same deal, he explained. The mediator helped both parties reach a peaceful resolution not only by seeing one another's point of view—which would have been impossible without intervention—but also by emphasizing the situation was not worth a life. CeaseFire maintains that regardless of the circumstances or cultural context the use of violence in the presence of a grievance can always be prevented if an interrupting intervention can be applied. By being aware of the persons and groups involved, those at the highest risk of being a perpetrator or a victim of violence, conflicts can be effectively mediated and efforts can be advanced to change the norms and social pressure that otherwise reinforce violence.

THE CEASEFIRE MODEL

CeaseFire is a "disruptive" innovation because it ideologically challenges the prevailing paradigms around the causes of violence and how it should be addressed. The CeaseFire model draws on key components of a disease-control methodology that are applied to violence. It is based on the understanding that violence is a learned behavior and that it behaves like an infectious disease. Research indicates that violence, like other behaviors, is acquired or learned—mainly through modeling, observing, imitating, or copying. We learn socially from those around us how to act, what to do, and what is expected of us. After the age of 10, these behaviors become unconsciously "regulated" not by family, but by peers. Social norms, the expectations of an immediate peer group, are the greatest indicator to predict how an individual will respond to a given situation, including whether or not they will react violently when "feeling" threatened, insulted, or wronged. Furthermore, the greatest predictors of violent "events," regardless of the specific political, religious, social, or economic motivations for violence or how it manifests (tribal conflict, militia warfare, street gangs), are prior events. Just as nothing predicts a case of influenza as accurately as exposure to a prior active case of influenza, nothing predicts a violent act as accurately as a preceding violent act—committed against you, someone close to you, or to your group. Accordingly, CeaseFire's successful approach to street violence focuses directly on those young people who are at the highest risk for initiating violence or being a victim of it, intervenes in conflicts likely to result in violence and then more violence, promotes and trains in nonviolent alternatives to conflict, insults, or events, and ultimately shifts community norms.

CeaseFire's clients usually are beyond the reach of conventional services and without effective intervention their next encounters with the system are likely to be law enforcement or prison, the emergency room, or the grave. The CeaseFire model approaches violence as an epidemic, and like all epidemics, it must (1) detect and interrupt all potential transmission, (2) determine who might transmit next, and likewise reverse the transmission potential (for violence, the thinking that violence is expected of them by their peers), and (3) change community norms. Violence interrupters keep the pulse of the community and are trained to be able to detect who has a grievance and might be thinking about or planning a violent event, and because of who is selected (persons from the same in-group) and how they are trained, they can intervene effectively to prevent the event from happening. This is not about law enforcement (or "snitching"), but rather the use of confidential health-based intervention methods for changing thinking. For the second part of the CeaseFire disease-control system, CeaseFire uses outreach workers, each of whom carries a caseload of 15 to 20 of the highest risk clients—person from the highest risk groups and situations who may not be planning events right now, but can be determined to be at risk in the next few weeks or months. The outreach workers engage with them to change their thinking about violence, as well as changing their level of risk for violence by redirecting them toward more positive paths. The third part of the CeaseFire system is work at community level to change overall norms of the community. This component includes motivating community-level responses to all violent events, involvement of the clergy and residents in specific actions, and a public education campaign to change the thinking. More detailed information about the intervention model in action is provided in the next sections.

BRINGING THE CEASEFIRE PROGRAM TO IRAQ

By 2005, Chicago's CeaseFire efforts already were reducing shootings and killings in highly affected communities in the United States, and cities from around the country, as well as internationally were beginning to visit Chicago to see how the new method worked. In June 2005, First Lady Laura Bush visited CeaseFire's Chicago project as part of the White House's Helping America's Youth (HAY) initiative. The goal of the HAY initiative was to highlight programs nationwide (in the United States) that were performing interventions and changing the lives of the highest risk young people. CeaseFire outreach workers and violence inter-rupters were soon to be profiled by the HAY initiative for their efforts on behalf of youth likely to be involved in violence. This June visit would prove to be the starting point for conversations on how the CeaseFire model might be adapted and used to change the overall situation in Iraq.

Although the purpose of the First Lady's trip was to visit and highlight youth intervention programs in U.S. cities, the First Lady had more than that on her mind: that summer there had been an increase of insurgent activity in Iraq and conversations rapidly turned toward application of the CeaseFire model to violence in Iraq. As the CeaseFire model is predicated on the understanding that violence is an acquired or learned behavior that escalates in an epidemic fashion, the cross-cultural applications were well worth discussing, and perhaps implicit.

Dr. Slutkin, founder and executive director of CeaseFire, said to Mrs. Bush during her site visit, "I've been thinking about the suicide bombings, and how they are frequently performed under peer pressure and responding to the expectations of the bomber's social group—and without sufficient social pressure and inter-vention from their own group occurring in the opposite direction."

Mrs. Bush responded, "I've been thinking about that same thing myself on the way to visiting with you." Later, Mrs. Bush would arrange a key meeting that would lead to other meetings with leading policy makers.

Even with the CeaseFire epidemiological model being a potential fit for some of the issues in Iraq, it would take a considerable amount of effort to move the thinking and a project forward. After some initial informal meetings with senior members in the State Department, Karen Volker, a long-term U.S. Department of State Foreign Service Officer, was tasked with looking into the applications for the CeaseFire model in Iraq. At the time, she was part of a high-level intra-agency government task force, including representatives from the Department of Defense, U.S. Agency for International Development (USAID), the Department of Energy, and others to focus on countering violent extremism. Volker became a strong advocate for adapting the CeaseFire approach for use in Iraq. Although she and others saw the potential for applying CeaseFire to the issue in Iraq, not everyone was convinced. Conversations between these groups would ensue, and many materials on the thinking behind the new approach to reducing violence would be developed and distributed to policy makers and to State and Defense Department officials sent to serve in Iraq.

It frequently was mentioned in Washington and in Iraq that "it is not a military solution, but a political solution that is needed." The CeaseFire intervention, however, fills the frequently not discussed, but essential, "third space"—the human space that is present but usually unfilled when a dispute or retaliation or violent act is resistant to both of these usual responses. This space exists because (1) the military or police cannot be in all places, and (2) all disputes are not political, and even when political solutions are developed, not everyone and all groups agree with the political solution. In other words, it frequently is hard to develop "political" solutions to a perceived need for retaliation—whether it is a provoked attack like the Samarra Mosque, or over a personal, family, or tribal conflict (see table 6.1). As a result of the new or "disruptive" ideas inherent in CeaseFire—that this is essentially about community-level change in Iraq—Volker would have to champion the project from within the Department of State through an

Table 6.1 Community Mobilization: The Missing Piece

How CeaseFire Adds to Military and Political Processes, and *Fills the Gap* in Iraq

1. Police and military efforts	2. CeaseFire campaign	3. Political and diplomatic negotiation
• Apprehends/kills some offenders	• Mobilizes the community itself	• Addresses grievances (some)
• Provides presence; deterrence	• Prevents retaliations	• But not everyone agrees
• Can't be in all places	• Offers face saving	• Not all conflicts are political
	• Reverses social pressure to perform acts	• Provocation can subvert

odyssey of many stops and starts. In some instances, the project was intentionally derailed with officials taking ownership over it for the sole purpose of burying it. At other turns, some agencies and departments saw the potential of the approach, but were not comfortable considering ideas or an initiative that was not developed in-house—or that followed the fundamental military or political paradigm. Volker's tenacity was instrumental in bringing the project to fruition. She saw the importance and the place for civil society's involvement in the solution.

In December 2006, Slutkin and Volker had a series of meetings with nongovernmental organizations (NGOs, for example, the International Republican Institute, U.S. Institute for Peace, the National Democratic Institute), the State Department (including the Office of Policy Planning, Senior Advisor for Iraq, Office of Counter Terrorism, Office of International Women's Issues), the Defense Department (J-5, deputy director for the War on Terror, advisors to Gen. David Petraeus), and USAID. Slutkin made a subsequent visit to STRATCOM (the US Strategic Command in the Department of Defense) and Volker continued to present the CeaseFire model to officials in relevant offices throughout the government. In all of these meetings, the main ideas promoted were (1) the focus in Iraq should consider fundamentally changing from winning a war to reducing violence, (2) persons from the groups or social networks themselves would need to be involved in the solution, and (3) jobs could be created in the process. Some of the interlocutors recognized the value of trying this new approach, others did not. On one occasion, a senior advisor to General Petraeus confirmed to Volker that the CeaseFire approach would indeed work in Iraq, noting that the tribal structure in Iraq was similar to the gang structure in large U.S. cities like Chicago. The ideas and the project started getting traction after Slutkin briefed a delegation from Iraq, including an advisor to the Council of Tribal Leaders and several female parliamentarians, and stated that an approach such as this would be worth trying. At various points over the next two years, Volker continued to present the CeaseFire model to multiple agencies and offices, including the National Security Council, the U.S. Foreign Service Institute (which trains all officials who serve in Iraq), and a visiting department official from the Basrah Provincial Reconstruction Team. (This official later wrote a cable to the department in support of AIC's proposal to implement the CeaseFire model in Basrah, a proposal that eventually was funded by the Department's Bureau of Democracy, Human Rights, and Labor.)

During this December 2006 visit, Zainab al-Suwaij, founder and executive director of the AIC, was introduced to the program. Al-Suwaij is no stranger to violence. In 1991, after a failed attempt to oust Saddam Hussein in the rebellion following the first Gulf War, she was forced to flee her home in Basrah, Iraq. Eventually, she found her way to the United States, carrying with her the desire to help her native country in whatever ways would be possible. This ambition led first to the formation of her organization, the American Islamic Congress (AIC) in the wake of the September 11th tragedy. At that time, AIC began a campaign to actively establish a two-way interfaith understanding between Christians and Muslims to counter strained relations between the two cultures. As the Iraq war started, AIC began actively reaching out to many other agencies, including the U.S. State Department, to find creative solutions to end the violence and stabilize Iraq. The collaboration with CeaseFire was the missing piece of the puzzle: an opportunity to empower Iraqi communities to take responsibility for reducing violence themselves.

IMPLEMENTING CEASEFIRE IN IRAQ

A three-fold process was used to make significant modifications to the model for adaptation to the Iraqi context. Initially, representatives from AIC visited Chicago and toured CeaseFire's flagship demonstration site on the west side of the city. They met with CeaseFire staff, interrupters, outreach workers, program coordinators, and program managers. Rather than a traditional presentation format, AIC was immersed in community-based activities in Chicago's West Garfield neighborhood to see the model at work firsthand. They accompanied outreach workers on walks through the neighborhood, attended a shooting "response," and participated in distributing public education materials. At the end of their visit, AIC staff were provided with additional CeaseFire materials for review to begin thinking through adaptation.

After AIC had the opportunity to sufficiently review training materials for several weeks and provide initial impressions and insights, CeaseFire staff traveled to Washington, D.C., where AIC is headquartered, for an intensive three-day session. Materials were reviewed step-by-step with the intent of "concretizing" the model's cultural shift from theoretical to actionable. For example, in the U.S. CeaseFire workers identify the high-risk individuals based on a set of specific criteria (for example, age, involved in a street organization, holding a significant role in a street organization, having a prior criminal history, engaged in high-risk street activity, recent victim of a shooting, or recently released from prison), but in Basrah these criteria required shifting focus. Reenvisioned for the Iraqi context, the team began to discuss application to religious leaders, community stakeholders, and tribal representatives. The key components of the model were morphed to match the situational context in Basrah.

Networking maps were constructed to identify inroads to connect with this indigenous structure. Job descriptions for outreach workers and violence interrupters were changed to reflect this approach to determine who was connected to the organizations on the ground. Similar revisions were made for the community mobilization components of the intervention. While in Chicago this component involves demonstrations, marches, and rallies, organizers had reservations about operating openly in Iraq. Based on the social and political climate, it was believed that conflict mediation staff might be marked for death, if operating publically. Community trainings were developed to engage all facets of society in peacekeeping efforts with these sensitivities in mind. Public education materials were developed to be highly culturally specific. Efforts were made to incorporate messaging that anticipated potential religious or tribal violence. Finally, general guidelines, revised training materials and job descriptions were presented to AIC staff.

CeaseFire staff worked intimately with the translator to ensure that presentations were conducted in Arabic to facilitate a free-flowing conversation. These discussions developed the specific details of what the program would look like on the ground. After the first five months of project implementation in Iraq, the staff reconvened to assess the project. What worked? What did not? What needed to be changed? An evaluation was conducted and changes were made to the next stage of implementation and materials were revised. Some surprising differences emerged between how the program had been envisioned and its actual implementation.

Following are the key points resulting from the evaluation:

• Tribal leaders played a larger role in mediations than initially had been anticipated.
• Conflict mediators acted more as meeting facilitators than their U.S. counterparts, convening meetings to get family, tribal leaders, and other individuals to the table to discuss events. Mediators served more as surrogate tribal infrastructure in the absence of these formal processes.
• Honor-killings or the challenges inherent in them were not sufficiently anticipated. They are so engrained in the cultural understanding that the entry-points that worked for other forms of conflict were not applicable.
• Similarly, militia-related violence was much more challenging to intervene on than initially anticipated. Conflict mediators were unable to make significant inroads to these groups and found such situations far more threatening to their personal safety to negotiate.
• Also, the active role community residents would want to play was underestimated. Community residents became instrumental in organizing and supporting events themselves and participating in messaging campaigns.
• As a result, workers were able to operate far more publically than they had anticipated. The was concern was that working out in the open could mark them, but that was not the case.

After funding to cover the elections was extended, priorities shifted to connect with a greater number of political groups. An additional 15 conflict mediators were added to the staff to think through and guide this aspect of the strategy, develop messaging specific to peacekeeping around the election, and develop inroads with these groups.

CEASEFIRE IN BASRAH: THE BASRAH ANTI-VIOLENCE CAMPAIGN

The Basrah Anti-Violence Campaign (BAVC) is focused on reducing the number of acts of violence in Basrah, Iraq. On a broader scale, it challenges and guides civil society actors and the broader grassroots community to take responsibility for decreasing acts of violence in Basrah, Iraq, including intertribal, interethnic, sectarian, domestic, and other types of violence. It represents the first community-centric effort of this kind in Iraq and implements a culturally specific adaptation of the CeaseFire Model in the Al-Jumhuriyah and Khamza Meel communities in Basrah, Iraq.

First, BAVC workers identify and detect potentially violent events, individuals, and groups by collecting information from a diverse variety of community sources. They engage political, religious, and tribal leadership who show up at mosques and community centers with bags of coffee or little gifts, sit down, and discuss nonviolence as a philosophy and an approach. Intertribal, interethnic, and sectarian approaches combined with the political, social, and economic tensions wrought by the war have created a climate of paranoia and fear through which personal conflict often gets mired in politics and misinformation, contributing to their escalation. To challenge these forces of influence in Basrah, outreach staff build coalitions of religious, tribal, and education leaders to endorse the concept that violence is dishonorable, rather than justified. In the past, some felt that violence was the only way to respond and that it showed strength, honor, and seriousness. The educational sessions created by the outreach staff challenge this notion and replace vindictive action with reason. BAVC workers focus considerable energy and effort on establishing trust and building rapport with leaders and citizens alike that can provide information, influence, and access.

Interruption and intervention of conflicts likely to lead to violence composes the second element of the model. BAVC workers focus on mediating conflicts between individuals before they escalate to violence or incorporate larger groups. One of the major differences in Iraqi conflict as opposed to street violence in the United States is the magnitude of casualties that can result, especially considering the accessibility of rocket launchers or bombs over handguns. A conflict between two students, for example, quickly grew to encompass both families and resulted in a shooting that could have produced a body count if not intervened in appropriately. Two students got into a fist-fight resulting in a black eye. The family of the injured student feared the worst, believing their child had been blinded, and retaliated by randomly firing a machine gun into the other student's home. Thankfully no one was hit. The family was understandably outraged that their home had been attacked and was prepared to respond violently, while the family of the injured boy was still bent on inflicting further damage to settle the score. An outreach worker was able to bring the student to the hospital to demonstrate the eye was not permanently damaged, and a second worker intervened with the other to deescalate the conflict. No further conflict or injury resulted from the event.

The third element of the model uses social marketing and public health communication strategies. CeaseFire has helped to shape an Iraqi messaging campaign to change thinking for the general public regarding violence. This approach uses empathy-based, culturally specific messages of peace, trust, and tolerance to challenge the dominant thinking about violence. These messages demonstrate how community members can play a crucial role in preventing violence and encourage citizens to get involved. It was crucial to the success of this campaign to incorporate input from Iraqi journalists, academics, and community and religious leaders in the development of messages and the coordination of the campaign. During a respected Shī'ah anniversary date, representing a divergence in religious thinking with the Sunni, it is common for some tribes to clash over defaced religious sites. Banners were hung in public spaces and leaflets emphasizing love and respect anticipated potential clashes and neutralized them before they occurred. A foreign NGO or externally imposed campaign would not have had as nuanced a response to anticipate these events.

Finally, data and monitoring is a fourth element of the CeaseFire model that runs throughout every step in the process. BAVC program staff analyzed violence trends in Basrah and focused the intervention specifically on violence hot-spots in Al-Jumhuriyah and Khamza Meel. Maps were developed with on-the-ground staff to identify tribal leaders that had prominence in each area and conflict groups that needed to be intervened on. Throughout model implementation, BAVC workers collect data on the number of conflicts mediated, the number of leaders recruited to become ambassadors for peace in their communities, and the number of trainings on nonviolence provided in the community.

EVALUATION OF CEASEFIRE IN THE UNITED STATES AND IRAQ

Over the past 15 years, the CeaseFire model has been tested and replicated in Chicago, throughout Illinois, and nationwide with considerable success. An extensive, independent three-year evaluation commissioned by the U.S. Department of Justice, and led by Northwestern University, found that CeaseFire reduced shootings and killings and made neighborhoods safer, with 41 percent to 73 percent drops in shootings and killings in CeaseFire areas, and demonstrated a 100 percent success rate in reducing retaliatory killings in five of the eight communities examined. Evaluation of the Baltimore-based CeaseFire replication conducted by the John Hopkins Bloomberg School of Public Health in 2009 reported similar outcomes, which suggested the program had led to fewer killings in those areas where the program was replicated with fidelity to model, and also saw the first signs of changes in the norms of the highest risk individuals in the intervention zones. The Kansas City replication also received a favorable initial evaluation of its first CeaseFire zone conducted by the Truman Medical Center in 2009, reporting a 38 percent reduction in homicides.

In a 2008 evaluation of the program, evaluators found that CeaseFire's outreach workers effectively assisted 85 to 97 percent of the youth served to find a job, enroll in school, access drug treatment, or get out of a gang. Furthermore, the survey indicated that CeaseFire workers were the second-most-important adult in their lives, second only to their parents. CeaseFire interrupters had been interrupting hundreds of conflicts and making neighborhoods safer, and shootings and killings were down in CeaseFire communities.

In the U.S. cities, CeaseFire is able to evaluate its performance and effectiveness based on changes in the number of shootings and killings in a given community or geographic area. Primarily because of many variables associated with the war in Iraq, it is difficult to have accurate baseline figures and to accurately assess the full success of the intervention and conflict mediation efforts; however, the BAVC measures the number of conflicts mediated, nonviolence training administered, numbers of community ambassadors for peace workers trained, the amount of public education material administered, and other qualitative measurements, while simultaneously compiling qualitative reports from the field staff.

In 2009, the BAVC provided intervention to 112 violent incidents and is thought to have prevented a potential killing in 105 of those cases. More than 30 nonviolence trainings were held to teach alternative strategies to resolving conflict and techniques for mediating common issues in a culturally acceptable and peaceful way. While culturally many people believe that violence is the only way to show your strength or the appropriate level of honor and respect in a given situation, these educational sessions and workshops, created by BAVC outreach staff, have challenged this notion, put workers and citizens into action, and repeatedly replaced vindictive action with reason—and potential violence with a peaceful result. Furthermore, more than 1,000 "Ambassadors for Peace" have now been specifically trained in these methods. These citizens have pledged themselves to nonviolence, have acquired new skills, now embody the philosophy and practice of nonviolence, and dedicate themselves to helping explore alternative means for resolving conflict. More than 1,500 key community stakeholders agreed to meet with BAVC and help the organization to realize its mission of peace in Basrah. In addition, more than 5,000 pieces of public education material were distributed throughout Al-Jumhuriyah and Khamza Meel.

Evidence of how deeply Basrah community members have eagerly embraced the BAVC was demonstrated during the recent BAVC-sponsored "BAVC Peace Soccer Championship." The event brought together 13 youth soccer teams, promoting peace between and among the Khamza Meel and Al-Jumhuriyah areas of Basrah. Each team and its coaches were required to participate in conflict resolution and violence reduction training before participation and were asked to become peace ambassadors in their communities. Sadly, one of the team coaches died of natural causes in the midst of the tournament series. After suffering this loss, the team debated whether they should continue playing or withdraw from the competition. In the end, the team unanimously voted to continue playing in the tournament because it was "so important to the community."

LESSONS LEARNED FROM THE CEASEFIRE PROGRAM IN IRAQ

Successful replication of the CeaseFire model in Iraq validates this implicit understanding that violence is a learned behavior that acts like an infectious disease. Regardless of cultural context, political circumstances, or social situation surrounding violence, an intervention can be applied to the use of violence in the presence of a grievance. The BAVC validates CeaseFire's understanding that by being aware of the players involved, specifically those at the highest risk for being a perpetrator or a victim of violence, conflicts can be effectively mediated and efforts can be advanced to change the norms and social pressure that reinforce violence. A second lesson is that harnessing the power of media and the use of visual aids has been crucial to the success of the BAVC. As a part of a BAVC public messaging campaign, posters with messages of nonviolence were created to hang in target neighborhoods. Early on, the organization expected that most of these posters would be torn down. Surprisingly, and on the contrary, neighbors poured out of their homes requesting copies of the posters and asking to be able to hang them at their homes, at their storefronts, and at other highly visible locations in their communities. Journalists and media professionals provided some of the most valuable knowledge resources. The media had strong connections with a wide variety of people and often heard firsthand of threats of violence or tense situations that they could relay to BAVC staff to intervene in before the threats escalated. Initially, it had seemed that requesting the cooperation and support of tribal leaders was little more than a formality, a cultural obligation for BAVC staff. It quickly turned out to be one of the most effective violence-reduction tools. The expertise of BAVC workers and the legitimacy gained as "independent" (that is, nonaffiliated mediators) in the communities, meant tribal leaders were soon calling on workers to mediate in serious conflicts involving shootings and honor crimes, traditionally handled only within the tribal structure. After the program launched, workers began fielding intervention requests outside of the Basrah target areas and even from beyond the city as word of successful mediations spread.

One of the biggest challenges facing the BAVC was shifting a cultural perception that the government, while deemed ineffectual, was the only entity that could curb violence. Citizens perceived themselves as powerless in this type of effort. Trust can be hard to earn in Iraq. The challenge was to prove that the BAVC was trustworthy and did not have ties to militias or political entities. Since launching the program, the BAVC has received numerous requests for training, conflict intervention, and mediation techniques to curb violence from other areas of Basrah, as well as other cities in Iraq, but right now, the project simply lacks the staff resources.

One of the BAVC's biggest facilitators is people, for example, tribal leaders and journalists. Journalists were open to promoting the work and writing positive news stories. AIC's reputation in Iraq, also facilitates BAVC's efforts. Since 2003, AIC has been running programs on the ground in Iraq, building a solid reputation, an established network of contacts, and a strong track record that made the organization a credible resource for violence-prevention work. Community institutions are great facilitators. The BAVC engages previously existing, locally organized groups and cultural institutions like mosques, churches, and soccer clubs in the campaign. Partnering with an organization that is part of the local community, perceived as politically neutral or unaffiliated and recognized as a credible messenger by the highest risk transmitters is integral to success.

Insights gleaned from the cross-cultural applications of the CeaseFire model to Iraq have served as a tremendous proof point for the underlying theories. Although CeaseFire had been proven effective for intervention with street organizations, transferring it to the Basrah context provided evidence that, regardless of the circumstances for the use of violence in the presence of grievances, an intervention can be applied. The Basrah adaptation provided a learning experience for the process involved. The organic method of reviewing and revising materials; implementation; evaluating, repeatedly assessing the project, and modifying accordingly has created a blueprint for subsequent international replications. This step-wise process has become the template for transferring the CeaseFire Model to other conflict regions.

NEXT STEPS

Currently, CeaseFire and AIC are seeking to continue the BAVC and to expand into other Iraqi cities at the request of provincial council members, members of parliament, and tribal leaders. Continued expansion will result in the full Iraq Anti-Violence Campaign (IAVC), a national campaign cantered on four strategically selected cities: greater Basrah, Baghdad, Kirkuk, and Baqubah. These cities represent a broad spectrum of Iraqi society—Shia, Sunni, Arab, Kurdish, Turkmen, and more—and much of Iraq's geography. The cities represent a microcosm of the types of violence that Iraq has suffered from for far too long—intertribal, interethnic, sectarian, and more. CeaseFire will continue to provide training and technical assistance in Iraq.

CeaseFire also is active in other regions. CeaseFire has partnered with the Citizen Security Programme to expand services to its first Caribbean-based site in Trinidad and Tobago, where the 2009 murder rate leapt to 42 per 100,000, nearly double the average of 18.1 per 100,000 for the rest of the Caribbean. Planning and discussions are under way in several other countries.

CeaseFire was named one of the top 25 organizations to work with the Ashoka network for global replication and reach. Ashoka is a global association of leading social entrepreneurs that works to address the world's most urgent social problems. Ashoka is working closely with CeaseFire to prepare further international scaling strategies. An organization interested in adapting the model to deal with their own violence issue can learn more through the CeaseFire website: www.ceasefirechicago.org/.

7

The Kingston Y™ Youth Development Program: An Effective Antiviolence Intervention for Inner-City Youth in Jamaica

Nancy G. Guerra, Kirk R. Williams, Julie Meeks Gardner, and Ian Walker

> Teachers here, miss? They look out for you and they treat me good because they like to see you grow, and they do not want you to be kicked out of the school so they look out for you and do good things to you. My teacher helps me with my school work . . . if I don't understand I just carry the book to her and say I don't understand, and she says in the afternoon stay back and I will show you . . . . She keeps extra lesson[s] in the evening.
>
> —Male participant, age 16, Kingston Y™ Program

BACKGROUND

IN DEVELOPING COUNTRIES such as Jamaica, harsh conditions and extreme environments present significant challenges for preventing aggression and violence. Children and youth face a myriad of personal, family, school, and community barriers to healthy development. When resources are scarce, adults and other caretakers often do not have the time or skills to provide for children's basic needs, and they have even less time for any type of remedial help for those who fall behind. For children growing up under these conditions, particularly for young males, aggression and violence may become, in essence, strategies or "tools" for self-help, providing access to resources, power, and status in a school or community, and psychological relief from the shame and humiliation caused by lack of opportunities, marginalization, academic failure, and exclusion. The slightest disrespect, absent contrary evidence of self-worth (such as respect from teachers as described in the example above) easily can lead to a violent response and, over time, to more habitual aggressive behavior in defense of one's honor, pride, and dignity (Harriott 2008; Levy 2010).

Indeed, for many young males in urban Jamaica, violence has become a way of life. Characterizations of disengaged teenage boys often describe youth who "go on like a bad man" or "kill fi fun." Examples abound of communities being renamed after notoriously violent regions of the world or former war zones such as "Gaza," "Tel Aviv," and "Viet Nam." This is reflected in extremely high rates of violence, particularly among young, urban males, with Jamaica now considered not only the most violent country in the Caribbean, but among the most violent countries in the world (World Bank 2007).

The Government of Jamaica (GoJ) is well aware of the economic, social development, and human costs from such high levels of violence. A number of studies and reports have been commissioned, and a range of individual and community-level programs have been established to target crime and violence. Typically, large-scale programs are funded through agreements with international development partners such as the World Bank, the Inter-American Development Bank (IADB), the U.K. Department for International Development (DfID), and the United Nations Development Program (UNDP). Some of these programs emphasize community development, including improving the built environment, enhancing citizen security and justice, and promoting social cohesion, trust, and a willingness to intervene for the common good. Other programs focus on providing opportunities, remedial education, job training, and skill building for individuals most at risk. These programs frequently serve poor, urban male adolescents through brief, targeted interventions (for example, teaching conflict resolution skills) or long-term, intensive services (for example, remedial education, high school re-entry, and job training programs).

A common challenge for youth violence prevention in developing countries is the lack of a credible "evidence base" for determining program effectiveness. When resources are scarce, funds are needed to provide basic services, and funding for systematic evaluation often lags behind program operations. Although a number of evidence-based programs have been developed in the United States and elsewhere, it is unlikely that these can be transported unchanged to countries such as Jamaica. Even standardized assessments for measuring outcomes need to be adapted for cultural fit through extensive pilot testing and refinement.

On the other hand, locally driven programs have been developed over time and in response to the needs of those they serve. These programs thrive because they are responsive to the local culture and fill a clear gap in services. In many cases, although they did not emerge from a theoretical model of risk and protective factors for youth violence as cited in the empirical literature, the key program components easily can be mapped on to logic models of expected program impact. Stated otherwise, intuitive models of what children and youth need to thrive and to reduce violence embedded in local programs frequently correspond with scientific evidence related to the causes of violence. More data on actual program effects on youth violence prevention clearly are needed, as well as a greater understanding of the most influential mechanisms of change (that is, did the program work, and how did it work?)

Fortunately, both the GoJ and international development partners have become increasingly interested more recently in commissioning systematic evaluations of well-developed and highly regarded local programs for youth violence prevention in Jamaica. Although these studies normally cannot use experimental methods such as randomized assignments, it often is possible to find plausible ways of measuring program effects through quasi-experimental approaches. This chapter draws on a recent evaluation commissioned by the World Bank and funded by the Trust for Environmentally and Socially Sustainable Development (TFESSD). The goal of the evaluation was to examine the effects of a comprehensive, multiyear intervention, the Kingston Y™ Youth Development Program, on youth violent behavior and related outcomes.

The evaluation developed a new survey tool to quantify systematically changes in behavioral propensities and actual behaviors of program participants. It then applied this tool in an evaluation of the YMCA program for at-risk adolescents in Jamaica. The study compared current attendees to a wait-list control group and included a tracer study of previous graduates to verify long-term effects. Surveys were conducted to assess changes in core social-emotional competencies, propensity for aggression, and aggressive behavior. In addition, individual interviews were conducted with youth attending the program to learn more about how the program affected their lives.

The Kingston Y™ Youth Development Program is a community-based program that provides alternative basic education and life-skills training for at-risk adolescent boys (ages 12 to 16) from disadvantaged urban areas who are not attending school because of academic or social problems. The overarching theme of the program is to promote the values and behaviors associated with Y™ principles: love, peace, service, and justice. The specific goals of the program are to educate, socialize, feed, reinstate in the educational system, maximize opportunities for employment, and achieve a passing score on the ninth-grade achievement test (required for entrance into high school equivalent).

The intervention provides daily supervision (from 8:00 A.M. to 2:00 P.M.), instruction, and socialization. Remedial education is provided in small classes (25 youth per teacher). Although there are no specific social skills curricula used, the program relies heavily on counseling, guidance, authoritative discipline (emphasizing rewards for positive behavior), and providing positive male and female role models. The average length of participation is three to four years, although some youth complete the program relatively quickly, and others cycle out and back in (because of circumstances such as dire economic need, excessive community violence, and so on) until they pass their ninth-grade achievement test and can be reintegrated into schools.

As is often the case with community-based interventions, core funding for program operations has been a continuing challenge. The Y™ operates as a non-governmental organization (NGO) and does not receive consistent funding from any one source. Given the intensity of services provided, costs are relatively low, estimated to be approximately US$650 per year per child. The administration has been able to bring in other partners to provide specific services but struggles to establish a reliable funding stream for the core program (that includes eight teachers and four administrative and support staff). For instance, the Human Employment and Resource Training Trust-National Training Agency (HEART-NTA) program provides vocational training for youth and offers access to programs for participants.

How effective is the program in reducing aggression and related behaviors? Did the program have a positive impact on social skills and core competencies for healthy development? Did it help participants feel respected and increase their self-worth and dignity? Did it actually reduce the incidence of violence? The results of the evaluation suggest that the program was highly effective in all of these areas.

The study shows that the program had a significant effect on positive sense of self and moral beliefs. Youth in the program experienced higher levels of self-esteem and hope for the future as well as stronger beliefs about the harmful consequences of aggression and violence. This indicates that the Y™ strategy of emphasizing self-worth and respect for others has had an impact on these outcomes.

But did these changes also translate into real behavior? Again, the answer seems to be yes. For the sample of youth who currently are enrolled in the program compared with those on the wait list, significant reductions were found in aggressive behavior, after controlling for aggressive propensity. For the graduate sample, significant reductions in *both* aggressive propensity and aggressive behavior were found several years after program completion. This suggests that, over a long-term period, improved patterns of actual behavior feed back into underlying propensities, in some sense "anchoring" in behavior the changes as a result of program participation.

These findings are particularly striking given that participants were well into their adolescent years, had fallen behind in school, and were from extremely disadvantaged communities in a developing country with few legitimate opportunities for positive engagement for these marginalized youth. It often is argued that it is difficult to make changes in behaviors for older youth and under such difficult conditions, but the Y™ program seems to underscore that remedial programs for adolescents can be effective.

The study also examined whether the degree of reduction in aggression and violence is reasonable in proportion to program costs. To measure this, the number of violent incidents avoided based on survey responses about the respondent's actual behavior in the previous month was calculated. Results indicated that manifest violence was reduced by 50 percent for the average participant (down from two incidents to one incident per month). Because the findings show that these improvements are sustained over time, it is reasonable to extrapolate this benefit over the young adult life of these men. This leads to the estimate that the investment of $2,600 made in each young man who graduates from the program after four years at age 18, has an average payback of 168 incidents of violence avoided during his young adult life up to age 30. The unit cost is a relatively modest $14 per violent incident avoided. This is in addition to the economic benefits that also will result from increased educational attainment of program participants and the savings on mainstream educational costs.

What did the youth think of the program? In the survey data, 96.9 percent of participants said the program "changed their life for the better." When individual youth were asked how the program helped them, responses included statements that the program helped in the following ways:

- Help others and deal with myself when I am angry
- Come up with creative ways of working out a problem
- Connect with other people on a deeper level (developing close friendships)
- Have a high opinion and being considerate of myself and others
- Manage my own life, and take responsibility for things and people
- Plan what I will be doing in the future

Overall, considering how youth who were interviewed discussed program benefits, four major themes emerged:

Improvements in learning and increased interest in schoolwork. The majority of boys interviewed reported that the teachers and programs at the Y™ helped them greatly to focus on schoolwork, learn things that previously were difficult, and increase motivation to do well at school. Many of the boys reported that in regular schools they were unable to follow assignments and just gave up trying to learn. As one student said, in the Y™ "they try to help us understand but if you don't understand they talk to you and say look this is how you're supposed to do it." Another student commented that when he did not understand something the teachers "try to break it down in parts and make it easier to understand." Many of the students complained that other schools just want them to get in line and do not really teach them—"you never get enough teaching at other schools." Or as one boy put it, "[t]he YMCA has given me a study mind-set." This suggests that the alternative lower-secondary education program offered by the Y™ is of relatively good quality, compared with the remedial components of mainstream public programs.

Being treated with respect. Many of the boys felt others treated them unfairly in their homes, schools, and communities, in part, because they were young and poor. When asked what they liked about the Y™ program, a frequent comment was that teachers and staff treated them with love and respect alike. They noted that the program emphasizes respecting yourself and others, and that they truly felt they were treated fairly. Comments such as "teachers treat you like they should treat students, they care about you and try to help you instead of getting mad at you and punishing you." Most of the boys interviewed mentioned that teachers were nice and cared about them. They also were happy that classes were small, and teachers are patient and encouraging, rather than negative and punitive. As one boy said, "I love the way they teach me."

Increased optimism for the future. Almost all of the boys noted that they now felt like they had a purpose or a plan for their life. Some have learned vocational skills, such as welding, that they will use to find work, others want to further their studies in careers such as mechanical engineering and computer science. As one boy noted, "I was slow, slow. When I came to the YMCA I was so glad that I came. I started picking up on more work, started getting high grades and just enjoyed the Y so if I wasn't here I don't know where I would reach. Now I have manners and respect and a future."

Time for fun. When asked what they liked best about the program, the most common response was "learning to swim" or "swimming." The boys generally appreciated the opportunities for fun and learning games, swimming, and so on. They suggested that more sports opportunities and programs (football, cricket) should be included in their daily activities. They generally felt that the students all got along (other than typical problems) and wanted even more time for fun and enjoyment. Many of the boys noted that they do not have these opportunities where they live because of circumstances, such as a lack of facilities and community violence.

The student comments give a good overview of characteristics that successful programs must have when working under extremely difficult conditions. The positive appraisals are even more impressive in the context of a program that struggles on a day-to-day basis with youth raised in extreme poverty, disadvantage, and community violence. These findings suggest that community-based programs such as the Kingston Y™ that promote positive youth development can help. Given the nuances of developmental contexts both locally and globally, youth-serving agencies may be best positioned to understand local needs and how to help youth adapt to their specific circumstances. Even under the most difficult living conditions, the findings from this evaluation suggest that just as it is never "too early," it also is "never too late."

LESSONS LEARNED

Following are the lessons learned from the Kingston Y™ Youth Development Program:

- It is important to identify respected community-based agencies that have in place the capacity to deliver high quality programs for youth.
- For at-risk youth, programs should be strength based and promote positive development, while at the same time providing education and skills remediation where needed.
- Not only must programs be comprehensive, they also must be extended in time. The Y™ program operated daily over a period of up to four years.

- Youth want to be treated with care and respect, features that frequently are absent in the schools they attend and the communities in which they live.
- The costs for the program are offset by the benefits of reductions in violence and increased productivity of youth involved. However, a stable funding stream is required, which should optimally be provided through a ministry such as education or youth development.

REFERENCES

Harriott, A. D. 2008. *Bending the Trend Line: The Challenge of Controlling Violence in Jamaica and the High Violence Societies of the Caribbean.* Professorial inaugural lecture, University of the West Indies. Kingston, July 2008.

Levy, H. 2010. *Killing Streets and Community Revival.* Kingston, Jamaica: Arawak Press.

World Bank. 2007. *Crime, Violence, and Development: Trends, Costs, and Policy Options in the Caribbean.* Washington, DC: World Bank.

8

No School Left Behind: Merging Israel's National Academic and School Safety Monitoring System and Matching Data-Driven Interventions for Each School

Ron Avi Astor, Rami Benbenishty, Hanna Shadmy,
Tal Raz, Ela Algersy, Michal Zeharia, David Ratner,
and Kris de Pedro

INTRODUCTION

ISRAEL IS THE only country in the world that has created a nationally integrated information system where each primary and junior high school receives up-to-date, site-specific data on various academic, school climate, and school safety issues. Gathered from students and other members of the school community, these comprehensive site-specific data are collected and distributed biennially. It is presented to school leaders in an accessible format alongside academic and school safety standards relevant to the school. Each individual school's safety data allows staff members to compare progress over time with other demographically similar schools and along specific school safety dimensions.

Israel's school-based psychological and counseling services system (about 7,000 educational psychologists, school psychologists, counselors, and social workers) has utilized these climate data and other surveys to help schools understand what types of problems they have, develop grassroots solutions to deal with their problems, find existing programs that match their specific situation or develop their own, and help monitor the implementation successes or failures of each site's adopted school safety policy and practices. Initial pilot studies suggest that this approach is promising at both the local and national level. Other states and countries may glean lessons from this centralized and coordinated data-driven response system.

This case study will demonstrate how a country can develop a national safety system that monitors all schools, and at the same time, can be sensitive to each school site—allowing local adaptation of programs aimed at specific violence issues (for example, sexual harassment, bullying, weapons use, verbal violence and social exclusion, teacher-child violence, and so on). This approach can identify a multitude of potential model sites with successful grassroots programs and implementation successes that other schools can emulate. This case study also will describe the background, historical evolution, political conditions, and components that contributed to this development and may be relevant to the implementation of such systems in other countries.

The effects of the U.S. school shootings during the late 1990s were felt around the world. Within Israel, the media, the general public, and politicians began to discuss the issues in more depth and with great concern. This chapter will tell the story of how Israel, as a country, dealt with the challenge in a positive and proactive manner.

BACKGROUND ABOUT ISRAEL'S EDUCATION SYSTEM

Israel has approximately 3,000 public schools in their K-12 population. An estimated 1.4 million students are educated in this system (about 1.1 million in primary and secondary level schools). The cultural, linguistic, and religious diversity in this small geographic area is staggering. Israeli public schools serve children with various ethnic and religious backgrounds: Muslim-Arab, Christian-Arab, Ultra-Orthodox Jewish, Secular Jewish, Modern Orthodox Jewish, Druze, Bedouin, and workers from many other countries, including the Philippines, Thailand, and China. Israel is a country of immigrants that came from diverse cultures in Africa, Europe, the former Soviet Union, North and South America, Australia, the Middle East, and Asia. The socio-educational-economic range of families is also quite diverse. Hence, the Israeli school system has a complex array of sociocultural issues important to each distinct community that need to be considered as part of the education process.

Israel's education is based on concepts of cultural pluralism rather than the "melting pot" orientation present in some Western countries. The education system is divided into four main basic "streams": Jewish-Secular, Jewish-Religious, Arab, and an Ultra-Orthodox stream that is not supervised by the national system, like the other three, but that is publicly funded to a large extent. Most of the schools are public, except for a small number of mostly religious private schools. This means that publicly funded schools tend to match the local culture, language, religion, and historical background. Families technically can attend any regional school they choose. However, the vast majority of families in Israel choose to go to local schools that reflect their own culture, religious form of expression, and language use. Teachers from these schools are also from the same cultures. Consequently, among Jews, modern orthodox students attend modern orthodox public schools, have modern orthodox public school teachers, and are educated using cultural texts that reflect this cultural orientation (in addition to a core curriculum shared by all). Similarly, secular Israeli Jewish parents (the vast majority of Jews in Israel) tend to choose Jewish nonreligious schools. Arab parents also tend to choose schools that reflect their own religion and community practices and have staff with similar orientations to their local community.

Israel's education system is centrally administered through the Israeli Ministry of Education. Local authorities at the municipal and district level have significant input on the curriculum. Standards, however, are established on a national basis. The responsibility for most services relevant to this case study, such as data collection, data interpretation, training of school-based data specialists, and psychological programming on school violence issues are developed and coordinated on the national level through the Ministry of Education. Nevertheless, local authorities have important input and supervisory power on local schools, especially in the secondary-level schools. Overall, municipal and district-level authorities greatly affect the delivery of services, but much of the funding and the overall structure of services are national. This is different from other countries such as the United States, where primary and secondary education tends to be funded through local taxes, and locally elected school boards and school districts create policy.

THE EVOLUTION OF SCHOOL VIOLENCE AS AN ISSUE OF WIDESPREAD CONCERN IN ISRAEL

It is likely that school violence as a phenomenon always has existed in Israeli schools, as it has within schools around the globe before the birth of the school safety literature. Within Israeli academic circles, school violence was a topic of concern dating back to the early 1980s (for example, Horovitz and Amir 1981). The Ministry of Education had an office on school safety staffed by one person for decades. The public awareness of youth and school violence waxed and waned and several public committees were established to address this problem. It was not until the late 1990s, however, that school violence was seen as a major problem within the Israeli public's consciousness. This shift in public awareness coincided with intense international media coverage and global international concern surrounding the highly publicized school shootings that occurred in the United States and Europe during the late 1990s.

Similarly, in the late 1990s, the print and television media in Israel began to show regular stories on issues of school violence. In 1998 and 1999, several potentially lethal stabbings on school grounds caught the attention of members of parliament and in particular, the minister of education—at the time, Itzhak Levy, who was a former school principal. He established a high-level public committee (the Vilany Committee) that made a series of recommendations.

Israel's concern led to an ambitious nationally funded research agenda to support the efforts to assess the magnitude of the problem and suggest new policies and interventions. The country embarked on the most comprehensive set of national studies covering issues of school violence. Five waves of studies based on large-scale representative samples were conducted between 1998 and 2005

(Benbenishty, Astor, and Marachi 2006). For instance, the 2005 wave studied 27,319 students, 1,861 teachers, and 420 principals in a nationally representative stratified sample (by stream and school level) of 526 schools.

Compared with research conducted in other countries, these studies were unique, because they covered in detail a wide range of violence-related issues, such as school climate, school victimization and perpetration, school organizational issues, and family and neighborhood effects (Benbenishty and Astor 2005). These inquiries explored the sometimes-divergent views of students, teachers, and administrators from the same schools (Benbenishty and Astor 2005; Stone, Astor, and Benbenishty 2009).

The findings suggested that Israel indeed had a serious school violence problem that was in some areas, such as moderate physical violence, twice as high as rates in the United States (Benbenishty and Astor 2005). These, and results of studies conducted by Harel and colleagues based on the Health Behaviour in School-aged Children HBSC of the World Health Organization (Harel, Kenny, and Rahav 1997) were reported in an intense manner by the Israeli media. These events made an indelible mark on the consciousness of the Israeli public education system. The normative shift in popular thinking and media coverage increased political pressure for the education system to respond in a comprehensive way.

In a parallel effort, Israeli Ministry of Education professionals began organizing systems designed to address the problems identified in the national surveys. The initial effort began in *Sheffy*, the office of psychological counseling services in the National Department of Counseling and Psychological Services, which oversees approximately 7,000 pupil personnel (counselors, psychologists, educational psychologists, and school psychologists). An early internal survey of these pupil personnel on school safety conducted in 1998 revealed that their perceptions of their roles were quite complex and ambiguous. They reported feeling conflicted about how they should be involved and ill-prepared to respond effectively.

Although concerned about the impact of violence on students' emotional and psychological well-being, the vast majority of pupil personnel at the time did not see school safety as their major role. Nor did they perceive that school safety was an integral part of their knowledge base or training. Many expressed frustration that the school called on them to intervene in cases of school violence without a realistic assessment of how helpful they could be in addressing this systemic problem. They found themselves involved in disciplinary actions that were not part of their professional identity, in response to the immediate needs of the principal and teachers. These findings within *Sheffy*, along with data from the national studies indicating that teachers and principals felt ill-prepared to cope with school violence and did not feel that their school counselors were helping them enough in this area, led to a decade-long reassessment, reorganization, and development of new ways in which *Sheffy* defined its role and *modus operandi* in the area of school climate in general and violence in particular. This process led to an overt understanding in the ministry that psychological and counseling services would take the lead in the national effort to reduce rates of school violence.

These processes led to major conceptual and organizational developments in how the Israeli education system is addressing many aspects of school climate, such as the development of national standards for several dimensions of school climate. In this case example, we focus on one central aspect: the systematic use of data to inform policy and practice on all levels. We will describe the important developments in this area and show how they are an integral part of the school safety efforts.

LOCAL DATA TO SUPPORT SCHOOL SAFETY INTERVENTIONS

The series of national studies provided detailed information on a range of violence types, presented separately by gender, age, school level, and educational stream. National monitoring was important in raising awareness and informing national policy on this problem. Still, these studies were less useful to local schools and communities that did not have any systematic information on school safety issues within their own local settings. School sites could not know how their school compared with the national norm, and therefore did not have the detailed local knowledge required to plan their school safety interventions. The awareness that each school needed local data to proceed properly was an important next step in building the national infrastructure for school safety monitoring.

There were several partial responses to this need. Some local authorities (such as Ashdod and Herzliya) commissioned efforts to provide school safety–related data on a school and municipal level. For instance, in the city of Herzliya, each school in the city conducted a thorough assessment of school violence and school climate. All these schools used the same instruments and method so that all of the information was aggregated to the city level. Each school site received a thorough assessment of violence in the school. This included student, teacher, principal and parent survey results and incident data. This information empowered the school leadership to plan interventions for the school on the basis of a valid and reliable assessment of the site. On the city level, a comprehensive and detailed picture of the region emerged. It described both the city as a whole and the relative situation of each school site within the city. Hence, the city's education leadership was empowered to make policy decisions and choices regarding what programs to adopt for the city as a whole and for particular schools on the basis of comprehensive and comparable data. Because this process was repeated annually for several years, it encouraged ongoing, shared learning and gradual improvements over time (Astor, Benbenishty, Marachi, and Meyer 2006). This local initiative was terminated after several years, however, mainly because of budget cuts.

In a similar vein, *Sheffy* began a nationwide voluntary data-driven approach with a survey instrument called the *Acham* (Hebrew for best educational climate). This instrument, which later became a Web-based survey, addressed an array of school safety questions, including many aspects of related school climate dimensions such as school connectedness, teacher-child relationships, participation in school, and an overall feeling of safety within the school. *Sheffy* helped administer the survey and worked with the school staff to help them plan their policy and interventions based on their data. School participation was voluntary and confidential—only the school leadership received the findings, and they decided whether and with whom to share the information.

This approach provided many schools with opportunities to develop their own school safety teams and guide their local efforts on the basis of their data. In an internal survey conducted in 2006 among principals who participated in this process, 75 percent expressed satisfaction with the information that they received from this process, and the ways in which it was presented to them. Furthermore, 80 percent said they were using the information for their planning processes to a large or to a very large extent. Most of the schools used the findings to identify a problem area that required a schoolwide response. Interestingly, only about 40 percent reported that they made major changes in their school safety policies. The rest either interpreted the findings as showing that they were doing well or thought that their current policies were effective.

The philosophy that guided the use of the school-level *Acham* emphasized the voluntary engagement and the confidential nature of internal processes. This philosophy had its advantages and limitations. On the one hand, the voluntary nature ensured grassroots buy-in and investment from the local school site; on the other hand, there were concerns that many schools with high school violence rates would not volunteer participation, because of their worries of being seen in a negative light.

Parallel to these voluntary system developments, Israel has created a sophisticated mandatory national system to monitor *academic* achievement in primary and junior high schools. This system had a major impact on school safety practices by providing a nationwide school-level data on climate and safety.

MERGING THE ACADEMIC AND SOCIAL-BEHAVIORAL DOMAINS ON A NATIONAL LEVEL

Internationally, during the last decades, governments have been mounting pressure to mandate every school to provide detailed academic standards-driven data. In the United States, this pressure culminated in the No Child Left Behind Act, which requires schools to monitor the academic progress of every student. Israel also created such a system, the *Meytzav.* With the *Meytzav,* the academic achievements of students in primary and junior high schools are tested, and detailed information is given to the principals and school staff with the goal of academic improvement.

This *Meytzav* system has existed for about a decade. In recent years, however, it has been revamped. It is now conducted through a new independent governmental agency—The National Authority for Measurement and Evaluation in

Education (*RAMA*). This highly professional agency is reassessing past practices and introducing major changes in the education measurement and evaluation system in Israel. These new developments in the instruments and methodologies of the national monitoring of schools provided an invaluable opportunity to integrate information on students' academic achievements with data on the school's social and pedagogical climate. It became clear to *Sheffy*, scholars, and the leadership of *RAMA* that including more detailed school social and pedagogical climate (including school safety) measures in the national academic monitoring system would create a stronger and more integrated reform context where every school had its own bi-annual academic, school climate, and school safety information.

Thus, the original school social climate elements of the *Meytzav* instrument were expanded and modified extensively on the basis of previous studies of school violence and climate in Israel and in collaboration with the *RAMA, Sheffy*, and academicians who had been studying this area for many years. These instruments are now included alongside the achievement tests.

Currently, there are monitoring versions for students, teachers, and principals. The instruments include sections on such issues as victimization in school, safety feelings, connectedness to school, school policies toward violence, staff violence, peer relations, and parental involvement (as assessed by the teachers). Students respond to paper-based questionnaires administered alongside the academic achievement tests. Teachers and principals are interviewed over the phone. This process is conducted in each school by outside personnel (supervised by the *RAMA*) every other year. Schools are encouraged to employ the instrument internally in the offset years. Whereas academic tests are conducted only in grades five and eight, the climate surveys include students from grades five to nine and teachers from grades one to nine. Every year, the process includes about 7,000 classes, 1,000 principals, 17,000 teachers, and 200,000 students.

This national mandatory system provides an extensive set of reports on the national, municipal, and school level. Each primary and junior high school (high schools may be included in the system in the near future) in Israel receives a school-level report that presents the prevalence of each type of school violence, and the distribution of multiple school climate indexes. The report compares the school with other schools with similar sociodemographic characteristics, and with previous reports of the school, to detect changes over time.

On an aggregated level, municipal- and national-level reports provide policy makers with important information on school violence and other aspects of school climate, comparisons between subgroups of schools, and changes over time. Furthermore, the national database supports a national priority setting with regard to schools that require special attention. Two groups of extreme cases are identified nationally: schools that experience high levels of violence, above and beyond what is experienced by all other schools that share similar demographics ("Schools in Focus"), and schools whose level of violence is so low compared with other schools, that they should be considered leaders in school safety ("Leading Schools"). Resources and interventions target the schools with high levels of violence, whereas leading schools are studied to identify effective practices that could be emulated and disseminated (for a similar process see, Astor, Benbenishty, and Estrada 2009).

The unique integrated national database that contains both academic achievement and school climate data is an important source for ongoing organizational and academic learning. It is being used to study the interrelationships between sociodemographic characteristics of the school's neighborhood and students, school's staff composition, pedagogical and social climate, school safety policies, and academic achievements of students. Currently, for instance, the *RAMA* is studying whether and how school social and pedagogical climate mediate and moderate the effects of the students' and schools' background on their academic achievements.

Additionally, the *RAMA* conducts periodic national-level studies to monitor school violence. These studies utilize more detailed instruments than the ones that can be used in the *Meytzav*, and employ large and representative samples of schools. This long-term monitoring maintains a longitudinal view of many aspects of school violence by grade level, culture and ethnicity, and gender.

THE USE OF DATA TO IMPROVE SCHOOL SAFETY

By itself, the availability of such rich information for each school does not ensure its effective use. Hence, it is not enough to generate relevant school-level data; it is essential to have a comprehensive conceptual and organizational model that maximizes the effective use of available information.

In Israel, both the *Meytzav* and the *Acham* reports are provided to each participating school. These reports are carefully designed so that they would be clear to nonsophisticated users, and they include graphics and explanations, so that readers can easily interpret the information. Furthermore, *Sheffy* has developed a system of supports for school counselors. This system consists of guides (*madrichim*), that is, senior counselors who accompany each of the counselors and the school climate team (headed by the school principal) throughout the processes of dealing with school climate and violence. The guides are specifically trained in the thorough understanding and interpretation of the information provided by both the *Acham* and the *Meytzav*. These guides are knowledgeable about the theory and practice in school safety. Furthermore, external supports for schools include in many instances the district-level supervisor and in a growing number of schools, outside consultants (such as academicians).

Thus, the interpretation of the information and the planning process are integrated in an interaction between the external supports and the internal school processes. School-level information is therefore an empirical, data-driven framework and a trigger for a series of interactions both between the external supports and the school and within the school. External supports offer feedback on school processes, interpretations, insights, and recommendations. These inputs go through internal processes that assimilate them into the school's culture, organization, and activities. In most schools the internal processes are initiated and coordinated by the school counselors. Nevertheless, the professional ideology of *Sheffy* is that counselors empower the school community to take responsibility for dealing with these issues, as part of the school's "way of life," rather than expecting counselors to introduce prepackaged manualized intervention programs.

The focus on grassroots interventions, and the preference for schoolwide approaches aimed to change major aspects of school climate, emphasize the need for an ongoing and long-term process of data-driven adaptations, rather than a "one-shot" evaluation of the effectiveness of a specific and well-defined intervention. In Figure 8.1, we illustrate a model of the iterative processes of schools that use

Figure 8.1   Data Driven School Safety Process

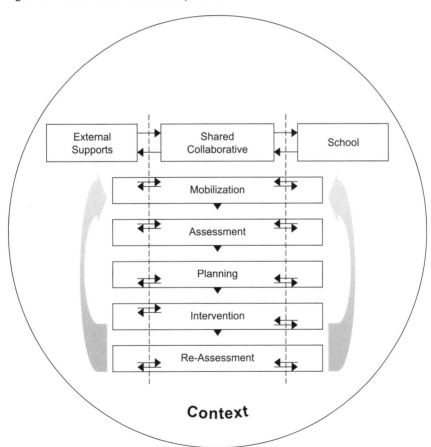

information to identify issues of concern, designing responses to these challenges and assessing progress toward the school goals.

In this model, schools engage with external supports and create a shared collaborative space. This space reflects what the external supports (such as guides and external supervisors) bring to the school as well as the contribution of the school to the dialogue. These interactions drive ongoing and iterative processes. It is essential to realize that all these processes are embedded within a local context. Each and every school is influenced by a myriad of factors, including its principal, staff, students, neighborhood, district, and school history. This context influences not only the information that the school gets from the various sources, but also how information is interpreted, what responses are desirable or feasible, and many other aspects that are relevant for how school safety is addressed.

The model describes ongoing processes that are driven by data. These include changing awareness as a response to pertinent information on the violence problem in school and the ensuing mobilization of the school community to address the issues. The information provided by the *Meytzav* and the *Acham* is used to assess the strengths and weakness of the school and the specific areas that may need attention.

The process of selecting school responses and policies should be based on a thorough familiarity with the available professional knowledge, and particularly what is known on validated evidence-based programs. Still, this knowledge is only one of the ingredients in the local decision-making process. A school may find a certain evidence-based program to be the best match for its needs and resources, but another school may realize that its current internal processes (for example, a new principal is not ready for major changes yet) may seriously impede the chances of effective implementation, and may select an alternative response, at least for the short run. Thus, similar findings may prompt different responses in different schools.

Even when a well-known and fully validated program is implemented, the question of whether this program would be effective in a specific local context and under specific circumstances is an open question to be answered by local data. Hence, the process of using the *Meytzav* and *Acham* data does not end when an intervention is chosen, as it continues to inform the ongoing evaluation of the changes in the school situation. Each time a school acquires relevant information, it is used to reassess the situation, evaluate ongoing efforts, and raise awareness to additional parts of the school puzzle.

In its brief existence, consistent use of the *Meytzav* and *Acham* data show promising results. *Sheffy* ran a pilot study and investigated 104 schools that have used the *Acham* more than once. An analysis of the distribution of changes over time in each of these schools, revealed that the number of schools that were able to reduce their levels of violence was three times that of the number of schools whose violence problem became worse. The range of improvement, however, was quite large: whereas about 45 percent of the schools improved up to 0.2 standard deviations, 16.4 percent of the schools improved 0.4 standard deviations or more.

CASE EXAMPLES OF HOW IT WORKED IN TWO SCHOOLS

The use of school-level monitoring information can be illustrated with two real-life examples. In the first example, the school provided students with a list of locations in the school and asked students to rate how dangerous they perceived that specific place to be. From the students' ratings it was clear that three locations were perceived as the most dangerous: (1) a small dilapidated area at the back of the school (an area not used officially by the school, (2) the school yard during recess, and (3) the students' restrooms. Following these findings and after deliberations among school leadership and the students, changes were introduced to address these concerns. First, after hearing the concerns of the students, the neglected area was adopted by an art teacher who worked with students to make the area a place for wall painting and wall-murals drawn by students. In addition, the janitor and science teachers partnered with student clubs to plant grass, shrubs, and trees in an effort to reclaim the territory. The formerly neglected space was thoroughly cleaned and became an "official" part of school grounds where students were allowed to go. In fact, it became a relaxing and positive place for students to "hang out" and express ownership over the space (with music and benches). Second, teacher presence and supervision (doubled) was enhanced on the school playground. The school chose to have positive and proactive supervision. The staff and student government initiated organized sports, board games, and music activities during recess. Finally, in a more radical move the problematic restrooms were moved right next to the teachers' lavatories (converting one of the teachers, restrooms to a student restroom). The new location was situated near the school office that had many people going in and out (thus higher visibility). The restroom was renovated with the help of students and parents to improve their appearance (for example, lining the walls with new ceramics).

The school conducted a similar survey a year later. The findings from students, teachers, and parents were mixed. Whereas the neglected "back of the main building" area was not seen as dangerous at all, and the dangerousness of the playground dropped significantly, the perception and incidence levels of violence within the new location lavatories remained quite the same as before. These somewhat-disappointing findings for the administration were then further discussed and evaluated by the school leadership and new ideas, such as having more teacher supervision in high-use time frames, were raised to address the problem identified by the survey. In the next round of surveys, violent behaviors in the restrooms subsided drastically (by half). These results demonstrate the fact that often it takes several rounds of data, discussion, ideas, and attempts to get to the root of the problem and gain any effects.

In another example, a new principal who entered a school with a negative reputation for violence decided to conduct parent surveys in addition to the student and teacher surveys. He introduced into each parent conference day a survey that was completed by parents while waiting to enter the teachers' room for the conference. The survey included a wide range of questions, some directly querying parents about their perceptions of violence and safety in the school. The principal shared the detailed and collective information with the teachers, and worked with the school staff and with the parent-teacher association to identify the top issues so that changes could be collaboratively planned. In the following years, the principal was able to show the school community that parents, students, and teachers had changed their views of the school climate considerably and correspondingly reported few violent events in their school. The collective survey information was later leveraged across the city in a successful marketing campaign to attract new students. Currently, the school has a waiting list of students who want to attend from all over the city.

CONCLUSION

In recent years, there has been a strong emphasis in the scientific literature on evidence-based policy and practice. The Israeli model presented in this chapter demonstrates a systematic way of creating policy and practice on pertinent evidence. This model is based on data that are collected and interpreted on multiple levels. Each school and region has current information on their local situation. This relevant evidence is interpreted, understood, and used for local decision making. These ongoing processes are the foundation of organizational learning and the identification of best practices. Current practices and role structures need to be developed further to support the integration of school social climate. The contributions of school safety to successful academic performance are critical goals for the future. Finally, because each school in the country is affected, the current system has created an infrastructure that, in the future, could support large-scale evaluation of evidence-based programs and randomized studies for different regions in the country.

REFERENCES

Astor, R.A., R. Benbenishty, and J.N. Estrada. 2009. "School Violence and Theoretically Atypical Schools: The Principal's Centrality in Orchestrating Safe Schools." *American Educational Research Journal* 46 (2): 423–461.

Astor, R.A., R. Benbenishty, R. Marachi, and H.A. Meyer. 2006. "The Social Context of Schools: Monitoring and Mapping Student Victimization in Schools." In *Handbook of School Violence and School Safety: From Research to Practice*, ed. S.R. Jimerson and M.J. Furlong, 221–233. Mahwah, NJ: Erlbaum.

Benbenishty, R., and R.A. Astor. 2005. *School Violence in Context: Culture, Neighborhood, Family, School, and Gender*. Oxford: Oxford University Press.

Benbenishty, R., R.A. Astor, and R. Marachi. 2006. "A National Study of school violence in Israel: Implications for theory, practice, and policy." In *Handbook of School Violence and School Safety: From Research to Practice*, ed. S.R. Jimerson and M.J. Furlong, 481–497. Mahwah, NJ: Erlbaum.

Harel, Y., J. Kenny, and G. Rahav. 1997. *Youth in Israel: Social Welfare, Health and Risk Behaviors in an International Perspective*. Jerusalem: JDC and Bar Ilan University.

Horovitz, T., and M. Amir. 1981. *Patterns of the Educational System: Coping with the Violence Problem*. Jerusalem: Henrietta Szald Institute.

Stone, S., R.A. Astor, and R. Benbenishty. 2009. Teacher and Principal Perceptions of Student Victimization and the Schools' Response to Violence: The Contributions of Context on Staff Congruence. *International Journal of Educational Research* 48: 194–213.

9

Community-Based Restorative Justice in Northern Ireland

Neil Jarman

IN NORTHERN IRELAND low-level crime, vandalism, and anti-social behavior remain a persistent problem in many working class communities, with young people identified as the dominant offenders and the cause of persistent problems and social tensions. Although Northern Ireland has been in a process of political transition for more than a decade, among the legacies of a generation of armed conflict has been willingness to use force to deal with social problems, the residual presence of paramilitary organizations, and a deep distrust of the criminal justice system. Collectively these factors have helped to sustain support for community-based initiatives in response to criminal and anti-social activities; and over the past decade community-based restorative justice projects have been established in a number of areas in an attempt to deal with local problems and build support for formal methods of justice. This paper describes the process of developing one such project in Belfast.

BACKGROUND

From 1969 to 1994 Northern Ireland was the site of an extended armed conflict over the constitutional status of the region and whether it was to remain part of the United Kingdom or to be reunited with Republic of Ireland in a single all-island state. The population of Northern Ireland was divided into members of the majority Protestant community who favoured the union with Britain and the minority Catholic community who were predominantly Irish nationalists. The conflict emerged from the failure of the Civil Rights movement to achieve political reforms and end discrimination against Catholics, and resulted in 3,500 people being killed, an estimated 50,000 people injured and tens of thousands being imprisoned. The armed conflict ended when the main paramilitary organizations, the Irish Republican Army, the Ulster Volunteer Force, and the Ulster Defence Association declared a ceasefire in 1994. These acts in turn stimulated a process of political dialogue involving local political parties, civil society groups, and the British and Irish governments that led to the signing of a peace agreement in April 1998. The peace process did not resolve the issues underpinning the conflict, nor did it bring an end to tensions and hostilities between the two main communities in Northern Ireland, but it did signal a change of approach and an agreement to resolve difference by dialogue, debate, and democratic process rather than by violence. However, the long duration of the conflict had created well-established patterns and justifications for the use of force to deal with a wide range of social and political problems and these had become deeply embedded in local culture and proved more difficult to address.

The paramilitary organizations were established primarily as military-like armies to fight against their counterparts and the British state forces, and although the British army was initially the front line of security and countering political violence, from the late 1970s the local police, the Royal Ulster Constabulary, took the lead in security matters. This ensured that the police were increasingly regarded as a key actor in the conflict, rather than being seen as primarily responsible for dealing with crime and public safety. This in turn created a vacuum in working class communities where the police were treated with suspicion and viewed as an unwelcome military presence.

This policing gap was in part filled by the paramilitary groups, who took it upon themselves (and it is often claimed, in response to demands from local residents) to 'police' the communities against various forms of crime and anti-social behavior and to impose 'justice' on those considered guilty of offences. Paramilitary justice took the form of kneecapping of perpetrators (shooting in the knees, plus legs, elbows, and ankles depending on the perceived seriousness of the offence), exiling people (from their immediate community or from Northern Ireland), or killing people.

The peace process and the agreement included a process of radical reform of the police, but even after the reforms were implemented from 2000 onwards, people remained suspicious and mistrustful of the police. One consequence was that the use of 'punishment' violence by the different paramilitary groups increased to levels that were higher than during the conflict, with around 270 people being shot or beaten by paramilitaries each year between 1995 and 2003. Furthermore, a growing number of such punishments were imposed on young people and even children, who were accused of criminal activities or anti-social behavior. Being targeted by the paramilitaries in this way further alienated some young people and their peers from adult authority.

Residents of some working class communities continued to support such actions by the paramilitaries, with people complaining of the failures of the police to deal effectively with crime and the criminal justice system working a slow pace and with a perception that too many prosecutions failed or that punishments were too lenient. Paramilitary 'informal justice' was in contrast tangible, visible, and immediate. However, other people argued that the process of transition should mean an end to all forms of paramilitary violence, and there was a need to find an alternative to the perceived limitations of the criminal justice system, and to create a process that responded to crime in an effective manner but that also had the confidence and support of the local communities. Growing numbers of people who were associated with the broad movements linked to the paramilitary groups (including politicians, community activists, and former prisoners) also became increasingly uncomfortable with the scale and nature of punishment violence and began to explore options that would reduce the number of punishment attacks while also responding effectively to social problems created by the policing and justice vacuum.

THE RESTORATIVE PROCESS

State criminal justice systems are based on a retributive process, one that responds to breaches of the law by some form of punishment or by exacting retribution, and where the nature of the punishment is to the scale or seriousness of the offence. Although the criminal justice system aspires to promote the rehabilitation of offenders, the re-offending rates in many countries illustrate how people who come into contact with the criminal justice system and obtain a criminal record tend to remain within its ambience. In recent years restorative processes have been put forward as an alternative to retributive forms of justice in certain circumstances. Restorative justice is a term that covers a broad range of activities and practices and which emerged from programs advocating mediation or reconciliation between victims and offenders developed in Canada and the United States in the 1970s. Others have cited parallels with models of dealing with social problems among indigenous societies in the Americas, New Zealand, and elsewhere. Restorative justice views crime not simply as an infraction of rules but as a form of interpersonal conflict which creates harm to real people. Restorative approaches aim to respond to crimes in a constructive and inclusive way and attempt to do so by repairing and restoring relationships between the offender, the victim, and the community at large.

Restorative approaches aim to be inclusive, insofar as they take into account the views and perspectives of all those with an interest in a case and attempt to bring both the victim and the offender into the process of addressing the problem. They also work to strike a balance between the needs and interests of the various parties to the process, with a key element being that participation must be voluntary rather than coercive. Participants utilize a problem-solving approach that is forward looking and strives to prevent future re-offending, as well as to reintegrate the offender back into the larger community. Thus restorative approaches acknowledge both the nature of the problem and the responsibility of the offender for his or her actions. Through this approach offenders are encouraged to take responsibility for the broader consequences of their actions and their impact on the victims. Offenders are strongly urged to initiate some form of reparation to the victim as part of a process of moving on. While restorative processes require an offender to take responsibility for their actions, participation in such a process generally allows the offender to avoid having a formal criminal record, thus further facilitating reintegration rather than re-offending.

In Northern Ireland there was considerable interest in the potential for restorative processes in the late 1990s. The state saw this as a means of responding to problems of offending, particularly by young people who did not have a long history of criminality. The Report on the Review of the Criminal Justice System in Northern Ireland (2000) which had been set up under the peace agreement recommended that restorative approaches be incorporated into the new justice system. Similarly there was considerable interest within sections of both the Protestant unionist and the Catholic nationalist communities, particularly among those with links to paramilitary groups who saw restorative approaches as a means of responding to anti-social behavior that had some level of community input and thus legitimacy, and that could also help reduce or eventually stop the use of punishment violence.

YOUNG PEOPLE AND VIOLENCE

The early years of the peace process saw the emergence of a significant problem of public disorder and rioting which was generally associated with the annual cycle of Orange parades and with tensions at the interfaces of segregated Protestant and Catholic residential areas. Young people were often prominent in such violence and disorder. Over the course of the conflict, rioting against the security forces had become generally accepted as a legitimate and acceptable activity in many working class communities. Many young people grew up in a culture where riots were a routine part of life, particularly during the summer marching season, and they readily followed their elders into the streets to confront the police or their counterparts in the neighbouring community. In the early years of the peace process young people were often encouraged to come onto the streets by adult members of the community and 'recreational rioting' soon became a popular pastime for the long summer evenings. If such behavior was initially accepted and tolerated, as political realities changed, the adult members of the community increasingly found it difficult to control such behavior. Inter-generational tensions began to equal and supersede sectarian inter-communal tensions in many areas and young people came to be classified as a social problem. They were readily accused of a variety of violent practices and the term 'youths causing annoyance' was adopted by the police to describe the main source of complaints they received from members of the public. In the early years of the new millennium the police in most if not all areas of Northern Ireland regularly claimed that they received the greatest number of complaints about problems with young people.

In most such cases the young people were doing little more than gathering together in public places to socialize. But some did cause persistent problems, particularly if drugs and alcohol were involved, and their behavior crossed the line into vandalism and crime such as burglary and car theft. Such young people often found themselves in confrontation with adult authority, whether this be the police or the paramilitaries, and this created a risk of being subject either to criminal justice or to paramilitary 'informal' justice. In either case the young person would be on a collision course with their wider community. In many working class communities there was concern at the increasing tensions, and in particular between adults and younger people, which grew in prominence as the peace became more solidly consolidated. Many community activists complained that they were expected to act as youth workers, which they were not trained for, and had to respond to disorderly and violent acts involving groups of young people, rather than dealing with tensions between neighbouring Protestant and Catholic areas. The community-based restorative justice projects were established in part to respond to this dilemma.

THE ALTERNATIVES PROJECT

Alternatives were initially established in the Protestant Shankill Road area of Belfast in 1998 (a similar scheme known as Community Restorative Justice Ireland was established in Catholic areas around the same time). Alternatives was initiated by individuals and groups associated with the Ulster Volunteer Force (UVF), one of the two main Protestant paramilitary groups. Tom Winston, an ex-prisoner working with EPIC (Ex-Prisoners Interpretive Centre), carried out research among local community activists, members of paramilitary organizations and workers with youth and community organizations to identify support for an alternative response to low-level crime that avoided the recourse to paramilitary punishment violence. The research identified that local paramilitary leaders were not enthusiastic at being involved in responding to crime and anti-social behavior and would be willing to support an effective alternative, if it could generate support among wider sections of the community. Tom's research outlined the model framework of a restorative justice program (see below) that was given the necessary community backing and he was charged with setting up Alternatives and initiating the project.

From the outset Alternatives included both former prisoners and former members of the paramilitary organizations as part of its staff team, although the organization always emphasized its independence and commitment to non-violence and drew in representatives of wider sections of the community. Since the beginning of the peace process many former prisoners had come to play a prominent and positive role in a range of peace-building activities and they were also seen as providing a public face to the wider paramilitary structures. In the case of Alternatives such connections ensured that the organization had a line of contact and an 'insight into the thinking' (to use a local euphemism) of the UVF, which enabled them to check out the veracity of threats on people who came to them and ensure the threat was lifted once they participated in the program.

The individual histories of people involved in Alternatives and the associations with armed groups necessarily raised some concerns among politicians within the state sector, among the police and within the criminal justice system. The response was to meet with key people to explain the aims and objectives of the project, set out the ideals and principles (including respect for human rights, non-violence, non-coercion, and consent) and to encourage an open form of engagement. From the outset Alternatives encouraged the police to send representatives to meetings and to participate on the board of management as a means of building trust and understanding in the approach that was being developed. But it was the work with young people that served to establish the benefit of the project.

The example of 'Billy' shows how Alternatives' Intensive Youth Support Programme works in responding to the problems of young people who are behaving in a violent, socially disruptive and criminal manner. The program aims to provide an alternative option to young people who are at risk of either being dealt with by paramilitary groups or through the criminal justice system.

Billy was an 18-year-old who was well known for drinking and abusive behavior, particularly towards older people. He contacted Alternatives after he had been threatened with 'kneecapping' by local paramilitaries following his abuse of a local woman. It was claimed Billy had broken windows in her house, thrown things at her in the street, and then stolen and crashed her car. The staff at Alternatives were also contacted by a senior paramilitary leader who said that it was felt that Billy had gone too far with the car theft and although no decision had yet been taken about whether Billy would be kneecapped, they would prefer that Alternatives deal with the problem if possible.

The coordinator at Alternatives met with Billy and an adult relative to outline his options, of which working with Alternatives was only one. He was advised that he could also go to the police, or another organization working with people threatened by paramilitaries. He was also told that participating in the Alternatives program would involve a mixture of service to the community, some form of restitution to the victim, and work on Billy's personal issues. Billy was given time to consider his decision, but he returned the following day having decided to work with Alternatives. While Alternatives staff began working with Billy, another member of the team, a volunteer trained in mediation, contacted the victim to inform her that a restorative process has begun and to ask if she had any immediate needs. In some cases victims and offenders are brought together as part of the restorative process but only if the victim desires this. In this case the woman was cautious about the potential of Billy making amends and stated that her main need was for the harassment to stop.

The work with Billy involved exploring the reasons for his behavior and building his understanding of the impact it had on the victim. Over a period of time and numerous meetings, Billy agreed to enter a 'contract' designed to respond to his previous behavior. This involved paying for the work to repair the victim's car, doing community service in a senior citizen's club, going to an alcohol awareness course, and refraining from drinking in public. Finally Billy was asked to present his proposal for approval to a panel of people who were not part of the Alternatives project but were representative of the wider community. Having received community support for his proposal, Billy was paired with another volunteer who mentored him through the process of making amends and restoring his position in the community, a process that took several months to complete. Although there is no formal compulsion to fulfil the contract, nor any retribution for failure to do so, around 90 per cent of people who begin the program complete it.

The Alternatives project, and the similar project run in Catholic areas, began receiving funding to develop their activities from an independent philanthropic source in 1999. An independent evaluation of the community-based restorative justice projects carried out in 2006[1] found that the projects had a significant impact on reducing paramilitary punishment violence, stopping more than 70 percent of punishments in Protestant areas where they were in place and more than 80 percent in Catholic areas. It also found that in 75 percent of cases, offenders dealt with by restorative approaches experienced no subsequent problems in their communities in the twelve months after their case was closed. The evaluation also noted that the projects had successfully promoted non-violent responses to crime and anti-social behavior, trained hundreds of volunteers in conflict resolution theory and skills, and had raised awareness of human rights issues among local groups and organizations.

DEVELOPING ALTERNATIVES

The relative success of the initial Alternatives project in the Shankill Road area led to similar activities being developed in north and east Belfast and in an estate in the neighbouring town of Bangor, with all projects linked under the umbrella structure of Northern Ireland Alternatives. In each case the projects were established in working class areas with a strong paramilitary presence and with problems associated with young people. In each case the local Alternatives group established a management committee drawn from a cross-section of the local community and also from statutory agencies. In North Belfast, for example, the management committee included community workers, the minister in the local church, representatives of the local school, the Northern Ireland Housing Executive (the body responsible for public housing), and the police.

One of the differences between the community-based restorative justice projects working in Protestant areas, compared with those working in Catholic areas, was their willingness to engage with the police. Police reform was a key component in the Northern Ireland peace agreement and in 2001, following an independent review and report on police reform, the Royal Ulster Constabulary

---

[1] Harry Mika (2006) Community-based Restorative Justice in Northern Ireland. Belfast, Institute of Criminology and Criminal Justice, Queens University.

became the Police Service of Northern Ireland. The new Police Service was based on a greater implementation of human rights principles and a focus on effective policing through working closely with members of local communities. Members of the Catholic community and particularly supporters of Sinn Fein remained wary of working with the police for some years after the reforms were initiated, whereas members of the Protestant community were willing from the outset to explore ways to work together. From the outset the Alternatives projects aimed to work closely with the police, and although there were suspicions about such projects within the wider criminal justice sector and among some political parties because of their association with paramilitary groups, the local police were engaged with from the beginning. Regular discussions and meetings meant that personal relationships were created and trust was built up on both sides, which helped establish the *bona fides* and credibility of Alternatives. Furthermore, the growing acceptance of Alternatives among the police in turn helped the organization create credability among other criminal justice bodies and the political establishment.

The value of the work being carried out at a community level was recognized at a higher level in 2006 when the government issued a consultation process on draft protocols for community-based restorative justice schemes. The purpose of this process was to incorporate such projects into the wider criminal justice sector and allow them to deal formally with cases of low-level crime on referral from the police. The protocols were approved in 2007 and this was followed by Alternatives being inspected by the Criminal Justice Inspector against five criteria before being able to receive their formal accreditation. The criteria were 1) openness and accountability; 2) partnership with other agencies; 3) equality and human rights; 4) training and learning results; and 5) value for the money spent on the program. Having received the formal accreditation, Alternatives was able to secure funding from a variety of government departments, statutory agencies, and independent funders in order to consolidate existing work and expand and develop into new areas with a degree of financial security. By 2010 the Northern Ireland Alternatives project employed twenty-two staff in four centers in the greater Belfast area and its programs were funded by a range of organizations including the Northern Ireland Office, the Department of Social Development, Social Services, the Northern Ireland Housing Executive, the Community Safety Unit, and the Probation Service.

As well as the intensive youth support program, which is based on referrals from the police for young people and young adults who have committed minor offences, the range of programs being delivered by Alternatives includes:

• Pupils and Community Together: An accredited peer mediation training and conflict resolution program run in a number of secondary schools in Belfast for 16-to 18-year-olds;
• Mediation and Community Support: A service level agreement with the Northern Ireland Housing Executive to intervene and support housing tenants who are involved in disputes; and

- Action for Community Transformation: A program which involves working with men who have previously been involved with paramilitary organizations with the aim of providing training in non-violent conflict resolution and the development of leadership and peacebuilding skills.

One of the major recent successes in Northern Ireland has been the development of the *Street by Street* project which was set up to challenge problems of persistent disorder by young people on the streets and other public spaces in east Belfast. The program draws on a network of staff and volunteers who work mostly at night and on weekends to engage with young people, challenge disruptive behavior, and provide reassurance to elderly residents. The relative success of this project has seen the police approach Alternatives staff with a view to replicating the project in a part of the city where Alternatives has not been previously active, thus highlighting how far the levels of trust and confidence in Alternatives had developed in a few short years.

CONCLUSIONS

The Alternative project has now been running for more than a decade and during that time has developed a wide range of programs to encourage restorative approaches to social problems affecting working class communities and in particular to respond to problems that are caused by, or impact the lives of, young people. Although there was some degree of suspicion about the potential of former combatants to take on a positive role in dealing with problems of crime and disorder, the organiszation has established sufficient credibility in its approach and its practice to have been able to secure funding from government and other statutory sources to deliver a range of projects that respond to crime, disorder, and social conflict. The organization has done so while remaining true to its original principles of following a community-led, non-violent, and restorative approach to social problems.

Over the past decade the approach adopted by Alternatives in seeking to involve the offender, the victim, and the wider community in developing an effective response to crime has contributed to the effective ending of punishment violence by paramilitary organizations and has helped to build more effective relationships between the police and local community groups and networks.

Having established a range of programs and projects, Alternatives now has to consider the most effective way of establishing its longer-term future. The devolution of police and justice from Westminster as well as the devolved government in Belfast may lead to some tensions and debate, particularly as some of the political parties remain wary of community-based initiatives in the field of policing and justice, which they still regard as the preserve of the state. But the track record of organizations such as Alternatives and the working relations that have been established with a diverse range of criminal justice bodies should ensure that the transition does not cause any sustained disruption to work that has been developed.

The more serious challenges that Alternatives faces relate more to internal organizational development and capacity to meet an increasing demand for services. It has been challenging to maintain the quality of its work and interventions in the face of ever greater calls on staff time and resources; and to maintain sufficient staff teams and collective organizational experience in light of the (currently) short-term commitment by agencies who are buying their services. In addition, it has been difficult to control the scale and nature of the future development of the organization given the large number of requests to establish new projects or develop new areas of work. While these challenges may pose demands on the organization, the experience that has been gathered by core staff members in building and consolidating Alternatives over the past decade will stand it in good stead for the future.

LESSONS LEARNED

Although Alternatives was established in a unique social and political context, it drew upon both theory and practice that had been developed elsewhere, and the experiences of the past decade can highlight lessons that might be indicative for projects in other jurisdictions.

1. *The value of a restorative approach*: The experience from Northern Ireland highlights the potential of a restorative justice approach as a response to youth involvement in low-level crime and anti-social behavior. Such an approach focuses on (re)building relationships rather than exacting retribution, and can offer people both a second chance and the opportunity to avoid gaining a record in the criminal justice system.
2. *Community-led initiatives*: Community or citizen-led initiatives that focus on independently responding to crime and disorder readily tend to be categorized (and criticized) as simply forms of vigilantism. The lesson from Northern Ireland is that community-led initiatives can work effectively and in a professional manner, while adhering to the principles of transparency and accountability and respect for human rights, and in doing so they can establish the respect and trust of the wider criminal justice system.
3. *Margins to mainstream*: The Alternatives example illustrates how a project which has been developed on the margins of, and as an alternative to the state system, and by people who have previously been involved in violent conflict with the state, can win over both critics and sceptics and become successfully mainstreamed, while still retaining its autonomy, independence, and community-level credibility.

REFERENCE

Criminal Justice Review Group. Review of the Criminal Justice System in Northern Ireland. March 20 2000. Belfast: Northern Ireland Office. Accessed online at: http://www.nio.gov.uk/review_of_the_criminal_justice_system_in_northern_ireland.pdf Accessed February 20, 2010.

The Groblershoop Youth Resilience to Violence Project

Patrick Burton

BACKGROUND

SOUTH AFRICA IS a country marked, both in reality and by widespread public perceptions, by high levels of crime and violence. Much debate exists whether South Africa occupies the rather dubious position of one of the world's most violent countries, but few dispute that the nature of crime throughout the country is unusually violent. The reasons for this have been explored in both academic and political literature, with the most common explanations providing some significance to the repressive and brutal nature of South Africa's history and transition to a democratic state culminating in the 1994 elections.

Although failing to provide a wholly adequate explanation for violence in South Africa, most explorations of violence, particularly committed by young people who constitute the largest percentage of violent offenders, relate to what Simpson referred to as "cycles of violence," or what more recently has been developed into the "normalization of violence," a constant bombardment of violent messaging and behaviors that serve only to further trivialize and entrench violent responses and emphasize violent means of achieving any desired end (Simpson 1998).

Most of the social characteristics that commonly are considered as correlates, or causes, of crime and violence coalesce in most urban and rural areas of South Africa. Despite positive attempts (and small successes) by the post-Apartheid government to address many of the social challenges left by Apartheid, factors remain that contribute to high levels of interpersonal and property crime. These challenges includes high levels of unemployment, with little scope for either formal or informal real employment growth in the town; increasing levels of substance abuse, particularly alcohol; high levels of teen and single mothers and pregnancy rates; poor social services and infrastructure; few recreational facilities; and poor education outcomes for many South Africans.

FROM YOUTH RISK TO YOUTH RESILIENCE

The risk factors, particularly relating to youth, for crime and violence, have been extensively studied and documented (Farrington and Welsh 2007; Hawkins et al. (2000); Maree 2003). These factors have informed the design and implementation of broad social crime prevention, safety, and youth policies, as well as the design of project interventions. These risk factors can be understood using an ecological approach that places an individual at the center of a series of systems that are interconnected and dependent. The innermost layer represents the individual, surrounded by the influence of family, schools, and peers, and then at the next level extended family, community neighbors, and friends, as well as more external factors like mass media, social and legal services, and so on. Each layer exerts some influence on, and in turn is defined by, the individual at the center, and determines or helps shape the developmental trajectory of the individual.

Within each of these layers, and the system as a whole, various risk factors exist that when present contribute to the likelihood that a young person will engage in crime and antisocial behavior as they develop. Most researchers agree that there is not a single risk factor that leads to child delinquency but rather an often-complex combination of conditions and factors that culminate in possible offending (Wasserman et al. 2003). Studies indicate that the greater number of risk factors a child is exposed to, the greater the possibility that he or she will display deviant behavior or commit a crime. The rationale of many programs is thus to minimize or mitigate as many of these risk factors as possible, thus reducing the likelihood that a young person will engage in crime, as well as improving the general quality of life of the person, or people.

The international movement, however, increasingly has focused more on identifying what the resilience factors are within young people that in fact protect them, or cause them to desist, from crime. Several reasons can be provided for this trend. First, many of the risk factors that have existed in literature and informed projects affect a large proportion of society. Yet despite the presence of these factors, the vast majority of individuals do not engage in violence. This suggests that there would be more use in determining what the factors that protect people from turning to crime might be, and then targeting these in programs and policies. Second, in the vast majority of program design and implementation, there is little assessment and prioritization of which risk factors are more pertinent within a particular context or time frame. Interventions aimed at addressing single aspects of the environment, or a single factor or a few risk factors, are rolled out with limited impact because other influential factors remain unaddressed. At the same time, debates exist on what constitutes a protective factor—whether such a factor is simply the converse or absence of a risk factor, or whether resilience exists as discrete variables (Farrington and Welsh 2007). The Center for Justice and Crime Prevention (CJCP) has built on the emerging international literature to identify and prioritize resilience factors within the South African environment, and through this research, has designed a demonstration youth project that builds the resilience of young people within a high-risk environment to violence. While using the broad layer of protective factors from the international literature as a departure point, the project was designed to focus in on those specific factors identified through the CJCP research as pivotal and most influential. Specifically, aspects of schooling and education, a peaceful home environment, non-exposure to criminal role-models (conversely, positive role models), abstinence from alcohol and other substances, neighborhood access to weapons, safety from youth victimization, attitudes intolerant of violence and antisocial behavior, and positive gender socialization, were identified as priority resilience factors that had a direct impact on proclivity to engage in crime and violence (Bonora, Burton, and Leochut 2009). Each factor, however, while affecting the likelihood to engage in crime, also strongly related to other factors—for example, youth victimization can affect positive education outcomes through the potential of crimes against youth to concentrate or form an attachment to school, or even to attend school. Similarly, positive education outcomes—an attachment to school and commitment to achieving—might mitigate the development of a violent masculine identity within a young person. It is these complexities and synergies between the various variables that necessitate a comprehensive approach to targeting each and every one of the resilience factors within a particular environment if any meaningful and sustainable impact is to be made in keeping young people from engaging in crime.

The encouragement of protective factors that deter young people from crime not only builds individual resilience but also contributes to the building blocks of a safer community and, ultimately, country. This strategy is arguably more cost-effective and yields more sustainable results than behavior modification following criminal behavior. To prevent the perpetration of crime and repeat offending among young people, it is important to offer young people long-term programming that focuses on mitigating risk factors and building personal and community strengths. In rural areas, in particular, where services are especially sparse, reactive and individual programs that run in isolation of sustained and proactive or preventative interventions have little success of creating positive change in young people.

It was from this departure point that the CJCP Groblershoop Youth Resilience to Violence Project was designed and implemented.

DESIGN OF THE PROJECT

The purpose of the CJCP Youth Resilience to Violence Project was to build resilience of young individuals across the key social institutions of the family, community, and schools, while also including support for the individual. Through this approach, the focus is on prevention and early intervention rather than later-stage, reactive response to violence and antisocial behavior.

Individual Level

On an individual level, the project offers activities that strengthen and expand existing diversion services to young offenders. The initiatives aim to enhance the key youth and child resilience factors of self-esteem, confidence, empathy, and self-control and teach children how to be responsible citizens. It is also a priority for the programs to promote healthy sexual identities and responsible health behavior. The projects are designed to provide access to information and communication technologies, thereby enhancing future employment opportunities. After-school and holiday programs are implemented to provide youth with constructive and enjoyable activities focused on sports and craft and culture. Leadership training is available in the form of workshops, specifically designed courses, and wilderness camps, and a mentoring program for at-risk youth has been established.

Family Level

On the family level, the project focuses on improving family communication and parenting skills through parent-child events and conflict resolution. The greatest achievements of child-focused interventions targeting violent and criminal behavior are those focused with children in their earliest years of development (Farrington 2007; Farrington and Welsh 2003). The family-level interventions have a particular focus on educating and supporting young fathers and teenage mothers. Family interventions espouse core principles of early childhood development (ECD), particularly those that focus on the role of parenting in setting positive examples for children. The groundwork for pro-social behavior and positive interpersonal relationships with peers and adults is learned through interaction with parents and relies on positive parenting skills. Family-level interventions support vulnerable families through the improvement of life skills and parenting skills that enhance the quality of life for children in the family.

Community Level

Community-level interventions seek to build social cohesion by strengthening community organizations and community structures. Rights-based awareness training workshops are conducted for community organizations. Young people, often excluded from safety and crime prevention interventions, are trained in community crime prevention and taught to identify potential dangers, unsafe areas, and safe community spaces. Through this process, young participants are encouraged to reclaim their community spaces and take ownership in making their communities safe.

School Level

School-level programming is an integral part of this program as schools form an integral part of community life and youth experience. A number of initiatives focus on reinforcing the positive role schools play in communities, especially for youth. Key nodes of care are implemented through international agencies such as the United Nations Children's Fund (UNICEF). A comprehensive meta-analysis of successful interventions focused on youth resilience highlighted the importance of including school-specific programs in a holistic approach to crime reduction (Farrington and Welsh 2003). The CJCP school-based interventions address violence and crime and explore how to build a culture of lifelong learning through the existing Hlayiseka Project.

The CJCP, in partnership with the National Department of Education and with support from the Open Society Foundation of South Africa (OSF-SA), had developed the Hlayiseka Early Warning System (HEWS), a school safety monitoring toolkit aimed at effective school management. The toolkit had been piloted, evaluated, and refined, and it has been rolled out at the ministerial priority schools nationwide, as well as at additional schools in a number of provinces, including Gauteng, the Western Cape, and the Eastern Cape. The Hlayiseka Project ensures that schools implement the necessary tools to address crime and victimization. The CJCP also advocated for the support of learners through afterschool activities and holiday programs. This ensures that opportunities for continued personal development and support are available for at-risk youth in the school. As such, the CJCP supports the integration of afterschool activities into school programming

---

Following are some stakeholder observations on the activities and their impact:

- **South African Police Service (SAPS):** The youth seem to have enhanced moral direction and violent crime committed by youth has decreased in Groblershoop.
- **Social development worker:** Youth now have opportunities for more constructive activities and fewer young adults and children appear in court for committing crimes.
- **Child welfare specialist:** The programs are enjoyable for young people while at the same time offering an education component to raise the consciousness of young people regarding social issues and crime.
- **School principal:** The CJCP programs develop the positive characteristics of young participants and parents—learners gain a sense of academic pride and parents become more interested in the development of their children.
- **Municipal manager:** The role of the CJCP as a major stakeholder in crime prevention is important because the municipality does not have a department specifically dedicated to those issues; the programs have positively changed the attitude of Groblershoop youth.
- **Social worker:** The initiatives have had a positive impact on the community as children now have access to services that did not before exist.
- **Kheis Municipality special programs officer:** The CJCP programs encourage youth leadership and train young people to act as role models for other youth.

and encourages schools to be responsive to community needs. The HEWS Toolkit provides a useful entry point to individual communities for further development of crime prevention work, engaging school leaders, learners, and educators, as well as parents. Although the Youth Resiliency to Violence Project was already firmly located within Groblershoop, the HEWS Toolkit is an essential component of the resiliency and school-based work of the project.[1]

Each of these activities are complemented by ongoing support to enhance the capacity of local projects to implement innovative diversion projects for young first-time offenders, targeting young people who have been in contact with the law for minor offenses. Targeted interventions at this stage in a young offender's experience minimize the risk of later, more serious offending and facilitate reintegration into society.

PROJECT SETUP AND CAPACITY BUILDING

The project initially was designed as a four- to five-year intervention that would be handed over to local stakeholders to implement in the long term. The setup, and institutionalization of project learning, as well as the buy-in and ownership of the project by the local community and partners, was thus essential.

The setup process included consultations and support from local community stakeholders, the development of a vision and mission statement, the identification of strong and effective leadership, and the mobilization and application of resources, as well as building the capacity for program implementation. At the outset of the project, the Northern Cape Department of Social Development facilitated a number of stakeholder and consultative meetings, drawing on school principals, nongovernmental organizations, local municipal councils, and community members. These meetings also provided an initial insight into some of the socioeconomic challenges faced by the community: poverty, alcohol abuse, domestic violence, lack of recreational activities, aggression and violence, housebreaking and theft, a high rate of school dropouts, and a lack of community involvement.

A local steering committee for the project was elected, consisting of the local ward councilor, a community development worker, a representative from the Structural Adjustment Program (SAPS), and a schoolteacher. After the steering committee was established, six volunteers were recruited to assist with program implementation. A baseline study was conducted by the research program of the CJCP, which collected data on key socioeconomic variables, victimization data, perceptions of crime and safety items, and service satisfaction variables. This data, together with stakeholder and service-provider interviews and analysis,

---

[1] The HEWS Toolkit has been expanded to include modules on parenting, offering positive parenting support to parents, as well as a xenophobia module.

provided, together with the information from the consultative meetings, an accurate profile of the community, as well as the specific needs.

From this baseline study, an initial set of project objectives, activities, and indicators was formulated. Central to its formulation are the vision and mission statements that provide overall guidance for the project. Similar guidance was provided to the project to select a name and develop its constitution. The Groblershoop Project adopted the name of !Kheis Youth and Community Development Project (KYCDP). The approval of the service plan, drafting of the constitution, and opening of bank accounts were prerequisites for the release of the seed funding.

Strong leadership is imperative to the success of a program. Leadership is required at every level of the projects; the ability to articulate and advance the vision and mission of the project enables the implementation of programs and services. The emergence of new leadership within the project surfaced via the steering committee and program coordinator. Solid and consistent leadership had a significant effect on other aspects of the project such as the number of project volunteers, the acquisition and management of resources, and the enhancement of networking activities.

The following training areas are included:

- Ongoing guidance, mentoring, and support visits
- Steering committee training
- Annual strategic planning workshops
- Facilitation skills
- Developmental assessment training
- Project management training
- Diversion and restorative justice training workshop
- Exposure to and internships with similar projects
- Facilitation of wilderness and adventure therapy programs
- Training toward compliance with the Minimum Norms and Standards on Diversion for adventure-based programs
- Training in compliance with the Minimum Norms and Standards for Diversion
- Financial management training
- Training on the implementation of mentor programs

With the steering committee structure firmly in place, focus turned to establishing a similar structure to support volunteers who, at times, were restless and frustrated because of the long delay in program implementation. As a result, program coordinators were appointed from within the existing project team to provide direction and leadership to volunteers. The CJCP placed strong emphasis on capacity building and support of the project and provided various training to support the implementation processes. Training was facilitated by the Northern Cape Department of Social Services. This training provided opportunities for sharing, connection, and teaching in an environment that counteracted the sense of isolation sometimes felt by members of small organizations.

CONCLUSION

Five years into the program, data collected from local probation officials reveal that the number of young people in conflict with the law in the area has dropped by almost 75 percent. The lack of any other interventions in the area at that time along with an unchanged policy environment, suggest that the changes evident in the data from those collected in the baseline study may possibly have been influenced to some degree by the combined, staged interventions rolled out under the program. Additional research will be needed to confirm this. A planned and staged handover of the project to local stakeholders is under way, with a phased exit strategy for the CJCP. Following complete withdrawal of the CJCP from the project, local stakeholders will receive ongoing mentoring and monitoring for twelve months.

The project illustrates how efforts to mitigate and respond to violence must be balanced by long-term systemic changes aimed at addressing the causes and drivers of this violence (Farrington and Welsh 2007; Jimerson and Furlong 2006). Rural areas present specific challenges for any type of development, often lacking services and infrastructure that support long-term and integrated initiatives. An important lesson learned in this project that can inform future social or developmental crime prevention programs, both rural and urban, is the importance of partnerships with communities and institutions and the need to identify and address community-specific risk and resiliency factors at various stages of youth development. The practices examined in this paper are intended to serve as an example that will increase the sustainability of future programs and, most importantly, shape innovative initiatives that provide the support, opportunities, and guidance youth need to become productive, happy adults, and to build safer communities for South Africa.

REFERENCES

Bonora, A., P. Burton, and L. Leochut. 2009. *Walking the Tightrope: Youth Resiliency to Crime and Violence in South Africa*. Centre for Justice and Crime Prevention Monograph Series No. 7. Cape Town, South Africa: Centre for Justice and Crime Prevention.
Farrington, D.P. 2007. "Childhood Risk Factors and Risk-focused Prevention." In *Oxford Handbook of Criminology*, ed. M. Maguire, R. Morgan, and R. Reiner. London: Oxford University Press.

Farrington, D.P., and B.C. Welsh. 2003. "Family-Based Prevention of Offending: A Meta-Analysis." *Australian and New Zealand Journal of Criminology* 36: 127–151.

Farrington, D.P., and B.C. Welsh. 2007. *Saving Children from a Life of Crime: Early Risk Factors and Effective Interventions*. New York: Oxford University Press.

Hawkins, J.D., T.I. Herrenkohl, P.D. Farrington, D. Brewer, R.F. Catalano, T.W. Harachi, and L. Cothern. 2000. *Predictors of Youth Violence, Juvenile Bulletin*. Washington, DC: U.S. Department of Justice, Office of Juvenile and Delinquency Prevention.

Jimerson, S.J., and M.J. Furlong, eds. 2006. *Handbook of School Violence and School Safety*. London: Lawrence Erlbaum Associates.

Maree, A. 2003. "Criminogenic Risk Factors for Youth Offenders." In *Child and Youth Misbehviour in South Africa: A Holistic View*, ed. C. Bezuidenhout and S. Joubert. Hatfield, South Africa: Van Schaik Publishers.

Simpson, G. 1998. "Urban Crime and Violence in South Africa." In *Justice for Children: Challenges for Policy and Practice in Sub-Saharan Africa*, ed. C. Petty and M. Brown, 66–71. London: Save the Children.

Wasserman, G.A., K. Keenan, J.C. Tremblay, T.I. Herrenkohl, R. Loeber, and D. Petechuk. 2003. "Risk and Protective Factors of Child Delinquency." www.ojjdp .ncjrs.org.

PART III

Multisector Interventions

Nothing Stops a Bullet Like a Job: Homeboy Industries Gang Prevention and Intervention in Los Angeles

Jorja Leap, Todd M. Franke, Christina A. Christie, and Susana Bonis

I wish people could understand what it was like to be in a gang. I have lived that life. I have held dead people in my arms. But Homeboy is the place that finally helped me. It leads you to a different direction. The knowledge you have from the streets—you use it here in a positive way—you wish there were places like this when you were younger, but now you can be someone's example—you can help save someone's life. You can tell them, everything is going to be all right and help them get the services they need. That's the thing about Homeboy—we mentor one another. There is the thing about Homeboy and the situation here—people feel love.

—Hector, age 24, Homeboy Industries

HOMEBOY INDUSTRIES (HBI) is one of the best-known anti-gang programs in America, offering a statement of purpose that also serves as a mantra: "Nothing stops a bullet like a job." Beyond this, its formal mission is to assist at-risk and formerly gang-involved youth to become positive and contributing members of society through job placement, training, and education. Originally founded in the Pico-Aliso housing projects of East Los Angeles by Father Greg Boyle—known to policy makers and gang members alike as "G"—HBI has developed a complex intervention framework serving thousands of youth throughout Los Angeles and its surrounding enclaves.

Los Angeles is often referred to as the "gang capital of the world." The label is accurate: this region is home to one of the largest and most entrenched number of street gangs on Earth. These gangs give rise to violence and criminal behavior involving young men as well as women at increasingly younger ages. Additionally, community fear and intimidation has affected both quality of life and public safety throughout Southern California for more than three decades. In this time period, three major approaches have been used to deal with gang violence: suppression, intervention, and prevention. Through trial and error, prevention and intervention strategies have been synthesized, and a comprehensive approach to this problem is now being applied to communities in which gang activity and violence is most likely to occur. For 20 years, HBI has played a significant role—alone and as part of the comprehensive approach—in both gang prevention and intervention in Los Angeles County. Its reputation now crosses borders: in one week, practitioners from as far away as Canada and Japan visited in order to study its program and varied components. Every year, in addition to policy makers and practitioners, more than 12,000 gang-involved individuals walk through its doors and receive help. The numbers show no sign of decreasing—in fact, the demand for services continues to grow: a visit to their headquarters any day of the week reveals a waiting room filled with people and a two-story center busy with activity.

So many people find their way to HBI for good reason. In Los Angeles and throughout the United States, few targeted prevention and intervention programs reach young men and women at highest risk of either joining gangs, youth in the early stages of gang membership, or gang members wanting to leave the gang lifestyle and reintegrate into the community. Such programs are vital to dealing with gang violence and reducing the attractiveness of gang life—but they continue to be woefully underfunded.

In Los Angeles, funding for anti-gang programs comes from a variety of sources, including the federal and state government, along with private foundations and individual donors. With the economic downturn beginning in 2009 and extending into 2010, however, and the increased demand for funding from newly organized city and county programs, a simple but vexing problem arose: demand far outstrips the available funding. Why is there such an incredible need?

Father Greg often explains that gangs and youth violence are caused by "a lethal absence of hope." This eloquent phrase serves as shorthand for the many factors at the heart of gang violence: dysfunctional families, inadequate schools, violent environments, and guns. Specific "risk" factors are at play: poverty, disorganization, and availability of drugs and firearms. But alongside these, there are also protective factors—that is, strengths within each community that work to inoculate children and youth against gang activity and violence—such as education, positive relationships and pro-social activities. Just as the seeds of youth violence are sewn in tragically disturbed families and impoverished environments, so too can the fundamentals of the solution be found right within the community where gangs evolve. The idea that the community is a resource and the importance of decreasing risk factors and increasing protective factors guide the theory of change at HBI. HBI interventions flow from the community and from the belief that a gang member is much more than the worst thing he or she has ever done.

From the start, the development of HBI has been inextricably tied to the community—emerging as part of a grassroots movement that arose in the *barrios* of East Los Angeles in 1988. All this occurred long before any systematic government response to the gang problem, during an era in which gang violence peaked and Los Angeles lived through "the decade of death" from the mid-1980s to the mid-1990s. Faced with this uncontrolled outbreak of gang violence, community members, a handful of probation officers, and a young Jesuit, Father Greg Boyle, joined forces to provide youngsters with an alternative to gangs. No one dreamed where HBI would be more than two decades later, in 2010. The population HBI initially served was based in Boyle Heights and composed mainly of Latino gangs. Three years ago, its headquarters and main training facility moved from a small storefront in East Los Angeles to a large, two-story building in the city's heart, serving at-risk and gang-involved youth from "every zip code in Los Angeles County."

In the beginning, there was no specific theory of change or rationale that drove the intervention offered by HBI. Father Greg has explained how organic program development was and sometimes continues to be, detailing how mothers in the community met and organized, "insisting we had to do something to stop all the violence and save their children from gangs." What was to become HBI began with the establishment of a middle school "for kids who had gotten into trouble." Once the school was up and running, there was a dual realization: something was needed for youth beyond the classroom to guarantee they would not join a gang and something was needed for active gang youth beyond the "neighborhood" that would allow them to leave the gang life.

As a result, the entire community became involved in creating a jobs program, pamphlets were printed, and the mothers in the community organized a march that was a crazy quilt of diversity. A member of the Homeboy Senior Staff recalled, "You should have seen it—the grandmothers were marching next to these gang members, probations officers, and social workers—everyone was there!" Father G added, "We asked these men and these women if they would give just one job to a homie or homegirl or to someone who needed it—a kid with problems or obstacles who just couldn't get a job anywhere else."

This grassroots movement and community organizing soon led to the development of an employment-training program, which Father G titled, "Jobs for a Future." The many community members—parents, grandparents, and stakeholders—also worked to establish a charter school at HBI to further reinforce the importance of education and work readiness. The theory of change at HBI further expanded to include the idea that an executive staff that includes former gang members in leadership positions is vital to the Homeboy program. Perhaps the development of a theory of change at HBI is best summarized by Father G, "As needs have presented themselves at Homeboy, programs were born." Everything that is here— both prevention and intervention—it is all organic and born from this population expressing what they need—and the place responds."

HBI works with "multi-problem" clients in a systemic and holistic way. Because of this, HBI involves virtually every sector of the Los Angeles community. But, there is an added ingredient that Father G describes, "Anyone who walks through those doors knows there is a feeling of acceptance, everyone can sense what is really the therapeutic elixir present in this building." For those who work or even visit HBI, it is more than a program. To explain this, G observes that HBI serves as a "symbolic representation of hope to all 86,000 gang members in Los Angeles county—whether they are ready to walk in our doors or not. And we represent hope to the kids who may feel they have to join a gang but don't want to. We seek to deal with the whole person now—not just employment."

The majority of Homeboy clients fall between the ages of 18 and 35, with a 3–2 ratio of males to females. These "homeboys" and "homegirls" have already faced and continue to face violence and conflict within their communities and families as well as within themselves. Most have been victims of violence, directly and indirectly; many have served time in the juvenile justice system and in probation camps and halls. Almost everyone at HBI suffers from post-traumatic stress disorder (PTSD). Additionally, substance abuse is an ongoing problem. But all are united in their desire, however new and untested, to find an alternative to gang life. The need for services at Homeboy far outstrips its capacity; a client selection process, led by senior leadership staff and Father G, takes into account numerous factors in hiring decisions, including client commitment to and readiness for change, urgency of a client's situation, obstacles faced as well as gang affiliation and its impact on the "pH" or balance of gangs represented at HBI.

The separation from gang life is marked by a long-term process, not a moment of immediate change. For this reason, Homeboy does not set a time limit on program participation. "We don't want people at Homeboy Industries for the next 25 years," Father Boyle insists, "but it takes whatever amount of time it takes. We require you to do certain things at Homeboy, we want to prepare you to move on into the world and work." HBI offers a broad spectrum of programs and services that will help clients develop new identities alongside work readiness and steps toward economic independence. Additionally, HBI recognizes that not everyone needs or wants to be a full-time Homeboy worker. Instead, HBI programs and services are available to the general public on a drop-in basis. It is the youth who are employed by HBI who receive structured support and for whom the intervention dosage is the highest and most consistent. Figure 11.1 represents the action theory of HBI.

The gatekeeper service is case management. The case manager conducts a client needs assessment and connects the client to appropriate programs and services at HBI, documented in an action plan with goals, benchmarks, and timelines. The case manager remains a central figure throughout one's stay at HBI. The possible programs and services available at HBI include the following:

- **Mental Health Education and Treatment Assistance Services:** HBI provides both short- and long-term individual and group therapeutic counseling through licensed clinical social workers, marriage and family therapists, and a psychiatrist. In addition, counselors dedicated to substance abuse and domestic violence abuse are on staff to provide support to clients. HBI's substance

Figure 11.1 Action Theory of Homeboy Management

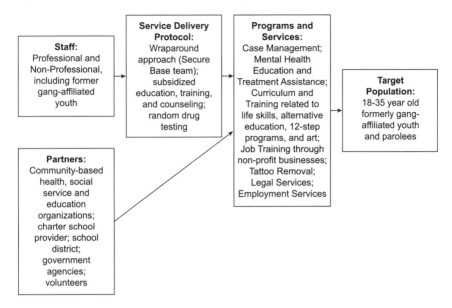

abuse service is offered on an outpatient basis and uses a cognitive-behavioral approach to substance abuse intervention, helping clients develop coping skills to deal with thoughts and emotions thought to either precipitate or maintain addictive behaviors. Clients requiring more intense services are referred to local residential drug and alcohol treatment centers.

- **Curriculum and Training:** HBI's wide range of courses fall into four categories: life skills (for example, leadership, sex education, parenting); alternative education (for example, General Education Diploma classes, charter high school); 12-step programs (for example, Alcoholics Anonymous, Criminals and Gang Members Anonymous); and art programs. Partnering with the Los Angeles Unified School District, HBI also provides training in solar panel installation. Many additional courses are offered in collaboration with local schools and community-based organizations. Additionally, HBI assists youth in applying to community colleges and state universities.
- **Job Training:** HBI oversees four businesses that employ its clients in a safe, supportive environment that teaches both concrete and soft job skills, while simultaneously building resumes and work experience. The businesses include *Homeboy Bakery*, which trains clients to become scratch bakers; *Homeboy Silk-screen*, which prints logos on apparel; *Homeboy/Homegirl Merchandise*, which sells clothes and items with the Homeboy logo; and the *Homegirl Café*, which trains female clients in the restaurant and catering industry. *Homeboy Press* and *Homeboy Music* are two pilot business projects that build on the skills and

interests of clients expressed in classes. HBI administrative and programmatic offices also offer job-training opportunities. Employment at Homeboy headquarters often precedes employment in one of the Homeboy businesses. The office setting permits a closer relationship between supervisor and employee, fostering development of work readiness in both attitudes and behaviors.

- **Tattoo Removal:** Using volunteer physicians, HBI offers laser tattoo removal to enable former gang members to remove visible tattoos that serve as an obstacle to obtaining employment.
- **Legal Services:** HBI provides support and referrals for clients facing myriad legal issues, including clearing warrants, expunging records, resolving child custody, and establishing immigration status.
- **Employment Services:** HBI employment counselors or "job developers" assist clients once they are ready to transition out of Homeboy. Job developers maintain a database of job openings and client qualifications to support employment matches. Working to increase this database, job developers seek out new employers, explaining both the challenges and benefits of hiring Homeboy clients.

The value of the Homeboy model is probably best evoked in the stories of the many homeboys and homegirls who have been part of the Homeboy organization. Jorge Perez[1] represents one such client.

Jorge Perez grew up within a fractured family, "My dad was a gang-banger and my mom's family were all gang-bangers." His childhood was marked by domestic violence, drugs, and criminal activity. "At my house there was always drama. People were selling drugs, partying and my family got caught up in it. But I was good at school and kept at it until I turned 12 years old—and then I changed. I told my mom, 'I want to go to prison one day'."

Jorge was arrested for the first time at 12 and shot for the first time at 13. At 14, he started drinking and doing drugs. By the time he was 15, he was supporting himself by drug dealing. When he reached his 18th birthday, Jorge had fathered two children and compiled an arrest record that included assault with a deadly weapon, second-degree robbery, and vehicular manslaughter. Jorge had finally made it to prison after a court-appointed psychiatrist declared him "a menace to society." Four years later, in 2007, he was paroled and went straight to HBI. It was there his life began:

> I got hired. In my head I was still institutionalized—but I concentrated on doing my job. I had a mentor—Marco—who really helped me. But I knew I was having a lot of problems—anger and anxiety—and I decided to see a counselor—there was one right there at Homeboy. That really helped me. I also took some computer training. I kept thinking, "I won't be able to do this," but everyone helped me and told me I could. My girlfriend was having some problems, she had a drug problem, she was pregnant with our third baby and she needed help. Homeboy helped her get prenatal care and sent her to rehab. After I was there for almost a year, an opportunity came up, and the

---

[1] Jorge Perez is a pseudonym and certain details of his story have been altered to preserve anonymity.

job coordinator at Homeboy asked me, would I like to be a case manager? I learned by doing that job—I don't preach—but I try to speak my truth. I know everything here—so if you're a new person who gets out—I am going to help you out. I got total job training being a case manager and just last week I was offered a job by Los Angeles County Probation—the same people who locked me up when I was 16. I am going to be a youth counselor. I feel excited, a little scared, and very happy. I was amazed that I got this opportunity. And G told me, "You'll always be part of Homeboy."

Jorge Perez exemplifies the "success case client" currently being studied in the evaluation described below. He succeeded in school at an early age, demonstrated skills and a willingness to learn, and ultimately was able to take advantage of the full range of services at HBI.

EVALUATION: CHALLENGES AND OUTCOMES

In such a dynamic environment, evaluation is a tremendous challenge. With any program built from the grassroots, outcomes are rarely well defined. In partnership with Father G and HBI, a research team from the University of California–Los Angeles (UCLA) have designed and developed a longitudinal evaluation of the program with the generous funding of the John and Dora Haynes Foundation. The evaluation, currently under way, combines both qualitative and quantitative measures, offering both "stories and numbers" to paint a picture of HBI. Before defining outcomes, the UCLA team considered both "success" and "struggling" cases to understand what individuals experienced as they participated in the Homeboy program. Measures are now being developed to assess whether HBI is truly successful, with whom, and why. But there have been lessons learned in developing and growing HBI, some with implications for implementation of this type of program in other settings. Based on the case of Jorge Perez and others like him, preliminary evaluation has revealed a pattern of impact as portrayed in figure 11.2.

The impact theory picks up where the action theory leaves off, outlining the cause and effect sequences that connect HBI programs and services to short-term and long-term outcomes. In this model, the primary mediators are highlighted in darker shading: hope, attachment, self-esteem, self-efficacy, emotion regulation, coping skills, and pro-social orientation. Also critical to understanding how the programs and services of HBI affect clients are the influences that can help or hinder progress. Moderators include addiction relapse and locus of control.

HOPE AND ATTACHMENT: THE FOUNDATION OF HEALING

The culture of HBI is warm, welcoming, and nonjudgmental. Staff abides by the motto that the young people they work with are "who they are meant to be," with strengths and potentials; staff work to help youth become better versions of themselves. This culture is felt immediately when one enters HBI, offering clients hope and attachment.

Figure II.2 Impact Theory of Homeboy Industries

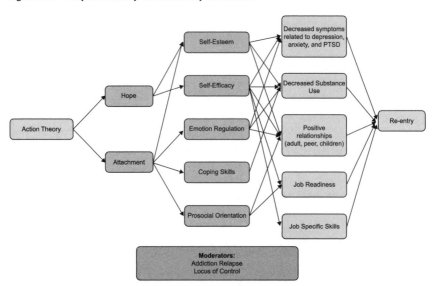

Snyder (1995) identifies hope as having two components, the cognitive willpower or energy to get moving toward one's goal (agency component) and the perceived ability to generate routes to get somewhere (the pathways component); in essence, there must be a will and a way. Homeboy offers youth a way; many come with the will—although with varying degrees of will, and this will may increase during one's time at Homeboy. Changes in levels of hope can occur over time through sustained interventions such as counseling and education.

In addition to helping to awaken hope in youth and young adults, HBI helps to repair or build a sense of security and trust. Erikson's (1963) stages of development and Bowlby's (1983), attachment theory inform Homeboy's efforts to provide a secure attachment relationship for its clients. Most young people at HBI experienced dysfunctional family life along with seeing negative, destructive relationships between adults around them. Many spent time in the foster care system. Through informal mentoring, counseling, and secure base teams, HBI fosters the development of consistent and caring relationships between youth and at least one adult. This positive attachment is the basis for subsequent development of youth and young adults at HBI occurring in two domains: intrapersonal and interpersonal.

INTRAPERSONAL DEVELOPMENT

In the intrapersonal domain, youth and young adults at Homeboy experience an increase in self-esteem, self-efficacy, and emotion regulation—through a variety of processes. From the beginning, clients observe former gang-affiliated youth progressing through Homeboy's various programs and career ladder; they interact with HBI staff members who once were gang members. One of HBI's strengths is its balance between professional staff and individuals who know first hand the struggles clients face. While self-esteem and self-efficacy begin with these early experiences, HBI structures situations that offer its clients "mastery experiences," through success in job training opportunities. This is portrayed in figure 11.2 as a two-way relationship between self-efficacy and job readiness and self-efficacy and job-specific skills.

Along with self-esteem and self-efficacy, many homeboys and homegirls are impulsive, angry, and have great difficulty regulating their emotions. "I got trouble feeling my feelings," one homegirl cried. Through counseling and training, HBI helps these youth to recognize their emotions, learn regulation strategies, and to express feelings in appropriate ways.

Emotional regulation along with self-esteem and self-efficacy are key components of socially competent individuals. Their development is key to the growth of positive relationships with adults, peers (including co-workers), and children, one of the expected outcomes at HBI. These intrapersonal variables are expected to lead to decreased symptoms of depression, anxiety, and PTSD, and to decreased substance abuse.

Substance abuse is one of the major coping skills used by youth attempting to leave the gang life. HBI provides its clients with alternative ways of meeting needs and modifying drug dependence through cognitive-behavioral approaches that introduce new coping skills. By teaching youth ways to refuse drugs, handle criticism, and express feelings, while building support networks, HBI helps its clients to grow and truly develop into their "best selves."

INTERPERSONAL DEVELOPMENT

Along with interpersonal coping skills, clients at HBI begin to develop a pro-social orientation and job readiness as part of their interpersonal growth. The secure connection to an attachment figure also influences the development of pro-social values. Pro-social behavior is further reinforced by the gratitude that many youth feel to their attachment figure and to HBI itself. Youth demonstrate pro-social behaviors as they interact with staff as well as with members of the general public who visit HBI. Homeboys and homegirls interact with the public at HBI, offering tours, making presentations, answering questions, and helping visitors to find their destination, even if this means having to ask multiple people at HBI or accompanying a person until their needs are met. Trainees often will watch out for one another, an act made all the more meaningful given that many youth come from rival gangs. In the impact theory model, this pro-social orientation is seen as leading to more positive relationships and to job readiness.

Job readiness is a central component to employability and it can include basic skills such as literacy and numeracy and social behavior such as punctuality and attendance (Eley 2007).

The HBI career ladder supports the development of job readiness. Trainees often begin their work at HBI administrative and program offices, instead of its businesses. In this setting, the supervisor-trainee ratio is lower and there is greater flexibility in time and duties. As individuals become more job ready, they move into the businesses, where they begin developing various job specific skills.

SUMMARY OF HOMEBOY MEDIATING RELATIONSHIPS

Following is a summary of HBI's approach to mediating relationships:

1. Hope leads to self-esteem and self-efficacy.
2. Attachment leads to self-esteem, self-efficacy, emotion regulation, coping skills, and pro-social orientation.
3. Self-esteem, self-efficacy, and emotion regulation lead to decreased symptoms of depression, anxiety, and PTSD, to decreased substance use, and to positive relationships.
4. Self-efficacy affects both job readiness and job-specific skills.
5. Coping skills also influence decreased substance use.
6. Pro-social orientation influences positive relationships and job readiness.

MODERATORS

Two moderators influence the Homeboy model: addiction relapse and locus of control. Addiction relapse can negatively affect almost every relationship in the model. In its most extreme cases, addiction relapse can cause a client to be "taken out" of HBI through suspension, referral to a treatment center, or even incarceration.

An internal locus of control is one of the most essential components of resilience. People with an internal locus of control believe that their own behavior and actions influence events, whereas those with a high external locus of control believe that powerful or unknown others, fate, or chance primarily determine events. Among Homeboy clients, internal locus of control is reinforced as the homeboy or homegirl accepts responsibility for their actions as a gang member. As HBI clients develop an internal locus of control they express fewer resentments toward others, including law enforcement and rival gang members. The internal locus of control is strengthened through experiences within the HBI program.

The hope that HBI offers and its model for gang intervention and violence prevention is entering a new phase. In the years ahead, as the longitudinal evaluation uncovers both processes and outcomes, research findings will accompany the many services offered by this remarkable place. As one homeboy explained, "This is the place that gave me my life."

REFERENCES

Bowlby, J. 1983. *Attachment*. Vol. 1, Attachment and Loss Series. New York: Basic Books.

Eley, S. 2007. "Job Searching with a History of Drugs and Crime." *Howard Journal of Criminal Justice* 46 (2): 162–175.

Erikson, E. 1963. *Childhood and Society*. New York: W. W. Norton.

Snyder, C. R. 1995. "Conceptualizing, Measuring, and Nurturing Hope." *Journal of Counseling and Development* 73: 355–360

12

Youth Violence Prevention around the World: The YouthBuild Case Study

Tim Cross

Everyone used to think I would wind up dead. But when I found people who believed in me, who showed me I could do something good and leave gangbanging behind, I began to see myself in a different light. When you are respected instead of feared, you are more powerful.

For everyone who experiences YouthBuild a seed is planted. Youth-Build made me stop hating the world. I discovered myself at YB. I am finally paying attention to what everyone at YouthBuild told me—that I can make something of myself. They've said it so often I believe I can do it. I challenge myself everyday to see if what they said about me is really true. To this day, I am still working on being a better person.

—Natalia, YouthBuild graduate and current staff member

ORIGINS

THE SEED FOR the creation of the YouthBuild was planted in East Harlem, New York, in 1978, and began, as all YouthBuild programs begin, with a question posed to young people by a caring adult. The question was simple: What would you do to improve your community if you had the resources you need to put your ideas for improvement into action? The young people who were asked this question had the same answer: We would rebuild abandoned buildings to create homes for homeless people and take back empty buildings from drug dealers. At the time more than 300 abandoned buildings blighted the East Harlem landscape, and thousands of idle teenagers and hundreds of homeless people roamed the streets. The young people's answers provided an obvious solution to all three tragic problems. Why not train and employ out-of-school unemployed young people to rebuild the buildings, creating affordable housing for the homeless? This is what YouthBuild does. At the same time, it educates and inspires the youth to become permanent community role models and leaders and educates policy makers regarding the valuable contributions young people are capable of making to the community development process. At the time, this question was posed to young people by Dorothy Stoneman, founder of an early childhood education program in East Harlem that serves low-income parents who are seeking quality, affordable education for their children. It took another five years for young people working with dedicated adults to rehabilitate their first building site. New partners had to be found to support the effort, including local residents, city officials, construction unions, public schools, and public and private donors. Many of these eventual partners resisted the proposed effort, not believing that poor kids from Harlem were up to the task, mistrusting the motives of other partners, and voicing skepticism of the "workability" of turning the completed structures over to formerly homeless adults. In adult-led forums where young people had organized their arguments and would speak up to describe and defend their vision, the presentations were dismissed as idealistic and unrealistic. This first effort, along with the many challenges and pitfalls that the leadership group confronted in those first five years, would provide essential lessons to guide the growth of what would come to be the national YouthBuild movement.

YouthBuild is grounded in the philosophy that given the right context—an environment filled with respect, a caring community, a positive peer group, a valued role in the neighborhood, an opportunity to develop skills, high standards of self-discipline and performance, and the means to a future education and employment—young adults with troubled pasts can transform themselves into productive citizens with viable futures. YouthBuild provides this opportunity through a unique combination of education, skill building, counseling, leadership development, community services, positive values and relationships, high standards of behavior, and clear pathways to a productive future.

YouthBuild students get a chance to build a positive track record that can outshine the difficulties of the past and to develop community ties as well as the skills and values that will enable them to succeed. YouthBuild meets their needs precisely and does so in a context that is not stigmatized, in which they can work alongside other youth as heroes in their community, building an important and visible community asset for their neighborhoods. YouthBuild demonstrates that marginalized young people—many of whom have been homeless, incarcerated, gang involved, or victims of forced migration and violence—can play a positive, contributing role in their communities when they are provided access to a program tailored to meet their many and varied needs. The program is infused with faith in the sacred value of every human being and guided by the knowledge that the power of love coupled with the power of opportunity can overcome enormous obstacles.

THE YOUTHBUILD DESIGN AND RESULTS

During the 9- to 24-month full-time YouthBuild program, youth spend half of their time learning construction trade skills by building or rehabilitating housing, schools, playgrounds, and community centers; the other half of their time is spent in a YouthBuild classroom advancing their basic education skills toward a recognized academic credential. Personal counseling and training in life skills and financial management are provided. The students are part of a mini-community of adults and youth committed to their mutual success and to improving the conditions of their neighborhoods.

In the United States, YouthBuild supports a network of 272 independent programs in 44 states, engaging 10,000 young people on an annual basis. Since 1994, more than 84,000 YouthBuild students have produced more than 18,000 units of low-income housing. In Canada, Mexico, Nicaragua, Guatemala, El Salvador, Honduras, Jamaica, Haiti, Brazil, South Africa, Israel, Bosnia, Serbia, and the United Kingdom, the YouthBuild model is moving through a culturally responsive process of adaptation, implementation, and scaling, with planning efforts under way in another five countries.

Outcome data collected across YouthBuild sites show that 62 percent of students complete the program; 71 percent of graduates went on to continuing education or were placed in jobs. Research has shown a return on investment of at least $10.80 for every dollar spent on any court-involved YouthBuild student. Between 5 and 15 percent of these young people who completed the YouthBuild program ended up reoffending, compared with a national recidivism rate of 67 percent. In a study conducted with 900 YouthBuild graduates, students reported an average expected life expectancy for themselves of 40 years before joining YouthBuild and after completing the program reported an expected life expectancy of 70 years.

THE YOUTHBUILD PROGRAM CONTEXT

YouthBuild programs experience virtually no violence from or among its students. Although the program sites are located in the most crime-ridden urban and rural communities, there simply has never been any pattern of violence within or against YouthBuild programs. Even when students from rival gangs join YouthBuild, they leave their hostilities at the door. Students feel safe, valued, and cared for. There are no metal detectors, no security guards. Feeling safe means the world to the young people; it enables them to drop their hostilities from the street and focus on their future.

The YouthBuild program has been shaped and transformed over a 30-year period by the direct input of young adults, the majority of whom, before joining YouthBuild, have been the victims or perpetrators of violence in their families, among their peers, and in their local communities. The most fundamental cause of the violence experienced by YouthBuild students are the conditions of poverty that YouthBuild students have, through no choice of their own, been born into. The physical manifestation of these conditions of poverty in the local communities where YouthBuild programs are located around the world include abandoned, dilapidated, or destroyed physical infrastructure affecting housing and all public gathering places; high incidences of crime; lack of access to public transportation, which reinforces a sense of isolation; lack of access to functioning schools and employment and training resources; lack of green spaces; and rampant degradation of the natural environment.

These physical realities exact a toll on young people, contributing to feelings of hopelessness and anger, driven by a sense of helplessness to affect change in their own lives and the world around them. Living in these conditions, young people develop an internalized sense of worthlessness borne out of the repeated experience of having few adult allies who are fully committed to their development and little or no access to the resources needed to acquire the basic elements of personal, social, and economic capital to enable them to break out of the cycle of poverty. These conditions of poverty conspire day after day to limit a young person's options for development and to drive them down a narrow track of illegal activities, negative behaviors directed at themselves and others, and in many cases, leading them to commit acts of violence. They simply see no other options, given the hand they have been dealt, and strike out both as a means of self-defense and as the only means of exerting some sense of control over the environment around them.

Ely, whose family members are refugees of the armed conflicts in El Salvador, found his way to a YouthBuild program in Los Angeles. His story is typical of many YouthBuild students:

> Like many people of color that are born and raised in L.A., I fit the statistics. At the age of eight I was abandoned by my father, so my two siblings and I were raised by a mother who fought with every bit of her strength to have not just a roof over our heads, but one in livable conditions. Due to her little time to discipline me and my brother, we took to the streets and found a gang lifestyle that embraced us and made us into so-called men. Once my life was in full force, initiating violent acts and lost in the midst of crime, the justice system came into my life and disciplined me with multiple incarcerations, and house arrest. But what they forgot to include in their discipline was love.
>
> When YB came into my life at the age of 17, I was facing three years of prison and about to be a father. They embraced me with love. Never was I reminded of the crimes I committed in the past, but rather I was directed towards the changes I was going to make in the future. A space was created for me to find self discipline and positive leadership. You can visit any YB site and hear stories like mine. YB began as an idea to empower youth to change their communities and now we are changing the world . . . . this transformation phenomena has become a reality to youth that were once trapped in cages of jail, oppression and failure, who can now provide for themselves and their families through positive means.

THE YOUTHBUILD APPROACH TO VIOLENCE PREVENTION AND CONFLICT MITIGATION

Ely's testimony illustrates many of the most powerful elements of the YouthBuild approach and program model that contribute to the process of transformation experienced by young people who participate in the program:

- Young people are introduced to an alternative learning approach that values their life experience, directly connects academic learning and advancement to real-world opportunities for the application of this learning; and demonstrates the connection of daily learning to future opportunity.
- Young people are given an immediate visible role in the community as leaders and creators of needed community assets and are given the opportunity to exercise their innate impulse to give back to their communities and derive the sustaining satisfaction of doing so.
- The orientation of the program is on the present reality of the young people who enter YouthBuild and on the development of a plan that will enable them to realize their future goals for personal, social, academic, and employment success; their history is not held against them, but is mined in productive ways for lessons that will instruct a productive pathway to the future.
- A strong program culture, starting with a two-week orientation called Mental Toughness, pushes and supports young people to discard the degenerative feelings of despair and hopelessness that previously imprisoned them and begin to take control of their lives.

Natalia, another YouthBuild student and now staff member at a YouthBuild program, elaborates on these parts of the YouthBuild approach:

Gangs controlled my neighborhood. If you were not with them, you were a rival. There were two ways to become part of a gang. You could jump in, and then get beaten up. Or you could get sexed in and get raped. I jumped in at 11, where they beat the girls for one minute. The gang leaders taught me how to fight with machetes and screw drivers and how to spit razors from my mouth. They made a fighter out of me. I saw people killed. After a while I was numb to it. It's just normal, nothing unusual about it. Why would you get scared or have any feelings for it? It was an everyday part of life.

I was 16 and had left high school, pregnant and homeless when YouthBuild came into my life. In YB, I had to learn to talk to people when they talked to me, to say hi when they said hi to me. I wasn't used to that being in a gang. I wasn't used to feeling safe either. But whenever I was in YB, I knew I would be fine for those few hours every day. I began to look forward to life.

The construction part of YB was the most amazing thing I ever did. We built a playground outside an apartment complex full of bullet casings, needles, drugs, and bottles. I kept at the work on the site until my body ached. As I dug up the ground I saw people looking out at us from their apartments. One old lady came outside and said to us: "I have lived here for 30 years and I have seen everything that has happened here. I have seen bodies carried out of here. But I have never seen anything like this. You are just a blessing."

The construction skills are not the most important skills I learned in YB. I learned to be thankful and tired. Not tired from running, not tired from crying, not tired from doing anything bad. Just tired from really working and making something good in a place that needed it . . . and people thanked us for it.

The YouthBuild program design consists of five components: education, technical skills training, leadership development, counseling support, and placement of graduates (placement in jobs, self-employment, or continuing education or training opportunities).

These five components, although distinct in their focus and outcomes, are experienced by young participants as tightly integrated and working in unison to support each young person's continual progress and eventual success. Taken together, the components comprehensively address the livelihood needs and aspirations of young people while addressing critical community development challenges. The core YouthBuild experience of young people creating tangible community assets, such as housing, community centers, schools, playgrounds, and so on, provides a vehicle for soft and technical skills training, applied learning, and leadership development, and is the best, most comprehensive, introduction to the world of work. Additionally, the young people have a direct, tangible experience of how their individual actions can make a real, visible difference in the world around them. Construction activities take place in the local communities where the young people, their peers, and their families live. As a result, the community at large starts to view young people as responsible leaders, taking responsibility for the development of their own lives and the life of their communities.

Again and again, YouthBuild students point to the program's ability, led by caring staff members, to create a mini-community rich in supports, responsive to students' needs, and infused with love and opportunity, and that calls young people to fully support each other as they move through a set of key developmental tasks. This mini-community often will stand in stark contrast to the communities in which the young people live, which often are highly fragmented, dangerous, and absent any activities that would prioritize the full development of young people. The success of many YouthBuild programs through the years has been compromised when the staff team hired to lead the program failed to coalesce around a shared vision of the role that young people are capable of playing in taking leadership in their own lives and in local communities and their abilities. Staff may not share a commitment to hold high standards for young people, while committing themselves to the task of supporting young people to overcome barriers to reach these standards. Lack of consistent communication among staff on these key points, so that all staff (teachers, counselors, construction staff, and executive staff) are deeply knowledgeable of the challenges and aspirations of each young person, has undercut program success.

A YouthBuild director has made this observation about the YouthBuild focus on community building:

> Gang community is very important, and you have to have a really strong community, built on trust in order for you to be able to compete with their former community. If you're asking them to do something different (to change their life), you have to offer them a better solution.
>
> Rival gangs get to interact at the YouthBuild program, and even become friends and begin to see each other in a different light. There was a case of a student that was recounting the story of a shootout, only to realize that another young man in the group, a friend of his in the program, had also been involved in that same shoot. In this sense, the program allows for a different kind of interaction for the young people, very different from their lifestyles outside of the program, in the streets.

Sitting at the center of the YouthBuild design is a focus on leadership development. Leadership development infuses all activities taking place within the other four program components. It is the YouthBuild belief that the most important investment that must be made to eliminate the root causes of poverty is to invest in the development of skilled, courageous, ethical young leaders who are equipped to address these causes with hope, vision, and resolve. YouthBuild provides students multiple opportunities to exercise leadership within the program context, in the classrooms, on the construction sites, on the youth policy council, as well as in their communities. These program-based lessons of exercising leadership, taking risks, integrating the learning from inevitable failures, and developing the internal fortitude to convert the learning from mistakes into assets for life-long leadership sustain YouthBuild graduates as they navigate challenges after graduation.

Wilfried, a YouthBuild graduate, has taken the leadership skills he learned in YouthBuild and applied these skills toward efforts to support the development of young people from Portland, Maine, to Southern Sudan:

> YB has helped shaped my life for the past 13 years. The oldest of seven children, I came to the US not by choice but as part of the lost boys of Sudan. Both my parents were killed in the civil war in 1997. My parents were refugees when I was born and when they were repatriated to Sudan, another war began. I was 11. By the time I was 17 I had lived displacement camps inside Sudan, jailed by the government in Khartoum, escaped and lived in refugee camps in Uganda and Kenya, finally coming to the US in 1994. Then I was introduced to YouthBuild. After completing my GED and receiving a certificate in construction, I graduated and began volunteering as a community leader in the Sudanese community. I have since received both my bachelor's and master's degrees.
>
> After 18 years, I returned to south Sudan to start a youth development project modeled after YouthBuild. It engages war-affected youth ex-combatants in reconciliation, conflict resolution and reconstruction of the country through building and construction while at the same time getting basic education, job training and leadership practice and entrepreneurship. Initially the pilot project was for 15 students but it has since been overwhelmed with more than it can absorb.

All the accomplishments and progress I have made would not have been possible without YouthBuild, to whom I offer all the credit of my success and of many other youth. It can also give hope to youth in post conflict Sudan and the world over, showing that we can be part of change we believe in.

In South Africa, a YouthBuild student has applied the leadership skills she has learned in YouthBuild to actively resolve conflict in her family and her country:

My participation in the YouthBuild program assisted me in dealing with my domestic conflict because I think if I was not in the program I wouldn't have healed. All I would do was to close myself in the house crying the whole day and not knowing what to do; feeling ashamed myself. The program opened my eyes and my mind for me to be able to take responsibility not only for my self but for my community. I was taught the skills to not jump to solve the matter, but get a clear picture on what went wrong; and to always try to solve a problem as a leader, not taking sides . . . not giving the blame to others but by coming up with ways to solve problems and misunderstanding and by looking at the root of the problem.

MAKING YOUTHBUILD AVAILABLE TO ALL YOUNG PEOPLE WHO WISH TO ENROLL

There's a lot of love in YB, and some day we're going to spread it around the world.

—Victor, graduate of East Harlem YouthBuild

According to the World Bank's *2007 World Development Report:* Development and the Next Generation,

The developing world's 1.3 billion young people ages 12–24 are its next generation of economic and social actors. Making sure that they are well prepared for their futures—as workers, entrepreneurs, parents, citizens, and community leaders—is thus enormously important to the course of poverty reduction and growth. Because human development is cumulative, missed opportunities to invest in and prepare this generation will be extremely costly to reverse, both for young people and for society.

YouthBuild has a long track record of bringing together a wide spectrum of stakeholder groups and working with these groups to find common cause in addressing the needs of low-income, marginalized young people. Since 1994, YouthBuild has raised more than $700 million in federal funding, from a total of seven different federal agencies, to support YouthBuild in local communities. This federal investment has in turn leveraged an additional $1.2 billion in local public and private resources for expanded support of programs for at-risk youth. This flow of investment in addressing the needs of at-risk youth in local communities has held steady through four presidential administrations.

This outcome is also a result of the program design, which is holistic, comprehensive, relevant to the learning and employment needs of young people, rich in supports, and maintaining high standards of achievement and, which is designed, implemented, and managed by local residents and community based institutions. Every YouthBuild program, both in the United States and in the 13 countries where the model is being adapted, is created, managed, and "owned" by local institutional partners from the nongovernmental organization, education, training, government, and business sectors.

As the YouthBuild program has been identified as a key resource by partners in countries outside of the United States, four consistent adaptations to the U.S. model have begun to emerge. First, the community assets that young people are creating overseas have diversified well beyond housing to include community centers, schools, orphanages, playgrounds, and sustainable, "green" infrastructure. Second, youth lending and adapted business development support services are being offered as part of a self-employment pathway within YouthBuild programs in settings in which existing jobs are insufficient to meet the youth employment demand. Third, there is a greater variation in the length of the program and in the mix of time spent in formal classroom learning and on the construction site. Length of program and cost per young person also are areas of adaptation. For many of the young people served by YouthBuild in the developing world, it is impossible for them to commit to a full-time training and education program for any more than four to six months, given the need for them to earn a livelihood to support themselves and their families. Moreover, YouthBuild and its overseas partners have had to find creative ways to reduce the program cost per student, while maintaining program quality, to attract institutional investors and to expand the impact of the program by reaching greater numbers of youth who want to join the program. Fourth, YouthBuild programs that serve only young women are being studied for implementation in several countries where the unique challenges facing young women require a highly customized set of adaptations.

Although the trajectory of YouthBuild's growth is admirable and a hopeful trend, the full scale of the challenge facing young people living in poverty-stricken communities around the world requires a much larger response. In the United States, according to the National Center for Children in Poverty, 29.2 million children or 40 percent are growing up in low-income families, and 18 percent or 13.5 million live at less than 100 percent of the federal poverty level. Some 3.5 million people live in communities with concentrated poverty that lack adequate affordable housing. There are 2.4 million low-income disconnected 16-to 24-year-olds in the United States and an additional 365,000 incarcerated youth. Crime, gangs, drugs, murder, and hopelessness characterize the street and community life of millions of American youth.

From the global perspective, we know that in the current decade the largest cohort of young people in history, 1.2 billion, will enter the job market. Ninety percent of these job-seekers will be under the age of 25 and will live in the developing world. The most optimistic projections show that only 300 million jobs will be created to meet this demand. Globally, 88 million young men and women are unemployed; young people represent 130 million of the world's 550 million working poor who work but are unable to lift themselves and their families above the equivalent of the US$1 per day poverty line. Violence affects millions of young people around the world. An estimated 59 million young people are engaged in hazardous forms of work. Approximately 35 percent of the world's 14 million refugees are young people ages 12 to 24. Twelve of the 15 countries with the largest youth bulge have been home to either brutal conflict or large displaced populations, or both, in the past 10 to 15 years.

It is estimated that by halving the world's youth unemployment rate from 14.4 percent to 7.2 percent would add an estimated US$2.2 to US$3.5 trillion to the global gross domestic product. The peace and security of the international community depends on solutions to respond to this dire global mismatch between available jobs and young people seeking employment.

LESSONS LEARNED

Success in designing, implementing, and managing a high-quality YouthBuild program is completely dependent on the vision, dedication, resourcefulness, and compassion of the staff assembled to lead the program. Staff must be dedicated to the success of each young person, they must combine an ability to listen to young people with a belief in the capacity of all young people, despite the difficulties of their past, to overcome these obstacles and succeed as healthy, happy, productive human beings. Young people in YouthBuild programs draw their strength and direction to make crucial changes in their lives from their relationships with the YouthBuild staff. They further depend on these relationships to help them co-create a developmental pathway leading to personal, social, educational, and employment-related advancement and success.

The program design is complex and can involve managing the participation of a wide cross section of local partners, all of whom have key roles to play in implementation. The executive leadership of a YouthBuild program must combine a fundamental love of young people with an entrepreneurial approach to building support for the program and sustaining its presence in local communities. The improvement of program outcomes can be shown to directly correlate to the longevity of the director's experience as he or she accumulates knowledge and experience running the program over several cycles. Success is tied to the ability of the director to consistently lead the agenda related to tight, consistent integration of each of the program design's working elements, and the alignment of partners in implementing these elements.

The most consistent challenge for YouthBuild programs continues to be securing placement for young people in jobs, self-employment, or continuing education upon graduation. This most critical point of transition, when young people leave the safe, supportive environment of YouthBuild and must navigate the workforce, has proven difficult to manage toward consistent success. Even those young people who are successfully placed in productive employment upon graduation often find it difficult to retain those first placements and must draw on their YouthBuild learning and graduate support network to manage their next transition. The challenge of placement has led programs to diminish their commitment to reaching the most marginalized young people who need the resources the most and instead choose young people who show a greater likelihood of success at orientation.

Three interventions have proven key to addressing this placement challenge. The focus on placement must begin from day one of the program, with staff focused on building relationships with employers that can lead to internships or jobs; follow-up support services should be an integral part of the program design for at least six months after graduation; and organized alumni networks of Youth-Build graduates can provide a powerful peer network of support and resource.

CONCLUSION

As stated by the National Alumni Council and Young Leaders Council of YouthBuild,

> Most people who have fallen off the track, suffered losses, and made mistakes can recover. If given a chance, they can learn to cope with obstacles and care effectively about themselves, their families and their communities. They can gain the skills and attitudes to become strong successful leaders who will help others.

From its earliest days of activity in East Harlem, New York, to its present-day work in communities around the world, YouthBuild's mission continues to be to unleash the intelligence and positive energy of marginalized young people to rebuild their communities and their lives with a commitment to work, education, responsibility, and family. The YouthBuild aim is not only to support young people to rebuild their lives, but also to inspire and train them to rebuild their communities through the creation of tangible community assets. As the program continues to expand internationally, YouthBuild maintains its commitment to work with partners to build livelihood pathways for all young people. Too often the experience of poor, marginalized youth is not given a voice in the forums in which decisions are being made to address the root causes of poverty. Because these youth are the victims of these conditions, failing to include their perspective in both the analysis of the root causes of poverty and in generating solutions to address these causes is a fundamental error. YouthBuild continues to multiply the numbers of young people who are prepared and inspired to raise their voices and provide leadership in addressing some of the world's most intractable problems; problems that they and their children will uniquely inherit, either as passive victims, or proactive change agents.

13

Reducing Alcohol-Related Youth Violence in Australia through Community Action and Multisectoral Collaboration: The Safety Action Project

Ross Homel

BACKGROUND

IN AUSTRALIA, AS in many industrial countries, crime rates are trending downward. Youth crime and youth violence, however, seem to be a disturbing exception. Much of the violence among older youth ages 18 to 22 is associated with alcohol use. Visiting pubs, bars, and nightclubs is the predominant form of nightlife for Australia's young people. Consistent with this, a significant percentage of youth violence and crime takes place in and around licensed premises such as pubs, bars, clubs, and nightclubs. Clubbing typically involves significant alcohol consumption. The connection between alcohol consumption, aggression, and impulsive behavior is well documented. In Australia, alcohol-related violence among youth remains confined primarily to the club environment, in contrast to the United States and other countries where it is often concentrated on campuses of universities. Two factors contribute to this: 1) most students in Australia commute to their universities and so by definition have fewer residential alcohol incidents on campus than in the United States; and 2) most Australian youth party culture is centered in inner-city entertainment districts rather than around or on campuses which form a big part of the life and cultural environment of the youth population in Australia.

Age 18 is young to be able to legally drink. Developmentally, adolescents this age may not yet be capable of making good decisions about the use of alcohol and may have difficulty setting personal limits regarding its use in the context of peers and a culture of drinking. Physically they are still maturing and can be more significantly affected by alcohol than older people. Cognitively they may still be slow to connect consequences and actions and may perceive themselves as invulnerable to the many risks such as physical injury, unprotected sex, automobile accidents, and violence that are associated with heavy and binge alcohol consumption. A young person's vulnerability to alcohol misuse is further exacerbated by the cultural norms among Australian youth related to drinking. Drinking in excess is viewed as a rite of passage, and drinking events typically begin with heavy pre-party drinking known as "pre-loading," and then progress to club-based drinking after the youth is already intoxicated. This progression over a night makes it highly likely that the young person will become intoxicated to the level that his or her abilities in decision making and impulse control are impaired. These drinking "parties" can be repeated many times over a single month, further increasing a young person's risk for negative outcomes at multiple levels.

Problem drinking is not limited to older adolescents. An increasing number of underage youth participate as well. Many parties occur in homes, but youths increasingly are renting halls or apartments to celebrate birthdays or other special events that involve significant quantities of alcohol, the costs of which are often paid for by their parents. With the advent of online social networking sites like Facebook, what once might have been a small gathering of friends now can grow to a significant size. These parties are large, involve significant numbers of under-age and older youths, offer significant amounts of alcohol, and have poor if any parental supervision, and have evolved to a point at which they present significant risks for alcohol-related violence.

The problem of adolescent drinking and violence occurs in a larger social context that has exacerbated the problem in recent years. Australia, like many European countries, provides an extensive social safety net for its citizens during periods of unemployment, a safety net that is available to the populace for support indefinitely; and culturally, the society places responsibility for addressing social problems such as youth violence, on communities and institutions, not just on the individual. Consistent with this, there is a tradition of progressive social policies for children and families in the country. Citizens support investment of tax dollars in strong social institutions. The Australian government invests heavily in programs designed to strengthen families and communities, investing heavily in nongovernmental organizations that support the early years of children's development in the form of play facilities, developmental play groups, parent support, and family empowerment programs; and the Labor government has introduced universal preschool so that *every* four-year-old child regardless of economic status will have access to and the right to attend preschool. Despite these advances, Australia, along with many other English-speaking countries, has underinvested in services for its younger citizens and their parents, and like many countries, Australia is struggling with the erosion of key supportive institutions in the society such as the church and the family.

In the 1980s and 1990s the concept of economic rationalism became popular in Australia. Economic rationalism tends to favor the free market, deregulation, and less government involvement in business. Economic rationalism in Australia emphasized the market over family needs. Many families were stressed by economic pressures, while being expected to protect their children from risks, such as drug abuse, unprotected sex, or heavy drinking, with insufficient help from external sources. Economic rationalism in Australia had a particularly heavy impact on low-income families who had fewer internal resources and economic options to draw on, but it affected more affluent families as well. These large-scale social changes have had a significant influence on youth violence. A leading predictor of violence is economic inequality, and although Australia has one of the highest per capita incomes in the world, it also has a high level of disparity between the affluent and the poor, driven in part by these theories underlying the country's economic policies.

THE SAFETY ACTION PROJECT

The Safety Action Project (SAP) was developed to reduce alcohol-related violence in and around nightclubs, pubs, and other drinking establishments. SAP involves collaboration across four sectors, including the community, law enforcement, business owners, and government licensing boards. It seeks to mobilize formal (police, licensing), informal (the community), and internal (the nightclub owner and staff) regulation to create environmental changes that promote responsible and safer use of alcohol and partying. The Safety Action model has been implemented successfully and evaluated in four cities in Queensland, Australia.

The SAP intervention is built around the concept that the most effective way to reduce a behavior such as violence around bars is to create changes in the context or environment surrounding the targeted behavior. Creating more civilized spaces for drinking and the behavioral norms within them can produce changes in rates of unwanted behavior. In our early work in this area, we were struck by the amount of abuse and violence young people put up with in the pub and nightclub environment, especially young women, that they would not tolerate in other settings. These young people would not tolerate these behaviors in their house or school environments, but they suspend these boundaries and rules once they enter a bar or club environment. "Partying" can and should occur in environments in which no one gets hurt, no rape takes place, and physical fights do not occur; and where staff in the drinking establishment support these norms rather than adding to the abuse, for example, by a "bouncer" losing control and assaulting a patron. Thus, the focus of the SAP intervention is not on educating patrons as many previous interventions have been, but rather on increasing the capacity of bar managers and staff to act responsibly, more fully engaging the police in preventive as well as reactive roles, and strengthening existing regulations and policies related to these institutions.

Building initially on the qualitative and quantitative data on risk factors for aggression and violence in licensed premises identified in a series of observational studies in Sydney (Homel and Clark 1994; Homel, Tomsen, and Thommeny 1992), strategies were developed to address the critical issue of management practices that allowed or encouraged serving to intoxication, the employment of aggressive crowd controllers (doormen and security staff), the dumping of large numbers of inebriated patrons onto the street with no safe transport options, and the creation of a generally permissive environment lacking clear rules about behavioral limits and respect for the rights of patrons. The theoretical bases of these strategies were situational prevention and responsive regulation, and the theory of change behind the strategies was to reduce these risk factors and hence observed rates of aggression and violence.

The strategies are designed to bring about change by combining pressure for better self-regulation by licensees with improved methods of formal enforcement by state agencies, namely, police and liquor licensing, supported by new forms of informal regulation based on licensee accountability to each other and to the local community through the creation of new organizational structures. The exact form and content of these three kinds of regulatory levers evolved with the projects. In practice, three of the strategies were implemented effectively in all four sites, but only partial success was obtained with regard to the fourth strategy (formal enforcement).

The central component of any SAP intervention is community mobilization. This creates the means for effecting change across the various sectors. Businesses and community residents located around the clubs and bars affected by alcohol-related violence and problems were organized and mobilized to exert pressure on local pub owners. The SAP supports, trains, and mobilizes these local residents and stakeholders (which includes some government agencies, such as health) to apply pressure to local bar operators, which creates the initial incentive for the bar operators to improve hiring practices, provide staff training, develop operating standards and policies, and adhere to licensing requirements. These same action groups are encouraged to reach out to the local police and encourage them to incorporate more preventive approaches in their responses in addition to traditional interventions such as preventing bars from exceeding their capacity and enforcing licensing and other bar rules. Bar owners and staff receive training, and managers are encouraged to revisit training and hiring practices.

A SAP intervention has four principal components: (1) creation of a community forum leading to development of community-based task groups and implementation of a safety audit; (2) the development and implementation of risk assessments in licensed premises followed by implementation of risk reduction strategies by managers; (3) training for community, managers, bar staff, security, and police; (4) and improvements in regulation of licensed premises by police and liquor licensing inspectors focusing on preventive rather than reactive strategies, such as preventing assaults by security staff, and improving compliance with provisions in the Liquor Act prohibiting serving of intoxicated persons.

EXAMPLE OF A SAP INTERVENTION: SURFER'S PARADISE

Alcohol-related violence was evident throughout Australia in the 1990s and was particularly pronounced in cities and entertainment areas along the Queensland coastline. The large and growing urban centers, such as the Gold Coast, Mackay, Townsville, and Cairns, drew tens of thousands of locals and tourists to the region each year. Gold Coast City is one of the largest of the regional urban centers with more than 500,000 inhabitants. Surfer's Paradise, an entertainment area within the city, has one of the highest concentrations of bars and nightclubs in Australia; and it is a popular site for young people looking to participate in alcohol-related rites of passage. Issues with drinking were further exacerbated by fierce competition among bars and clubs for these young patrons. To attract customers, the bars offered low-cost and sometimes free drinks. Managers of these establishments seemingly lacked management experience. Neither did they have a sense of responsibility for the high-risk drinking environment that was being collectively created in the area. Finally, police and licensing authorities failed to enforce drinking regulations; and Surfer's Paradise received ongoing negative publicity about crime and safety problems.

The business and residential communities surrounding the Surfer's Paradise entertainment district were negatively affected both by the disorder and violence and the negative news stories, so they were ready to engage in organized action to improve the situation. The frustration of the surrounding community and their readiness to act was a critical element to getting the Queensland intervention off the ground in this region.

A pilot of the SAP was conducted at the Surfer's Paradise region of Queensland in 1993. The first step of the project was to conduct a public forum. More than 100 people participated in the forum and indicated they wanted to see a change. These participants then formed task groups that were assigned different activities. One group was tasked with observing the clubs and bars and making reports about the incidents there. A second group was tasked with reaching out to club managers and leading training for the staff. A third was tasked with engaging and working with the police to promote incorporation of measures to prevent violence around the bars.

Twelve different organizations and 17 individuals participated in the forum. The groups met once or twice a month during the project and extensive training was offered, including half-day courses for the forum members on structure, content, process, and accountability; five-day courses for participants on project theory, structure, responsibilities, and processes; seven-day training by specialist police in liquor licensing law and investigations for police and project officers; a two-day course for security staff on best practices; and courses of variable length on management practices, development of house policies, responsible serving practices, and management of security staff.

The intervention team began work with a bar or club by conducting needs and risks assessment at the establishment. They would then work collaboratively with bar managers and staff to identify areas of greatest risk and develop a strategy for addressing them. In one instance, a club in the Surfer's Paradise area was experiencing a particularly high level of sexual harassment from male patrons toward its female patrons. The Community Action Group for Surfer's included a women's sexual violence organization, and the police and local business owners put pressure on the owner and manager to reduce the incidence of these events. Working with the intervention team, the manager and staff in this and other clubs decided to establish a code of behavior for patrons and staff that fostered respect of persons. Licensees and managers designed, implemented, and then enforced this code of behavior for their facilities. Two years after intervention, the clubs were still adhering to the policies and rates of harassment and sexual violence as well as other forms of observed and officially recorded aggression had declined.

PROGRAM OUTCOMES

Students were hired as observers and paid to go to the clubs and observe over randomly selected two-hour time periods. These students were not to drink and were trained to fill out an observation form that identified aggressive behaviors in the institution. Between pre- and post-test observations, the research team found a dramatic reduction in aggressive behaviors and violence. Similarly, crime statistics showed significant drops in reportable violent and aggressive behavior in the area. Finally, rates of reports filed by local businesses and residents concerning disorderly conduct and vandalism also declined significantly from pre- to post-intervention.

System-level effects included increased capacity in the formal regulatory system, including greater specification in legislation of responsible alcohol policies and practices, increased knowledge among licensees and licensing officers of sound and responsible alcohol policies and practices, improved communication and engagement between licensing officers and community stakeholders, increased involvement of community stakeholders in informal regulatory enforcement, greater engagement by local government in licensing enforcement, and creation of a permanent community safety officer position charged with responsibility for licensed premises.

The SAP was replicated in three additional communities in Queensland with similar positive outcomes. Unfortunately, funding for the project was cut after three years and not renewed. Within 12 months, 50 percent of the bars as well as police enforcement methods had returned to pre-intervention status.

LESSONS LEARNED

Unfortunately, although the intervention in Surfer's Paradise had a significant impact on violence in and around drinking establishments that was replicated in three additional sites, the state and federal governments did not provide funding to support or expand the program after its initial implementation. The project team learned several important lessons from this.

First, leaders and elected officials need to be educated on complex multi-sectoral interventions so they are ready and able to support innovative and complex programs such as SAP. If this readiness does not exist, then it must be developed. Decision makers and government leaders need time and repeated exposure not only to the specific intervention but also to the scientific context of these interventions to understand the value of complex multi-sector efforts over modest ones. It can be difficult for individuals who are not experts in a specific area or intervention to understand multi-sectoral efforts. Policy makers are most familiar with simpler intervention models, which are less expensive, easier to coordinate and publicize, and easier to enact, but also often less effective. Substantial time and effort must be invested in this type of multisector education. For example, the concept of problem-oriented policing, which is a key element of SAP, was new to the Australian law enforcement community at the time of the SAP pilots. Our team engaged Herman Goldstein, a leader in this area, to inform state leaders about the approach.

Readiness also needs to be developed in frontline workers like the police. This requires spending time in local police stations and departments talking about the program, developing persuasive informational materials about the approach, and equally informing other key stakeholders such as the licensing division, local councils controlling fire and safety regulations in pub settings and the surrounding areas, and health officials.

Another lesson learned is the importance of building the capacity of grass-roots organizations that are able to push forward change efforts such as this. Community groups can be pivotal to creating this understanding by repeated and persistent messaging and education. Mothers Against Drunk Driving (MADD) in the United States is one example of how a community movement can create readiness for significant collaborative social change. In Australia, community groups are less empowered. In general, groups like MADD that are capable of pushing initiatives like SAP forward are absent.

Finally, reliable data systems play a critical role in providing support for these types of programs. Good data collection systems involve multiple sources of data ranging from police reports to emergency room data, and they are difficult and expensive to implement. Without data, however, it is impossible to understand the extent of a problem, advocate effectively for solutions, or evaluate the impact of interventions with any consistency or reliability.

REFERENCES

Homel, R., and Clark, J. 1994. "The Prediction and Prevention of Violence in Pubs and Clubs". In *Crime Prevention Studies*, ed. Clarke, R. V., Vol. 3., 1–46. Monsey, NY: Criminal Justice Press.

Homel, R., S. Tomsen, and J. Thommeny. 1992. Public Drinking and Violence: Not Just an Alcohol Problem. *Journal of Drug Issues* 22 (3):679–697.

14

Youth Violence Prevention in Canada: Exemplary, Collaborative, and Evidence-Based Efforts

Laura Dunbar, Irvin Waller, and Kate Gunn

BACKGROUND

RECENT HIGH-PROFILE incidents of gang-related violence involving young men with guns have drawn attention to the problem of youth violence in Canada (Bania 2009; Waller 2009b). While the federal government continues a traditional discourse of making "get-tough" changes to the Criminal Code, increasingly, Canada is pioneering exemplary, collaborative, and evidence-based efforts that will prevent gang-related and youth violence, particularly at the provincial and municipal levels.

WHAT WE KNOW ABOUT GANGS AND YOUTH VIOLENCE IN CANADA

The sensational media headlines reflect to some extent real increases in gang-related homicides since the early 1990s. In 2008, about one in four of the 600 homicides in Canada was reported by police to have been gang-related (Beattie 2009). The rates of these homicides tend to be highest in cities such as Calgary, Edmonton, Regina, Saskatoon, and Winnipeg (Li 2008) where there is a growing concentration of young men with the classic negative life experiences known to predispose them to violence. Of the reported homicides in 2008, 32 percent of the incidents involving a youth accused were gang-related compared with only 11 percent of incidents involving an adult accused (Beattie 2009), demonstrating the prevalence of violence perpetrated by youth gang members in Canada (see figure 14.1).

In 2002, the results of the *Canadian Police Survey on Youth Gangs* estimated that there were 434 youth gangs in operation across the country with a total

Figure 14.1   Gang-related homicides continue to increase

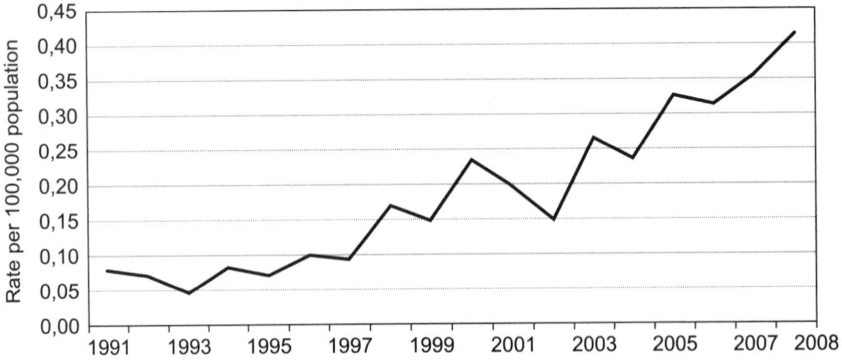

Note: These data became available beginning in 1991.
Source: Statistics Canada, Juristat, 85-002-XIE 2009004 vol. 29 no. 4 Released October 28, 2009.)

membership of 7,071 (Chettleburgh 2003). In Canada, almost all young gang members are male and almost half are 17 years old or younger (CISC 2006). Most gang members are African Canadian or black (25 percent), followed by Aboriginal (22 percent), and 18 percent are Caucasian or white (Totten 2008). According to official sources, street gang activities consist primarily of street-level illicit drug-trafficking and prostitution, but also involve weapons-trafficking, robbery, home invasions, extortion, and fraud, as well as both strategic and tactical violence (CISC 2006).

CAUSES OF GANG-RELATED AND YOUTH VIOLENCE IN CANADA

The vast majority of young men in Canada live positively and never become involved in crime or join gangs. A small group of teenage and young adult men, however, are involved in frequent and persistent violence, and they tend to have had a series of negative experiences in certain areas of their lives that differ from those of other young people (National Research Council 2001; Waller 2009b). To effectively prevent these youth from joining gangs and engaging in violence, the National Crime Prevention Center (NCPC) of Public Safety Canada has focused on identifying and addressing the risk factors that may influence involvement and membership in gangs (NCPC 2007b). Additionally, the Institute for the Prevention of Crime at the University of Ottawa has focused on ways to harness the significant amount of international scientific knowledge on the factors that influence the likelihood of a young person becoming violent and ways to address those risk factors to prevent violence (Waller 2006). Table 14.1

Table 14.1 Risk Factors for Youth Involvement in Violent Behavior and Gangs

Individual	Peer Group	School	Family	Community
• Prior delinquency	• High commitment to delinquent peers	• Poor school performance	• Family disorganization, including broken homes and parental drug and/or alcohol abuse	• Social disorganization, including high poverty and residential mobility
• Illegal gun ownership	• Street socialization	• Low educational aspirations	• Family violence and neglect	• High crime neighborhood
• Drug trafficking	• Gang members in class	• Negative labelling by teachers	• Family members in a gang	• Presence of gangs in the neighborhood
• Limited social and cognitive abilities	• Friends who use drugs or who are gang members	• High levels of anti-social behaviors	• Lack of positive adult and parental role models	• Availability or perceived access to drugs and firearms in the neighborhood
• Anti-social attitudes and behavioral problems	• Interaction with delinquent peers	• Few teacher role models		• Cultural norms supporting gang behavior
• Aggression	• Exposure to stress	• Educational frustration		• Feeling unsafe in neighborhood
• Alcohol and drug use	• Low attachment to school			
• Early sexual activity	• Learning difficulties			
• Violent victimization				
• Dropping out of secondary school				

National Crime Prevention Centre (2007b), adapted from Howell (2005); Waller (2006)

Aboriginal Youth and Gang Membership

Particular attention should be paid to the life experiences of Aboriginal youth. In Canada, research has demonstrated that Aboriginal people are more disadvantaged and concentrated in high-crime areas (such as inner cores of central metropolitan areas) than non-Aboriginal people (Fitzgerald and Carrington 2008; Fitzgerald, Wisener, and Savoie 2004; La Prairie 2002) and tend to be overrepresented in youth gangs. As noted, an estimated 22 percent of known gang members in Canada are Aboriginal youth (Totten 2008), despite making up only 6 percent of Canada's total youth population (Milligan 2008).

Although Aboriginal youth engage in violence and join gangs for the same reasons that non-Aboriginal youth do, the problems are more acute (Monchalin 2009). Aboriginal people experience a disproportionate burden of suffering, and this may explain their increased membership in gangs. Additional factors related to the involvement of Aboriginal youth in gangs include racism, marginalization, and dispossession; the loss of land, traditional culture, spirituality, and values; and the breakdown of community kinship systems (Totten 2009).

represents the major risk factors for youth crime, violence, and gang involvement that have been identified (Howell, 2005).

Those who are affected by these negative life experiences are two to four times more likely to join gangs (Hawkins and Pollard 1999) and to become persistent offenders (Farrington and Welsh 2007; Waller 2006).

Additionally in Canada, research has confirmed that gang-related violence is not randomly distributed; it is perpetrated and experienced by a small number of people concentrated in certain areas of its cities (Bania 2009). So, although gang members in Canada come from a variety of ethnic, demographic, and socioeconomic backgrounds, the majority of youth at risk or already involved in gangs tend to come from groups and areas that suffer from the greatest levels of economic inequality, disadvantage, and social disorganization (Chettleburgh 2003; CISC 2006; Wortley and Tanner 2004). For these disadvantaged youth, the motivation for joining a gang can range from seeking money to looking for prestige, protection, and a sense of belonging (Totten 2009; Wortley and Tanner 2004).

LIMITATIONS OF TRADITIONAL TOUGH-ON-CRIME APPROACHES

In Canada, the most common response to youth violence, and especially in the case of violence perpetrated by members of youth gangs, is suppression by the criminal justice system. These "get-tough" responses focus on identifying persistent offenders and aggressively pursuing them with additional police officers, more prosecutors, and harsher sanctions (Chettleburgh 2007; Totten 2009).

As the rise in gang-related homicides illustrates, these suppression measures are failing. Critics suggest that not only have these policies been ineffective in reducing crime and preventing victimization, but also have lead to counterproductive impacts on individuals and communities, including the following: increasing the cohesiveness of gangs and making them more attractive to vulnerable youth, undermining the reputation and legitimacy of the police when few arrests turn into serious charges, and creating a damaging cycle of release and imprisonment for young adults, especially young males (Bania 2009; Chettleburgh 2007; Wortley and Tanner 2004).

CRIME PREVENTION THROUGH SOCIAL DEVELOPMENT

Although tough-on-crime measures continue to remain prominent in Canada, in the last 25 years, there has been an increasing acknowledgment in the political discourse of the role that crime prevention through social development (CPSD) can play in addressing various crime issues. In 1994, the federal government launched Phase I of the National Strategy on Crime Prevention and Community Safety. The centerpiece of this strategy was the creation of a National Crime Prevention Council, which focused its limited resources on designing prevention initiatives aimed at children, youth, and families and addressed the socioeconomic risk factors linked to criminality. In 1998, Phase II of the National Strategy was launched and included the creation of the NCPC and the investment of $32 million per year in support of prevention activities (Hastings 2005; NCPC 2009).

Generally in Canada, the CPSD approach has been endorsed but without significant energy or funds. Only within the past decade have we begun to see evidence-based prevention approaches to gang-related and youth violence being encouraged and tested by the federal and some provincial and municipal governments. Based on an orientation to CPSD, they address multiple risk factors, are administered at different points in the lives of youth, and are expected to reduce gang-related violence and increase positive youth development.

LEADERSHIP IN CPSD IN CANADA

National Crime Prevention Center

The NCPC provides $70 million a year in federal funds for local projects that test effective and cost-efficient ways to prevent and reduce crime by addressing risk factors before crime occurs (NCPC 2009). The NCPC works closely with partners and stakeholders in the provinces and territories to develop and implement results-driven programs that target their identified priority areas, such as at-risk youth and Aboriginal populations (NCPC 2007a). In January 2007, with a focus on equipping Canadian youth with the supports they need to resist joining or returning to gangs, the NCPC established an $11.1 million Youth Gang

Prevention Fund to provide support to community-level programs across Canada (NCPC 2007b; Public Safety Canada 2007). To address youth- and gang-related violence, the NCPC is encouraging the implementation of programs that tackle known risk factors, such as Youth Inclusion Programs and Stop Now and Plan, as well as problem-solving partnerships that address gun violence, such as Boston's Operation Ceasefire and its replication in the Strategic Approaches to Community Safety Initiative (NCPC 2008, National Institute of Justice 2008).

Safe Communities Secretariat of the Alberta Government

Safe Communities Secretariat of the Alberta Government (SafeCom) is an important new and exemplary strategy to reduce crime, prevent victimization, and enhance community safety across a province. It was created in 2007 to oversee a three-pronged crime reduction strategy, balancing enforcement, prevention, and treatment to reduce crime and make communities safer. SafeCom orchestrates collaboration among nine social development and enforcement ministries to implement initiatives aimed at reducing crime based on evidence about what works (Government of Alberta 2009).

In 2008, the Alberta government allocated $468 million in new funding over three years to support and implement the key recommendations made by the Crime Reduction and Safe Communities Task Force. The overriding recommendation was to develop a long-term strategic plan to achieve reductions in crime. One of the specific recommendations of the task force was to "provide mandatory, early and ongoing education for children and youth to build their skills and reduce the risks of them getting involved in gangs, violence, drugs or other crimes" (Alberta's Crime Reduction and Safe Communities Task Force 2007, 57). The province also has created a new $60 million Safe Communities Innovation Fund (SCIF) to develop and support community-based projects and community-police partnership projects. In 2009, several projects were funded under the SCIF to address factors that give rise to gang activity (Government of Alberta 2009).

NATIONAL MUNICIPAL NETWORK OF CRIME PREVENTION

The Institute for the Prevention of Crime (IPC) seeks to bring together the best scientific knowledge from the most authoritative sources so that Canadians will enjoy the lowest rates of crime and victimization possible (Waller 2009a). The annual *IPC Review* provides state-of-the-art reviews on what works to reduce crime and how to deliver it successfully. In this journal, Canadian and foreign academics and experts bring together the latest knowledge on a variety of crime prevention topics aimed specifically at Canadian policy makers and practitioners. Several of the articles focus on the relationship of youth violence and gangs and insist on the importance of locating these phenomena within their social contexts and wider social and structural arrangements (Hastings 2009). To harness this knowledge, and with the recognition that municipalities have a key role to play in reducing crime and enhancing community safety (Janhevich, Johnson, Vézina, and Fraser 2008), the IPC has formed a National Municipal Network on Crime Prevention consisting of major Canadian municipalities from coast to coast.

Municipalities are the order of government best able to collaborate with local agencies and neighborhoods and are in a strategic position to engage and provide focus to these multiple sectors (Waller 2009c). They have a key role to play in mobilizing stakeholders, identifying the needs for service, developing action plans that tackle local areas of need, and implementing short- and long-term solutions (Johnson and Fraser 2007; Shaw 2001). As such, municipalities may be the order of government best equipped to undertake solutions to reduce instances of gang-related and youth violence and to enhance positive youth development and overall community safety. Several effective initiatives currently are under way in Canadian municipalities to address gang-related violence perpetrated by youths.

Ottawa

In 2007, the Ottawa Youth Gang Prevention Initiative, a multistakeholder collaboration, was created to address the issue of youth gangs in the nation's capital. With a group of 60 stakeholders, Crime Prevention Ottawa, in partnership with the Youth Services Bureau and the Ottawa Police Service, published the report *Now Is the Time to Act: Youth Gang Prevention in Ottawa* and is working toward a prevention strategy based on a four-component approach: healthy neighborhood cohesion, early prevention, intervention, and suppression. Canadian experts have been hired to diagnose the problems, look at what is currently under way, and explore what else may work (Chettleburgh 2008).

Toronto

In 2004, Toronto City Council unanimously approved a Community Safety Plan, which emphasized neighborhood-level actions to address gun and gang violence among youth. One key element of this plan was the creation of an intergovernmental advisory panel to the mayor that provides strategic advice and support for strengthening neighborhoods through the city's targeted, place-based approach to community safety and neighborhood investment. Toronto has focused on advancing partnerships across various sectors and institutions, advancing youth employment opportunities, and piloting innovative program models that reach out to youth (Community Safety Secretariat 2004).

THE ROLE AND RESPONSIBILITY CENTERS IN CANADA CRIME PREVENTION STRATEGIES

Properly focused and well-designed prevention strategies can reduce levels of violence and victimization and increase the safety and well-being of communities

(Janhevich, et al. 2008). Key elements of these successful municipal prevention strategies include assigning the responsibility of coordinating community safety to a specific unit and engaging in a long-term strategic planning process that will ensure that programs implemented in a community will result in reduced crime and a better quality of life for residents (Waller 2009c).

Establishing a Responsibility Center

Assigning the responsibility of coordinating crime prevention efforts to a specific unit within the municipal organization is a key element of success. This notion of a responsibility center is essential to follow up and effectively implement strategic orientations, policies, and priorities adopted by the municipality and its partners (Vézina 2009). In general, these coordination units should have a mandate to achieve the following:

- Support the partnership structures in place and work with municipal elected officials, senior management, and other institutional and community stakeholders.
- Provide a focal point for sharing strategic information and making the links between projects.
- Contribute to the analysis of crime and insecurity issues and trends.
- Provide strategic and technical support to the development, implementation, and follow-up of municipal strategic vision, community safety policies, action plans, and projects.
- Develop strategies to mobilize financial resources.
- Develop indicators, monitor implementation of action plans and projects, and report on the progress made to municipal authorities and other stakeholders.
- Design communication strategies and tools.

Strategic Planning for Crime Prevention at the Municipal Level

The development of a strategic plan is a key element for a successful crime prevention strategy. It identifies where current resources and new investments would decrease crime and enhance community safety and where populations (NWG 2007, adapted from Waller 2006) and neighborhoods within a municipality have special needs. It provides a basis for priorities, implementation, and evaluation (Waller 2009c). The strategic planning process involves four key steps (see figure 14.2):

The first step is to identify the particular crime and disorder problems facing the municipality. The information gathered at this stage will help to establish priorities and targets for intervention, which crimes and which communities should be targeted. Focusing on specific problems will help to determine who should be involved in the programs. It is much easier to coordinate the work of different agencies if everyone is clear about the nature of the problems and knows their role in preventing them (Linden 2009).

Figure 14.2   Four Key Steps for Crime Prevention

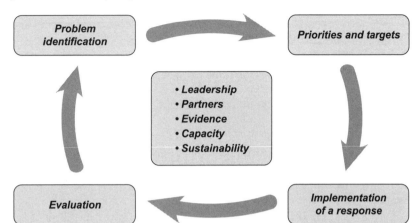

At this point, it is important to bring community members together to develop solutions. It is better to involve people at the planning stage rather than to develop programs and then ask for their help and cooperation. Initially, a planning group will have two tasks. First, they must decide on the best strategies to use to prevent crime in the target communities. Second, they need to develop ways of involving the rest of the community in the implementation of the selected programs (Linden 2009).

The final steps are to implement the selected response and to evaluate the implemented programs. Implementation must have clear objectives and will require extensive coordination. Evaluation will ensure that the program has been implemented as planned and that it has had the desired impact (Linden 2009).

Strategic Planning in Edmonton

The City of Edmonton, Alberta, is the most recent and exemplary case of a municipality taking responsibility and planning strategically for the prevention of gang-related and youth violence. In September 2008, Mayor Stephen Mandel created a Taskforce on Community Safety with a mandate for change based on a preventative approach to issues of safety. The recommendations of the taskforce have been approved by City Council and now are being implemented. The City of Edmonton deserves international attention for their courage and skill in investing in actions that will prevent gang-related and youth violence across a municipality of approximately 1 million residents.

Building on Edmonton's strong local initiatives, the taskforce first conducted a thorough environmental scan to assess existing assets, gaps, and trends. Next, a robust community engagement strategy invited diverse citizen and community partner input. Examining and rethinking community safety in Edmonton meant involving people from all walks of life, not just the "experts." It meant giving a voice to newcomers, immigrants, business owners, the victims, youths, families, and other at-risk individuals. In March 2009, the taskforce hosted a comprehensive series of interviews, panels, and focus groups that engaged more than 500 stakeholders. Overall, there was a strong consensus that change is imminent. Edmontonians called for leadership change, new approaches, and an overarching leadership to provide a shared purpose and vision for the city. Finally, they articulated a clear commitment to a new, citizen-driven approach to community safety with key champions.

Where there are currently silos, Edmontonians envisioned a more coherent strategy to network pathways and links to coordinate the effort to reduce crime. They called for a plan focused on the root causes of crime in their community that supports their most vulnerable children, diverse families, and neighborhoods.

Three critical approaches were identified in the community engagement process as vital to reaching this goal: providing sustainable funding to power long-term change, transforming civic institutions to meet the needs of the 21st century, and targeting resources to those vulnerable times of transition when people most need a helping hand. Finally, citizens advocated for an overarching coordinating body—community driven and inclusive—to galvanize a culture shift that imbeds prevention and citizen engagement into civic life.

In September 2009, Edmonton City Council unanimously approved the taskforce's final report, titled *REACH: Building a Culture of Community Safety in One Generation* (www.reachreport.ca). The REACH report reflects a truly made-in-Edmonton blueprint for a new approach to community safety, one that focuses on investing in prevention to effect change.

The nine REACH recommendations blend vision and practical solutions to reframe Edmonton's approach to community safety. The evidence-based recommendations focus on preventing crime before it happens and offer innovative new ways of coming at old problems. They fall into three strategic areas for action:

Investing in Children, Youth, and Families

The taskforce heard clearly that family dynamics create risk for children and youth, which in turn place the community at risk. Diverse community participants in the taskforce engagement workshops expressed a sense of urgency. They stressed that the time for change and more effective, coordinated support for at-risk youth is now: "This needs to happen very soon. We are losing our youth quickly. If we can just make the connections so we can work together for those kids and find opportunities, we can make success happen."

Accordingly, the REACH report identifies that we need to help families do the best job they can to raise healthy, caring, responsible children who are less likely to be drawn to criminal behaviors and to become victims of criminal activities. Four critical REACH recommendations offer ideas for new ways of supporting and engaging at-risk youth and families:

- Build and nurture a more integrated model of families and neighborhood safety that positions schools as community hubs and key access points for social supportive services and for citizen engagement.
- Lead development of comprehensive, coordinated access to 24/7 services for those most at-risk youth, sexually exploited individuals, gangs, and so on.
- Facilitate development of a communitywide strategy on Fetal Alcohol Spectrum Disorder (FASD) that supports a coordinated outreach model for high needs individuals.
- Source sustainable funds to develop and evaluate targeted actions that focus on turning at-risk youth away from gang involvement.

New Leadership

REACH also recommended the creation of a new, overarching leadership body for community safety. The community-driven coordinating center will integrate, promote, and sustain community safety in Edmonton. An arm's-length membership-based organization, it will offer a leadership vehicle to engage ordinary Edmontonians, diverse sectors (including business, education, enforcement, and health), and all orders of government around a shared vision. The center will be ensured of sustainability through the "incubation" of redirected resources from the municipality's Community Service Department, in addition to accessing some significant one-time funds to kick-start a long-term strategy based on the REACH report.

Catalyzing Change

The responsibility center will steer the implementation of the new models presented in the REACH recommendations in the years to come. Perhaps most important, it will generate a sustained culture shift around citizen engagement in community safety in Edmonton. A key task will be to shift Edmontonians from asking, "What can be done?" to instead asking, "What can I do?" REACH will foster a cultural and behavioral shift so that every Edmontonian has a shared responsibility to one another, to the community, and to future generations to ensure that the city is safe.

These recommendations will help us address the root causes of crime and ensure at-risk individuals get the support they need so they don't resort to crime. By investing in crime prevention, we'll realize a substantial shift in one generation towards an Edmonton where citizens feel safe, but most importantly, where they are safe.

—Taskforce Co-Chair Fred Rayner

We all must understand that while we can look for short term solutions, we must take our first steps towards the real solution too, the one that will take a genera-tion to accomplish and thus will require our focused and continued commitment to stay the course.

—Mayor Stephen Mandel

Edmonton's REACH report lays out a clear road map, based on the belief that a focus of time, energy, and funds on prevention and innovation, particularly in relation to the children and youth of tomorrow, will produce a safer community today and in the years ahead.

LESSONS LEARNED

If we are serious about addressing the issue of gang-related and youth violence in Canada, we need to shift to an evidence-based, comprehensive, and colla-borative approach to the issue. A more effective response to the challenges posed by youth involvement in gangs in Canada requires a greater investment in the research and development of effective evidence-based prevention strategies and programs that address gang-related and youth violence. There is already a great deal of knowledge on what has and has not worked in the prevention of youth offending internationally, and Canada is leading the way in harnessing this knowledge so that it may play a greater role in decision making at the public policy level.

A shift to a more comprehensive and long-term solution requires the creation of a responsibility center to increase collaborative partnerships, policies, and investments and to oversee the implementation of an integrated action plan. To create an action plan to target gang-related and youth violence, a strategic planning process is necessary to identify priorities, select the best strategies, develop an implementation plan, and determine how to evaluate successes. Even as the initial Canadian responses to youth gangs relied too heavily on "get-tough" policies, the pioneering nature of the federal NCPC investments, the exemplary model of the Province of Alberta, and the innovation demonstrated by the City of Edmon-ton, each facilitated by an orientation toward CPSD, are expected to inspire many more jurisdictions to undertake policies that will reduce crime, prevent victimization, and enhance community safety in a cost-effective, responsible, and successful manner.

More can be done at the municipal level to reduce gang-related and youth violence by coordinating and investing in prevention strategies, which strengthen and adapt successful programs to reduce violence. Following are important actions for municipal stakeholders:

- Closely examine municipal strategies in Canada and abroad that have been successful in reducing the number of persons victimized violently by members of youth gangs.
- Implement programs that address underlying causes for gang involvement and membership, including issues of child poverty, inadequate housing, barriers to education, unemployment, mental health, racism, and discrimination and that are both culturally and gender competent.
- Target programs and investments to areas in the cities that have disproportionately high levels of economic inequality, disadvantage, and social disorganization and that lack services.

Finally, the increasing governmental support for evidence-based prevention approaches to gang-related and youth violence in Canada is not a result of a difference in public attitudes toward crime and punishment between this country and other Western nations (Waller 2006). The key difference is the way that crime issues have been framed in terms of reducing harm to victims and saving taxpayers' money (see Waller 2006). This is not about being soft on offenders, it is about being tough on causes, getting results that stop victimization, and saving money. Furthermore, in Canada, support for prevention is the result of increasing confidence that these evidence-based initiatives, once implemented, will reduce gang-related and youth violence and prevent future victimizations.

REFERENCES

Alberta's Crime Reduction and Safe Communities Task Force. 2007. *Keeping Communities Safe: Report and Recommendations*. Edmonton: Government of Alberta.

Bania, M. 2009. Gang Violence among Youth and Young Adults: (Dis)Affiliation and the Potential for Prevention. *IPC Review* 3: 89–116.

Beattie, S. 2009. "Homicide in Canada, 2008." *Juristat* 29 (4). Ottawa, ON: Statistics Canada.

Chettleburgh, M.C. 2003. *2002 Canadian Police Survey on Youth Gangs*. Ottawa, ON: Astwood Strategy Corporation.

Chettleburgh, M.C. 2007. *Young Thugs: Inside the Dangerous World of Canadian Street Gangs*. Toronto, ON: Harper Collins Publishers.

Chettleburgh, M.C. 2008. *Now Is the Time to Act: Youth Gang Prevention in Ottawa*. Ottawa, ON: Astwood Strategy Corporation.

CISC (Criminal Intelligence Service Canada). 2006. *Project Spectrum: 2006 Situational Overview of Street Gangs in Canada*. Ottawa, ON: Criminal Intelligence Service Canada.

Community Safety Secretariat. 2004. "Community Safety Plan." www.toronto.ca/community_safety/index.htm. November 1, 2009.

Edmonton Taskforce on Community Safety. 2009. *REACH: Building a Culture of Community Safety in Edmonton*. Edmonton, AB: City of Edmonton.

Farrington, D.P., and B.C. Welsh. 2007. *Saving Children from a Life of Crime: Early Risk Factors and Effective Interventions*. Oxford: Oxford University Press.

Fitzgerald, R.T., and P.J. Carrington. 2008. "The Neighbourhood Context of Urban Aboriginal Crime." *Canadian Journal of Criminology and Criminal Justice* 50 (5): 523–557.

Fitzgerald, R., M. Wisener, and J. Savoie. 2004. *Neighbourhood Characteristics and the Distribution of Crime in Winnipeg*. Crime and Justice Research Paper Series, 4. Ottawa, ON: Statistics Canada.

Government of Alberta. 2009. "Safe Communities." www.justice.gov.ab.ca/safe/. November 1, 2009.

Hastings, R. 2005. Perspectives on Crime Prevention: Issues and challenges. *Canadian Journal of Criminology and Criminal Justice* 47 (2): 209–219.

Hastings, R. 2009. Sustaining the Momentum: Crime Prevention at a Crossroads. *IPC Review* 3: 7–10.

Hawkins, J.D., and J.A. Pollard. 1999. Risk and Protective Factors: Are Both Necessary to Understand Diverse Behavioural Outcomes in Adolescence? *Social Work Research* 23 (3): 145–158.

Howell, J.C. 2005. Moving Risk Factors into Developmental Theories of Gang Membership. *Youth Violence and Juvenile Justice* 3 (4): 334–354.

Janhevich, D., H. Johnson, C. Vézina, and J. Fraser. 2008. *Making Cities Safer: Canadian Strategies and Practices*. Ottawa, ON: Institute for the Prevention of Crime.

Johnson, H., and J. Fraser. 2007. *Making Cities Safer: International Strategies and Practices*. Ottawa, ON: Institute for the Prevention of Crime.

La Prairie, C. 2002. Aboriginal Over-Representation in the Criminal Justice System: A Tale of Nine Cities. *Canadian Journal of Criminology* 44 (2): 181–208.

Li, G. 2008. "Homicide in Canada, 2007." *Juristat* 28 (9):1-26. Ottawa, ON: Statistics Canada.

Linden, R. 2009. "Plan Strategically." In *Making Cities Safer: Action Briefs for Municipal Stakeholders*. Ottawa, ON: Institute for the Prevention of Crime.

Milligan, S. 2008. "Youth Custody and Community Services in Canada, 2005/2006." *Juristat* 28 (8): 1–22. Ottawa, ON: Statistics Canada.

Monchalin, L. 2009. "Aboriginal Peoples' Safety." In *Making Cities Safer: Action Briefs for Municipal Stakeholders*. Ottawa, ON: Institute for the Prevention of Crime.

National Institute of Justice. 2008. "Gun-Violence Programs: Operation Ceasefire." www.ojp.usdoj.gov/nij/topics/crime/gun-violence/prevention/ceasefire.htm. November 1, 2009

National Research Council. 2001. *Juvenile Crime, Juvenile Justice*. Washington, DC: National Academies Press.

NCPC (National Crime Prevention Centre). 2007a. *A Blueprint for Effective Crime Prevention*. Ottawa, ON: Public Safety Canada.

NCPC (National Crime Prevention Centre). 2007b. *Youth Gang Involvement: What Are the Risk Factors?* Ottawa, ON: Public Safety Canada.

NCPC (National Crime Prevention Centre). 2008. *Promising and Model Crime Prevention Programs*. Ottawa, ON: Public Safety Canada.

NCPC (National Crime Prevention Centre). 2009. "Supporting the Successful Implementation of the National Crime Prevention Strategy." www.publicsafety.gc.ca/res/cp/res/ssincps-amosnpc-eng.aspx. November 1, 2009.

NWG (National Working Group on Crime Prevention). 2007. *Building a Safer Canada: First Report of the National Working Group on Crime Prevention*. Ottawa, ON: Institute for the Prevention of Crime.

Public Safety Canada. 2007. "Youth Gang Prevention Fund." www.publicsafety.gc.ca/prg/cp/ygpf_index-eng.aspx. November 1, 2009.

Shaw, M. 2001. *The Role of Local Government in Community Safety*. Montreal, QC: International Centre for the Prevention of Crime.

Totten, M. 2008. *Promising Practices for Addressing Youth Involvement in Gangs*. Vancouver, BC: British Columbia Ministry of Public Safety and Solicitor General, Victim Services and Crime Prevention Division.

Totten, M. 2009. Aboriginal Youth and Violent Gang Involvement in Canada: Quality Prevention Strategies. *IPC Review* 3: 135–156.

Vézina, C. 2009. "Take Responsibility." In *Making Cities Safer: Action Briefs for Municipal Stakeholders*. Ottawa, ON: Institute for the Prevention of Crime.

Waller, I. 2006. *Less Law, More Order: The Truth about Reducing Crime*. Westport, CT: Praeger.

Waller, I. 2009a. "Invest Smartly." *Making Cities Safer: Action Briefs for Municipal Stakeholders*. Ottawa, ON: Institute for the Prevention of Crime.

Waller, I. 2009b. "Safe Streets." *Making Cities Safer: Action Briefs for Municipal Stakeholders*. Ottawa, ON: Institute for the Prevention of Crime.

Waller, I. 2009c. "Why Invest." In *Making Cities Safer: Action Briefs for Municipal Stakeholders*. Ottawa, ON: Institute for the Prevention of Crime.

Wortley, S., and J. Tanner. 2004. "Social Groups or Criminal Organizations? The Extent and Nature of Youth Gang Activity in Toronto." In *From Enforcement and Prevention to Civic Engagement: Research on Community Safety*, ed. B. Kidd and J. Philips, 59–80. Toronto, ON: Centre of Criminology, University of Toronto.

15

Tambou Lapè (Drums for Peace): A Positive Experience for Young People Previously Involved in Armed Violence

Daniela Bercovitch

THIS CASE STUDY of Tambou Lapè (Drums for Peace) describes the activities of social mobilization, community development, and prevention of armed violence, implemented in the neighborhood of Bel Air, Port-au-Prince, Haiti, carried out in a joint Haitian and Brazilian effort. Viva Rio, a Brazilian nongovernmental organization (NGO), was instrumental in bringing together former armed gang members (from Solino, Bel Air, Delmas 2, La Saline, and Fort Rond) to sign an accord in 2007 in support of the government's national commission for disarmament, demobilization, and reinsertion program (that is, the National Commission of Disarmament, Dismantling and Rehabilitation, CNDDR, in French). These ex-gang members are now engaged in community cultural projects under the Viva Rio project Tambou Lapè (Drums for Peace). Residents of the previously violent zone are working together to manage community projects. This joint Brazilian and Haitian project illustrates the implementation strategy of an integrated safety, development, and humanitarian effort, as part of the stabilization and reconstruction of a community in a postwar context.

SIMILARITIES BETWEEN THE RIO DE JANEIRO AND PORT-AU-PRINCE CONTEXTS

Viva Rio, a Brazilian NGO, has been operating in Haiti since 2006, focusing its activities in Bel Air and surrounding neighborhoods. There are many similarities between Port-au-Prince, and Rio de Janeiro, where Viva Rio was established 15 years ago: a high incidence of armed violence in a context of poverty and socio-economic disparities can be found both in the *favelas* in Rio de Janeiro and the slums in Port-au-Prince; youth living in slums are the most at-risk group for violence victimization and perpetration in both cities; and the availability and use of weapons that exacerbate conflicts, fear, and insecurity is a common risk factor. The participation of boys, girls, and young people in organized armed violence is not a new phenomenon in Latin America and the Caribbean. Easy and widespread access to firearms, insufficient job opportunities, the lack of access to basic health and education, inadequate urban infrastructures, and disorder are characteristics of many urban communities throughout the region—found in the *favelas* (slums) in Brazil, the *comunas* (slums) in Colombia, or the disadvantaged neighborhoods in Haiti, among others—where organized armed violence groups flourish. These groups are known as gangs, *maras*, *bandas*, drug trafficking groups, and by other names, depending on the country and local contexts (Pérez 2008).

In Haiti and Brazil, children and youth are at the greatest risk of the most serious forms of urban violence, as both victims and perpetrators. The teenagers and youngsters are more aggressive when victimized in violent contexts; this heightened risk is largely due to external factors and not individual character-istics. Moreover, youth have the energy that eventually may lead them to rebel against society in difficult situations. Therefore, the interaction between security and youth networks is crucial to Viva Rio's project, in both Rio de Janeiro and Port-au-Prince.

Slums in both cities are vulnerable to external factors and generators of violence, and to the growth of parallel armed groups. Although loosely organized, youth engaged in organized armed violence have a significant impact on margin-alized areas. Furthermore, subject to the local powers that impose and reproduce themselves by the direct use of violence, poor neighborhoods become the scene of equally violent actions by the state and, in the case of Haiti, by the United Nations Mission for Haiti's Stabilization (MINUSTAH). Violence is a serious problem for all the children and youth in these neighborhoods, particularly for those adolescents and youth who do not attend school.

These marked similarities, and the accumulated experience in addressing urban violence through social development in Rio de Janeiro over the last 15 years, led to the Bel Air project, and Viva Rio's engagement in Haiti. The mission of the work in Bel Air is to reduce violence and upgrade and renew urban areas, with a focus on safety, development, and human rights of its inhabitants. This integrated approach includes increasing access to water, solid waste management, and the creation of alternative energy sources, as well as education, sport, and school health. Viva Rio's principal objective is the maintenance of community peace, and as such its efforts are particularly centered on women, young people and children, community leaders, and groups whose role is critical in the organization, stability, and prosperity of the local community. They not only are the victims of much of the violence, but also are the potential change agents, with the power to transform their community and keep the peace.

The historical and cultural neighborhood of Port-au-Prince, Bel Air lived a period of great prosperity until the 1940s. However, a demographic explosion led to the proliferation of informal settlements and popular markets, paving the way for the formation of slums. The local problems took on a political dimension in 2004. Bel Air had become a lawless area, in which politically motivated violence and confrontations did not spare either the churches or the schools: an enclave where the armed groups devoted themselves to a war without regard for the local inhabitants, held hostage by the violence. According to the census conducted by Viva Rio,[1] 40 percent of the population fled Bel Air during the periods of conflicts and confrontations.[2] The demographic pyramid of the neighborhood in early 2007 shows that families withdrew their children from the area during periods of violence. A second study in December 2007 showed that two-thirds of the children removed by their parents had returned. According to those who were surveyed, the reasons for their return were as follows: (1) 23.2 percent recognized that MINUSTAH had restored a secure environment and (2) 14.3 percent attributed the safer environment to the work of the national police of Haiti (Fernandes and Nascimento 2007). Another important reason cited was the return to normalcy and the ability to continue to work, study, and be reunited with family members. Stability remains fragile, however, because of structural political, economic, and social challenges as well as the more visible, environmental challenges.

THE PROJECT IN HAITI: TAMBOU LAPÈ

Designed to be implemented over four years (2007–2011), the goal of Viva Rio's project Tambou Lapè in Bel Air aims to reduce community violence and to manage and transform conflict in the intervention area. As a stabilization strategy, the project works with local power structures through a process of peace negotiations between local community leaders; it also facilitates the implementation of other community projects, thus solidifying the process of stabilization and development as well as the presence of Viva Rio in the neighborhood.

In May 2007, the first peace agreement was signed, articulated by Viva Rio among the rival bases (areas that represent complex groups) of Delmas 2, Bel Air, Solino, La Saline and Fort Rond at the CNDDR headquarters in the presence of the CNDDR president, Alix Fils Aimé; the director of Viva Rio, Rubem César Fernandes; the rival leaders of four areas of Bel Air; and a large number of journalists. After one month free from homicides or confrontations (with firearms or other weapons) resulting from conflict among the bases or with the Haitian authorities, Viva Rio offers scholarships to children and adolescents of every locality (11 in the first agreement). A drawing is used as the selection instrument for the scholarships. If a violent death occurs, the drawings are suspended for the month in question.

---

[1] See www.haitiici.com or http://blog.comunidadesegura.org/haitiici/recensement-de-bel-air-2007/, http://www.comunidadesegura.com/fr/node/42434.

[2] 74.3 percent of the population studied reported having lived there.

After two months without violent death, the program offers grants for vocational training to the young members of the groups of each locality. The offered courses include French, English, music (percussion, guitar, and electric piano), handcrafts, poetry, and production of cultural events.

Every two months, Viva Rio promotes cultural events in one of the four areas of the neighborhood. The young people trained by the program are responsible for the production of these events. Every month without violent death—resulting from collective or personal reasons—an award is granted, by drawing, to the leaders of the bases, in recognition of the advances made for the safety in Bel Air. Once a month, organized meetings are held between the National Police of Haiti, the CNDDR, and Viva Rio, as well as the Brazilian military to discuss the safety of the community and to identify whether a violent death occurred by knife or gun. Those encounters encourage a fertile debate among the local leaderships and the forces of law and order, during which the basic needs for each locality are discussed, the distributions of food on the part of the MINUSTAH are organized, and gaps in police presence and other relevant subjects for the community are identified.

To achieve peace, all parties in opposition should be included. To part the territorial definition, other elements should be considered. After the period of strong conflicts between 2004 and 2006, the project identified 14 localities articulated in five rival areas: Bel Air, Delmas 2, Solino, La Saline, and Fort Rond. These areas are articulated in bases that represent complex groups that combine the following four characteristics (Fernandes 2008):

- Local Leadership: These form a community leadership de facto, unelected but recognized as the organized "basis" of the local society. Indeed, these often are entitled "*Basis*" (a nomenclature maximized by the address of the Theology of the Liberation in the 1980s.
- Political Affiliation: This category includes the heirs of the time of president Aristide,[3] who gave them sufficient weapons to be able to arm some bases. These groups are sensitive to the policy and hope to obtain benefits.
- Cultural Expression: Every locality has one or more *bandes à pied*, street bands, called RARA, that practice a traditional style on edge and dance. A RARA band can have an average of 50 regular participants (men and women).
- Criminal Activity: Groups that run parallel to a recent history of armed violence.

The four characteristics are crossed dynamically. The members usually are associated with one dimension more than another. The "Basis," however, contains all the types. Together, these characteristics form the profile and the internal dynamic of the "Basis" and its impact on the territory.

---

[3] The president of the republic in 1999, from 1994–1996, as well as 2001–2004, before his departure from Haiti, in exile.

In December 2007 and January 2008, after the first signing of the peace agreement, an increase in tension caused by the liberation of ex-prisoners was registered in Bel Air. One of these former prisoners, called Ti Djo, was murdered by the local leaders of the *ligne lasts*,[4] which felt threatened by his return. After signing a peace agreement—between May and December 2007—additional deaths were not registered. During January, however, five murders were registered, all caused by violent disputes.

A repressive response on the part of the military controlled the situation, but the members of *ligne lasts* positioned themselves against the community leader of Viva Rio, accusing it of altering the military and issuing a death threat. The presence in Haiti of the Brazilian minister of the human rights created an opportunity for an encounter between Viva Rio and the local community leaders, including the most radical line. The presence of the military commanders gave a political importance to the encounter. The encounter provided a space in which the local leaders were capable of presenting formal complaints against the Brazilian military in the presence of officials, of the ambassador, and of the minister, representing a positive experience with regard to conflict resolution. The leaders were satisfied to have an opportunity to express their views and the military was asked to reduce its pressure on the community.

A second peace agreement was signed on May 15, 2008, by 14 leaders in the CNDDR in the presence of its president, members of the MINUSTAH program for a Reduction of Community Violence, the director of Viva Rio, the Brazilian ambassador, representatives of the Ministry of Foreign Matters of Canada, and representatives of Norway and the Canadian International Development Agency (CIDA). Various innovations were added to the rules of the first agreement, as the inclusion of two areas—Fort National and Corridor Bastia—gave more responsibility to the community leaders with regard to maintaining safety. The celebration of the Peace Agreement Tambou Lapè II occurred in La Saline, with the participation of rival bands of RARA music being presented in an environment of harmony for all the neighborhood.

For the second agreement, a new stimulus was proposed the community leaders: an award of a motorcycle (value up to US$1,000) was offered by drawing in the absence of violent death, regardless of the causes. The community leaders were equally responsible for maintaining a peaceful environment in the local society.

A year later, urban violence and homicides in Bel Air reduced from 26 deaths per 100,000 people in 2006–2007 to 17 deaths per 100,000 population in 2008–2009. This number was lower than in many cities in Latin America and comparable to the homicide rate in U.S. cities in the 1980s (Viva Rio 2009, 20–21). On May 16, 2009, a third peace agreement was signed. The project team evaluated

---

[4] "Ligne Dure," or hard line, is an armed military group, increasingly involved in criminal activity, that dates back to the time of Aristide.

the criteria for the agreement, with the participation of school directors, relatives of beneficiary children of the scholarships, beneficiary musicians, community leaders, and project funders.

Between 2007 and 2009, the community leaders included only men. For the third agreement, feminine leadership was identified and six women also signed the agreement. New rules were added to this agreement: the children of the 29 leaders would receive classical fellowships which also were offered to the leaders and members of the CNDDR, including informatics, languages (Creole, French, English), report drafting, and conflict management in the community center Kay Nou.[5]

Violence is a complex multidimensional phenomenon, but some factors help to reduce collective violence in the area of intervention of Viva Rio, including the following: (1) a strong but interactive presence of the military (Brazilian Battalion), (2) the presence of the Haitian National Police, also following an interactive trend, (3) the education and cultural incentives to the members of bases and local families, (4) mediation of conflict over the territorial leaders with the support of the CNDDR, and (5) investments in public goods in the area (water, solid waste) and in recreational activities (sports and popular parties) that together create an improvement in the living conditions.

With the positive impact of the project and the decline in the indexes of crime in the area, on May 1, 2009, Via Río launched the campaign called "Bel Air Verde" that has a double objective: (1) ecological, with the creation of a plant cooperative for the reforestation of Bel Air; and (2) safety, with a petition signed with more than 3,600 people in support of Bel Air Verde, requesting that the MINUSTAH change the categorization of the area from red to green.[6]

HIP HOP

The circles of hip hop in the red neighborhoods are at times associated with youth violence. Following the same line of work of street culture and of inclusion of different youth groups, Tambou Lapè promotes competitions of rival hip hop groups among the communities at several public events, using the subjects of violent themes, sexuality, and AIDS prevention. More than 100 groups from several violent neighborhoods in Port-au-Prince (including Cité Soleil, Martissant, and peripheral areas of Pétion Ville) as well as others, participated in the last competition. The 15 best groups had the opportunity to record a disc that

---

[5] Kay Nou is Viva Rio's community center in Bel Air. The 25,000 square meter facility is under a 10-year lease and houses the recycling, sports, and training centers, as well as Viva Rio administrative facilities.

[6] Bel Air continues to be considered a "red" zone by MINUSTAH. United Nations personnel cannot visit the zone unless they are in armored vehicles and accompanied by military escorts. Cité Soleil, however, is considered a "green" zone by day and a "red" zone by night.

is played on different radio stations. A series of programs were presented at schools to strengthen the AIDS prevention campaign and condoms were distributed during the events. The project strengthened not only the *Rap Creole,* which facilitated the young talents of the ghetto neighborhood to promote art in the musical and cultural market, but also broadcast a message of behavioral awareness for young people about sexually transmitted diseases. The *raperos* (that is, young people of the bases) have the opportunity to be guided toward new subjects such as peace, love, honesty, tolerance, prison, crime, abuse of all types, and nonviolence. But above all, the music is heard by all and has a considerable impact on Haitian youth. The artists leave the state "*underground*" to reach an *amador* level. The economic capacities strengthened the group, as well as the national institution of the *Rap Creole.*

CAPACITY FOR IMPLEMENTATION

Three major factors facilitate the implementation of the project. The first factor is the capacity and style of Viva Rio to design and implement urban rehabilitation and reduce armed violence in poor neighborhoods. Viva Rio believes that the increase in armed urban violence in a context of poverty and social exclusion generates a vicious cycle in which basic living deficiencies aggravate the situation. It is fundamental to face the problems simultaneously, creating policies for safety, social inclusion, and development. The program integrated in Bel Air, which in a deliberate way generates safety and development and strengthens the capacity for stabilization of the MINUSTAH, offers a quantity of services to the community that cannot be offered completely by the Haitian government because of the country's economic and political fragility.

Another positive aspect of the work of Viva Rio is the willingness to understand the local context before planning its activities. That attention paid toward the local conditions permits the adaptation of the projects to the country context and facilitates the adaptation for local development priorities. The first activity was the implementation of the 2007 household census (applied in more than 10,000 homes),[7] and a study of the Bel Air water market before the water supply project was structured. Viva Rio concentrates its activities in Bel Air to avoid diluting efforts in other areas. Its organizational structure permits flexibility and fast adaptation. The Haitian government and civil society organizations have been involved in the approval of its work plan and implementation. The style is operationally pragmatic and intuitive, with an evidence-based program based on the census and other studies that are quantitative and ethnographic (Neiburg and Nicaise 2009).

---

[7] See Viva Rio, Censo de Bel Air www.haitiici.com or http://blog.comunidadesegura.org/haitiici/recensement-de-bel-air-2007/, http://www.comunidadesegura.com/fr/node/42434.

The project Tambou Lapé represents an example of participation at the local level. The fact that Viva Rio works from the inside, based in the same Bel Air neighborhood, facilitates the intercultural dialogue with community input, avoiding the exclusion of community actors. Taking into account the fluidity of the identities and the complexity of the partnerships in the Haitian context, Viva Rio elected to deal with that multiplicity of identities which can cause tensions depending on the interpretation. Considering the bases as purely criminal neglects the dynamic of the different identities. Except for the CNDDR, state agencies are absent in Bel Air and a dialogue with the members of recently disassembled parties, which are still present and powerful, is absent. Integration of this sector in networks is essential, and the incentives offered can provide the only realistic driving force to maintain the commitment to the peace agreement, especially in a poor environment like that of Bel Air.

Among the different actors of the state that proposed to address the problem of violence affecting children, a special unit of the Haitian National Police was created in 2003 specifically to address crimes against children. It is financed and trained by the United Nations Children's Fund (UNICEF). It is difficult to attract children engaged in armed violence because it does not have an integrated action plan. The brigade depends on the Institute of Social Welfare and Research. The latter works with children in conflict with the law and with children who are victims of abuse and rapes mainly committed by adults. The institute also does research on the history of children, ultimately to reunite them with their families or legal guardians, when possible.

After two years, it is evident that the situation in Bel Air has changed: territorial conflict no longer exists among the different areas. Violence results, instead, in other forms, such as rapes, violent games, and lynching. Small violent groups continue to be organized in acts of crime, mainly in the area of the market where different groups dispute the control of the businesses. The participation of different groups of the community in the struggle against violence (directors of school, church, families, groups of RARA bands), the integration of the forces of law and order in the community, and the reinforcement of the political role of the community leaders constitute a test of the significant impact of the project Tambou Lapè on Bel Air. The participation of Bel Air in the demonstrations of April 2008[8] was passive in contrast with the emerging aggressive signs of Martissant, Pétion Ville, and other neighborhoods. During the demonstrations of 2009, led by students, people, and the community, they looked to the streets of Bel Air for a more peaceful route to arrive and depart from the downtown.

The program of Viva Rio contributes to the increase of pride in the local culture through support toward Creole music and sports activities. With an

---

[8] Protests following the sharp increase in foodstuff prices across Haiti resulted in 6 deaths, hundreds of injured people, and the fall of the Alexis government.

increase in self-esteem, the general attitude toward violence can be changed. Some weaknesses of the project include low attendance of the victims of violence, the criteria for identification of the community leader and its legitimacy, and little work on violence tames and of gender. Although the statistics of homicide represent a fundamental indicator for the control of violence, they do not capture other aspects of the safety.

Another identified problem has been the low participation of the target groups, including school directors and relatives of beneficiary children. The intent, with the evaluation, was to incorporate these groups through the formation of school committees in charge of raising the awareness of the students, the parents, and directors on the subjects of "peaceful resolution of conflicts," hygiene, and health.

As an objective for the two coming years, Viva Rio wants to give continuity to the peace agreement signed by the territorial leaders to radically reduce lethal violence in the area. The incentives to the participation of the members of the "Basis" in the peace agreement will benefit 504 children from scholarships for basic education, 84 young members of RARA bands with vocational training, and 14 community leaders with a public recognition award. The Community Center Kay Nou will promote the musical entertainments and cinema to increase entertainment and promote micro businesses in the area. The street celebrations stimulate the cultural aspect of the organization of the "Basis," as a professional alternative for youth of the street. This represents a change in the terms of the original agreement. Six celebrations were planned in 2009.

The program also attempts to include the hip hop groups in the process of the peace agreement. Although the rap, graffiti, and street dancing usually are associated with a culture of violence, hip hop does not have territorial roots like the RARE groups. In this case, Bel Air functions as a catalytic neighborhood for the hip hop groups of other neighborhoods of Port-au-Prince, including other cities, to address peace maintenance. In 2008, matters of violence of gender and of prevention against HIV were the object of a hip hop competition, with the participation of more than 100 different groups. In 2009, rap competitions concentrated on matters of violence against nature.

Viva Rio intends to train the Brazilian military in community relations and to facilitate implementation in the area of practical military-civil cooperation), engage the National Police of Haiti in regular, interactive patrols in Bel Air, with a positive contribution to the environment of peace agreement, train local leaders (members of bases and others) in conflict mediation and democratic practices, and identify and give voice to women without losing the support of those who traditionally hold the power.

The case of Haiti challenges traditional concepts of war and postwar environments. For this reason, different efforts in establishing conventional disarmament, demobilization, and reintegration (DDR) programs have failed. The existence of a formal peace agreement between bases is a good precedent: it promotes the dialogue and comprehension of the roots of violence by means of the strengthening of the community. Furthermore, the capacity to work with the military, the police, and the bases enables Viva Rio to facilitate the search for objectives of mutual interest, encouraging life and the local talent.

REFERENCES

Fernandes, R.C. 2008. *Honor and Respect for Bel Air Youth, Street Culture and Peace Accord*. Port-au-Prince, Haiti.

Fernandes, R.C., and M. Nascimento. 2007. "A Violência em Bel Air, Porto Príncipe, Haiti." www.comunidadesegura.com/fr/node/42434.

Neiburg, F., and N. Nicaise. 2009. *The Social Life of Water: Bel Air*. Port-au-Prince, Haiti: Nucleo de Pesquisas em Cultura e Economia/Viva Rio.

Pérez, R. 2008. *Mobilization, Disarmament, and Social Incorporation*. MDI.

Viva Rio. 2009. "Narrative Report of the Project Honour and Respect for Bel Air." www .comunidadesegura.org/files/Bel_Air_report_20081.pdf.

Viva Rio. "Honour and Respect for Bel Air." www.vivario.org.br/publique/cgi/cgilua.exe/ sys/start.htm?sid=22&infoid=1676.

16

Latin America and Caribbean Experience in Urban Youth Violence Prevention: Citizen Security and Regional Responses

Jorge C. Lamas and Joan Serra Hoffman

CONTEXT

LATIN AMERICA HAS the highest murder rates in the world for people between 15 and 24. Figures from 2002–2005 in a study of youth homicides in 83 countries estimate the murder rate for young people was 36.6 for every 100,000 people in Latin America, with the Caribbean a close second at 31.6 per 100,000. In Africa, the murder rate was 16.1 per 100,000, Asia was 2.4, Oceania was 1.6, and Europe was 1.2. The corresponding figure for Canada was 2.5, and in the United States, the murder rate of young adults was 12.9 per 100,000. These continent-wide averages hide substantial divergence in rates between countries and cities in Latin American and the Caribbean (LAC). In El Salvador, the country studied with the highest youth homicide rate, the annual death toll is 92 per 100,000, and rising. The lowest youth homicide rates in Latin America were in Chile, Cuba, and Uruguay, all with around 7 deaths per 100,000 (Waiselfisz 2008).

The countries with high youth murder rates in Latin America and the Caribbean also are among the countries in the region with the worst overall murder rates. Regional overall homicide figures record the highest rates in Honduras (58 per 100,000; see OCAVI 2008), El Salvador (56; UNDP 2008), Venezuela (52; OAS 2009), Jamaica (49; United Nations 2008), and Trinidad and Tobago (42; TT Crime Statistics 2008). Inversely, Peru, Argentina Uruguay, and Chile have homicide rates of 5 per 100,000 or lower (United Nations 2002). Within-country differences show that the highest rates of violence tend to occur in the poorest, urban communities with the fewest resources to cope with the financial, social, and psychological strains produced by the resulting deaths and disabilities. Pervasive violence and deprivation form a vicious circle that stifles economic growth and democratic governance and results in further social exclusion for many youth and urban communities in the region.

There are no empirically supported explanations as to why youth violence in Latin America and the Caribbean is the highest in the world, and why youth violence has increased so sharply in the last decades. Available evidence at the societal level links the high levels of violence in the region with the demographic transition that has boosted the segment of the population that is most prone to aggression (that is, youths). Some of the underlying risk factors that lead to such behavioral problems include high inequality fueling increased opportunities to commit crimes; social exclusion by ethnicity or race, which is closely linked to inequality; being raised in areas with high levels of poverty; inadequate parenting skills; complex household arrangements; high levels of community disorganization; poor quality education in the public school system; high youth unemployment levels and lack of recreational and income-generating opportunities; the rapidly growing trade in weapons and drugs, linked to globalization and organized crime in drug trafficking; and the availability of firearms and other weapons. Furthermore, institutional weaknesses of the penal system, courts, and the police, including serious problems with police and corruption; situational triggers to crime and violence in poor urban slums with deteriorated urban infrastructure; and an authoritarian culture that grants authority to men in the family and condones violence against women and children are variables linked to the high regional violence rates.

Given the high rate of youth and overall violence in the region, there has been a considerable amount of pressure on governments, at all levels, to take action. Over the past 20 years, important prevention and reduction efforts surfaced in the region, with an early characteristic being the emphasis on multisectoral responses and coordination, and a multidimensional approach to the prevention of violence. The pioneering efforts in the region combined a range of approaches, and this case study focuses on those implemented at the municipal and national levels, with a particular focus on national citizen security programs financed by the Inter-American Development Bank (IADB). The approach is intended to be epidemiological in nature in the sense that different risk factors are assessed and factored into an integrated risk management approach that relies on contributions from many departments and many sectors—health, education, family welfare, urban infrastructure, law enforcement, justice sector reform, police reform, and the media. This approach rests on the belief that violence is often a learned behavior, thereby positioning domestic violence as a precursor of violent behavior in the street. IADB projects, therefore, in many cases address issues or aspects of youth violence as well as child maltreatment and domestic violence, which can condition young people for violent behavior.

MUNICIPAL EXPERIENCES IN VIOLENCE PREVENTION

Experience in the region (in particular from Bogotá, Medellín, and Cali in Colombia, and São Paulo in Brazil) suggests that one of the most effective entry points for crime and violence prevention is at the municipal level. Locally designed and managed programs have certain advantages: they allow inputs and involvement from citizens and communities in analyzing the problems; encourage agreement on a course of action and assign responsibilities; make it easier to achieve inter-institutional coordination of agencies involved in prevention and assistance efforts (such as justice, health, education, media, police, social services, and nongovernmental and religious organizations); and make it easier to collect information for specific areas on different aspects of the problem. The devastating effects of violence often are felt most directly by cities, communities, and neighborhoods. Local governments have received great pressure to address the problem and to develop highly localized responses. The best known of these initiatives has been in Bogotá, Colombia.

Under the leadership of four different mayors (with varied party affiliations), Bogotá, Colombia, has been laboring mightily for the past 18 years to change its reputation as a lawless, dangerous city. The city leadership has supported and continued to implement a multifaceted set of violence prevention policies and programs, including restrictions on the sale of alcohol and firearm carrying on weekends and special occasions, community mobilization, infrastructure development, and improved policing and social services. Bogotá's success with violence reduction illustrates the importance of political commitment, sustained across three different administrations, and of the allocation of sufficient resources to address the risk factors for youth violence at the individual, relationship, community, and societal level. During this period, safety and living conditions in the city have improved dramatically. Murder rates have fallen to levels even lower than some U.S. cities. Bogotá reduced its homicide rates from a peak of approximately 80 per 100,000 inhabitants in 1993 to 18 in 2006 and continues to be hovering around 20.[1]

Other dimensions of the municipal transformation significantly affected the quality of life and development opportunities for many of the city's youth and young adults, reducing social distance and some dimensions of inequality. The 1993–2003 violence reduction efforts in the city enabled subsequent mayors to deepen social development efforts and expand the social safety net with programs, such as *Bogotá sin hambre* ("Bogotá without hunger") and *Bogotá sin indiferencia* ("Bogotá without indifference") coupled with a focus on education and improving public health. Currently, 98.5 percent of school-age children are enrolled in schools in Bogotá. A major public transportation system improvement and an extensive expansion of the public library system has earned Bogotá UNESCO's 2007 World Book Capital City award in addition to the Bill and Melinda Gates Foundation's 2002 Access to Learning Award for the Bogotá's Network of Public Libraries whose vision is to foster peace in a more equitable

---

[1] For comparisons to various cities in North America; in 2007, for example, the homicide rate for the city of Detroit was 33.8.

society by creating access for all. In a section of the city without parks, without malls, and few options for a young person to pass the time, BibloRed's libraries serve as a beacon of hope.

Luis, a 12-year-old boy who once was not enrolled in school, describes the Tintal Public Library as "a large white building" that "appeared without warning" in the area where he lives. After BibloRed's Tintal library opened, Luis became a regular visitor almost immediately. He got involved in reading-incentive programs and technology workshops. As the time Luis spent at the library grew, the librarians took note of his curiosity and eagerness to learn, and approached the Bureau of the Secretary of Education to help Luis register for school. So next year, Luis will be attending school. He says the library has given him the "opportunity to learn, to know the world, to become someone, to dream, to travel in time and space—without spending money."

Alexander, age 19, currently is unemployed. He travels by bus to the library to look for jobs online. Alexander says that Internet access in the library has helped him learn more about the world. He hopes to continue his education. Among many of the city's youth, the perception of political leadership as committed, competent, and inclusive has given many young residents new confidence in their government and a growing sense of civic pride.

The city of Medellín, Colombia, also applied a combination of similar situational and social development policies over several mayoral administrations starting in the mid-1990s and they were able to steadily reduce the level of youth and urban criminality. Efforts to reintegrate thousands of former combatants, many of whom were youth, were carried out in partnership with the national government. A dramatic drop in homicides occurred in Medellín, from 381 per 100,000 inhabitants in 1991 to 32 per 100,000 in 2008. Cali, Colombia, on the other hand, has experienced a more uneven pattern in crime reduction over the same period related to constant changes in policy orientation from one mayoral administration to another.

CRIME OBSERVATORIES: INTEGRATED INFORMATION SYSTEM FOR DECISION MAKING AT THE MUNICIPAL LEVEL

A key component in developing informed policy responses was made possible by the development and implementation of low-cost and highly efficient geo-referenced violence and crime information systems, or Crime Observatories. Modeled after the mortality surveillance system developed in Cali by the mayor in 1993, the observatories were implemented through a collaborative process at the municipal level with the participation of national institutions. Since 2002, 60 observatories have been established for the documentation and prevention of violence and unintentional injury in Colombia. A study of the impact of policies based on observatory data in seven small Colombian municipalities found an average decrease in homicides over the 2002–2004 period to be

What Worked in Bogotá

Among the strategies implemented, the available evaluation data links the following to reductions in violence (Buvinic, Alda, and Lamas 2005; Llorente and Rivas 2004):

- *Campaigns to Promote Citizen Disarmament and Control of Alcohol Consumption.* Effective information systems provided detailed information on violent crime events, resulting in the formulation of the *Plan Desarme* that controlled the circulation of firearms. In 2001, for instance, around 6,500 firearms were returned voluntarily to the police as a result of the plan. In addition, with the implementation of *Ley Zanahoria*, alcohol sales ended at 3:00 A.M. on weekends to reduce the rates of violent crimes. Firearms and alcohol control had a significant (although not large) effect in violence reduction.

- *Actions to Recuperate Decayed Urban Spaces.* In 2003, the Mockus administration provided 1,235,000 homes with sewage service and 1,316,500 with water services. The city's provision of drinking water rose from 78.7 percent of homes in 1993 to 100 percent in 2003. The sewage service rose from 70.8 percent of homes in 1993 to 94.9 percent in 2003. Two of the most violent areas in Bogotá underwent urban and transport infrastructure renewal. As a result, levels of crime and violence declined substantially in both areas. In Avenida Caracas, the levels of homicide declined by 60 percent from 1999 to 2003. At the same time, in the Cartucho zone, robbery went down by 70 percent between 2000 and 2003.

- *Neighborhood Crime-Monitoring Committees.* These committees encourage collaborative relationships between community police officers and local residents, which have reversed the levels of mistrust between police and community. These included the creation of Schools of Civic Security and local security fronts. In 2003, Bogotá had about 7,000 local security fronts. "It is very important to understand that the Schools and Fronts respond to a civic ideal. They have nothing to do with firearms but basically promote community organization," points out Mayor Mockus.

- *Family Police Stations.* Evaluation data show that protective measures available through these police stations established to control family violence were more effective than conciliation measures in reducing physical violence against women in the family.

- *Professionalization of the Police.* Police reform and modernization were accomplished through a plan emphasizing results-based performance. An epidemiological approach was introduced to monitor crime and violence data, which allowed the design of crime prevention actions. From 1993 to 2002, traffic accidents were reduced in half; and the police increased capture rates by 400 percent without an increase in the size of the police force. Training in preventing policing has been accepted widely by citizens as an efficient alternative to reduce violence and improve coexistence.

nearly 50 percent, with a significant decrease in events between 2002 and 2003 (Gutiérrez-Martinez et al. 2007). Community responses included improved collaboration between police, the district attorney, technical investigation body, and the army; mobile police controls; firearm disarmament programs; targeting of juvenile gangs; and restrictions on alcohol sales and consumption.

Observatories routinely obtain descriptive information on a small number of key indicators that can be accurately measured to monitor trends in violent victimization. These data are recorded in response to direct violence prevention efforts and their indirect impact on youth violence of traditional development activities in such sectors as employment, education, and economic and urban development. They gather basic information on incidents, such as what occurred; when, where, and how; and victim information, including the day of the week, type of weapon, and context of assault (interpersonal violence, domestic violence, confrontations with law enforcement bodies, organized crime, or gang involvement).

Observatories are demonstrating commonalities between different types of violence in terms of factors such as the groups at greatest risk, the time and place where the acts took place, and the involvement of alcohol, illegal drugs, and weapons, enabling the formulation of policies that can have an impact across various types of violence. Information is georeferenced to identify hot-spots of crime and violence that need critical interventions. The observatories are a high-level policy committee and an integral feature of this system. Decision makers (ministers or municipal department heads) routinely meet ranging from weekly to monthly, depending on the volume of incidents, to review the findings and information produced by the observatory technical staff, permitting timely, flexible, and integrated policy responses.

These uniform monitoring systems have been developed in municipalities of varying sizes in Colombia, Mexico, and Central America, and at the national level in Guyana and in Trinidad and Tobago, and a regional south-south collaboration project has increased the number of countries with comparable systems and has enabled cross-national comparisons.

The poor quality and lack of reliable and timely data has been an obstacle to developing informed policies to address youth violence and to evaluating the impact of much of the reduction and prevention efforts carried out in the region to date. The observatories provide the core information infrastructure needed for impact evaluation of the current and future youth violence prevention efforts under way across many cities and governments in Latin America and the Caribbean, enhancing government accountability to its citizens.

REGIONAL AND NATIONAL-LEVEL GOVERNMENT SUPPORT

Municipal efforts in the region were further enhanced when supported by higher levels of government, and in cases in which strong links exist between the local, regional, and national levels. São Paulo, Brazil, illustrates how states and municipalities can work together in establishing focused targeted programs, research, and monitoring of lethal violence that address more immediate aspects such as those associated with managing public security policy and police institutions, as well as socioeconomic and demographic elements. Since 2000, São Paulo has enjoyed similar results to those cited in Bogotá. Based on health records, a steep rise in violent death rates was followed by a subsequent fall from 43.2 cases per 100,000 inhabitants in 1999 to 22 cases per 100,000 in 2005. This decrease brought São Paulo rates to below the national average (26.2).

The reasons for this drop have been attributed to (1) improvement of the technical aspects of police activity, including management of justice as well as the public security institutions; (2) the redefinition of the role of the municipal authorities in preventing crime and violence, a change in the approach from repressive to preventive, a shift in the focus from crime to violence, and a focus on implementation in urban settings (for example, developing city security plans, and the passage and enforcement of laws restricting the operation of bars and sales of alcohol); (3) increasing social participation and recruiting the vulnerable populations such as youth; (4) curbing turf wars among criminal factions; (5) providing near-universal access to schools, with schools serving to educate and socialize previously excluded children and youth, as well as serving a protective role, especially for those students residing in high-risk areas, and aiding the entry of various previously excluded groups into the job market; and (6) prioritizing the imprisonment of individuals responsible for multiple deaths (de Lima et al. 2008).

At a national level, several countries in the region responded to the crisis of youth and overall violence by establishing large-scale, national citizen security programs, typically of five to six years, duration. The IADB was the first development bank to systematically lend for programs explicitly designed to address the underlying causes of violence, justifying the inclusion of this new arena based on the economic and social benefits of investments in reducing violence, and to ensure that violence does not undermine the benefits of traditional developmental activities and governance of countries. Early cost studies estimated that violence costs countries in the region anywhere between 5 and 25 percent or more of their annual gross domestic product (GDP) (Londoño and Guerrero 2000). Moreover, prevention interventions are found to be more cost-effective than control interventions. Another innovative dimension of these national efforts was that the defining element was a focus on the prevention of violence rather than on crime or solely violent crime. This stems from the recognition that the fight against violence needs to include criminal as well as noncriminal (culturally accepted) forms of violence and that the solutions go well beyond those related to the courts and the police.

Since 1998, when the first program was established in Colombia, ten citizen security programs have been established in LAC. In just over a decade, the IADB has developed an extensive lending portfolio of national and urban-level programs that currently totals just more than US$275 million in loans to member countries (IADB Loan Reports). The goals of these projects are to promote "peace and citizen security/coexistence" through the reduction and prevention of crime and violence. The types of strategies that are supported are (1) violence prevention through social development; (2) situational prevention (attempting to eliminate the opportunity for this to happen, making it more difficult and risky for the offender to commit the crime);[2] (3) enforcement and justice; (4) reducing reoffending; and (5) community mobilization.

A strong emphasis on capacity building is another key component in all efforts, to strengthen the effectiveness of institutions responsible for youth violence prevention and to increase the numbers of staff trained in youth violence prevention program development and evaluation. Efforts have been made to increase the knowledge base on legislative, regulatory, and program strategies that have been successful in reducing levels of violence in other parts of the world. Another salient characteristic of work supported in this region has been the early integration of that research and prevention efforts for the various types of violence and disciplines, offering considerable scope in the future for more comprehensive and effective interventions (see tabel 16.1).

The citizen security programs in the region draw from various disciplines. Programs incorporate an epidemiological approach to violence prevention, identifying the dominant risk factors associated with violent activity and attempting to reduce them through specific interventions informed by various disciplines and sectors. As such, a variety of actors, who often do not have a tradition of working together (for example, law enforcement officers and social service providers, education, employment, housing, justice, safety and security, social action, sports and recreation, trade and industry, and welfare) are needed to implement these projects. They have emphasized, with varying success, building partnerships and engaging a range of potential partner sectors with valuable contributions to make, including both public and private (that is, for-profit) organizations, as well as civil society and nongovernmental organizations.

Typically, the citizen security efforts are housed in Ministries of National Security, Interior, or Home Affairs, or at the municipal level in government secretariats, in contrast with the experiences in North America, and other regions of the world, where efforts are led by other government ministries, departments, or agencies, such as health and social services. This has been in large part because of the urgency of the violence problem, the immediate threats to governance and security, and the recognized need to bring a range of resources, perspectives, and greater political coordination to reduction and prevention efforts at the national level.

The choice of ministries as a lead agency affects the approach and implementation focus. Citizen security efforts typically have concentrated on remedial interventions, information and surveillance systems, and actions with the police—

---

[2] These actions include, among others, erecting physical obstacles, controlling the access to places, and improved urban design.

Table 16.1 IDB Work on Violence Reduction

Country	Name of Project	Amount (US$ mill)	Components
Argentina	Citizen Security and Inclusion Program–Province of Buenos Aires	25	**Institutional strengthening of the Security Ministry** **Strengthening of community participation** **Improvement of violence prevention programs related to intra-family and youth violence**
Colombia	Peaceful Coexistence and Citizen Security	95	**National government** Strengthening of Dirección Nacional de Planeación as Coordinator **Municipal (Bogota, Cali and Medellin)** Social prevention of violence and juvenile delinquency
Uruauy	Crime and Violence Prevention Program	25	**Institutional capacity strengthening** **Youth as prevention agents** **Community initiatives for the promotion of preventive interventions**
Chile	A Safer Chile Program	16.6	**Strengthening of the citizen security policy** **Safe municipality** **Safe neighborhood** **Strengthening of carabinero (police)–community integration**
Guyana	Citizen Security Program	16	**Capacity building of Ministry of Home Affairs** Formulation, implementation and evaluation of preventive strategies **Capacity building of Guyana police force** Comprehensive training scheme in crime investigation and detection **Community action** Strategies to engage communities Violence preventions services inclusing youth violence, delinquency and anti-social behavior, child abuse and neglect and domestic violence,
Honduras	Sula Valley Citizen Security Program	22.2	**Institutional strengthening** **Social prevention of violence and juvenile delinquency** **Support for the community police and crime prevention project in the RVS** **Communication and social awareness strategy**

(continued)

Table 16.1 (Continued)

Country	Name of Project	Amount (US$ mill)	Components
Jamaica	Citizen Security and Justice Program I	21	**Elaboration of a national crime and violence prevention strategy** **Capacity building on the MNSJ** **Strengthening the criminal justice system** **Community action**
Jamaica	Citizen Security and Justice Program II	21	**Community action** Support community mobilization and governance Prevention services in improving parenting skills, youth training (life and skills training, anger management and conflict resolution) and situational crime control **Strengthening of the Ministry of National Security** Development of evidence policies
Nicaragua	Citizen Security Program	28	Institutional strengthening Legislation update Prevention
Panama	Integral Security Program	22.5	**Institutional strengthening for the Ministry of Government, National Police, Ministry of Social Development (social prevention policies), Ministry of Education (school violence policies)** **Citizen security interventions** Extracurricular activities for youth attending school Interventions for at-risk-youth not attending school Community situational prevention
Trinidad and Tobago	Citizen Security Program	24.5	**Community actions** Strategies to engage communities Violence preventions services including youth violence, delinquency and anti-social behavior, child abuse and neglect and domestic violence, **Support for TT police service** Activities to enhance police-community interaction and increase public confidence **Strengthening of the Ministry of National Security** Policy analysis and evidence based formulation

the areas of competence of such ministries. A key component of such programs is the improved performance of the police and justice system, often housed in such ministries. Lack of confidence in state capacity to control or prevent crime, and the problems of police and judiciary systems not only add to the violence, but also create deep mistrust among citizens. Countries perceive citizen security projects as a window of opportunity to improve how their police function; these projects have supported civil police training and community policing.

The rapid expansion of nonstate forms of social governance, extrajudicial killings, and vigilante justice has placed a high priority on improving access to justice, especially in communities with high levels of violence. Some of the notable regional responses include the establishment of Justice Houses (or *Casas de Justicias*) in Bogotá, Medellín, and Cali, Colombia.

A Justice House is a community center where neighbors find traditional and nontraditional justice services to resolve conflicts. Formal justice sector authorities are present, but alternative dispute resolution mechanisms are also available, including those based on Afro-Colombian or indigenous traditions. Other social services are available for youth, children, and women, providing swift assistance to community residents. Extrajudicial conflict resolution services also are provided. In Jamaica, multipurpose centers were established in high crime communities to centralize service delivery of different prevention initiatives for youth and community residents. In the near future, some of these centers will include Community Justice Centers to resolve disputes between citizens, which will be heard with the consent of the disputing parties and enforceable by the Courts.

YOUTH VIOLENCE PREVENTION

Youth violence prevention efforts in the region have been aided by international advocacy and coordination. The Inter-American Coalition for the Prevention of Violence (IACPV) founded in June 2000, and first hosted by the IADB, brought together multilateral and bilateral organizations working in Latin America to advance knowledge and action on violence and its prevention in the region, fostering donor cooperation and coordination, and quicker uptake of the most promising and best regional models of violence prevention.[3] The need for programming for high-risk youth groups was understood from the start. Without this youth programming, regional efforts are unlikely to reduce national rates of violence-related mortality or rein in violence-related expenditures, and will do little in developing countries to bring down high homicide rates. This is the first

---

[3] Current members include the Organization of American States (OAS), the Inter-American Development Bank (IADB), the Pan American Health Organization (PAHO), United Nations Educational, Scientific, and Cultural Organization (UNESCO), the U.S. Centers for Disease Control and Prevention (CDC), the World Bank, and the U.S. Agency for International Development (USAID), and UN-Habitat.

violence prevention effort of its kind on the American continent, and it may provide a model for similar regional initiatives in other parts of the world.

For close to a decade, coalition members have provided technical support in the design, implementation, and evaluation of local and national programs to prevent youth violence, encouraging the incorporation of tools and perspectives on a range of disciplines (such as public policy, development economics, public health, and urban planning, among others). The coalition also elevated the prevention of violence as a regional policy and development issue. At the April 2001 Summit of the Americas, convened by the Organization of American States, heads of states of the Western hemisphere identified violence prevention as a prerequisite in regional efforts to strengthen democracy, create prosperity, and realize human potential. The Summit Plan of Action encouraged national institutions to work together, and with the Coalition, to implement long-term comprehensive violence prevention initiatives.

An expanding body of literature on youth violence in the Latin America and Caribbean region has begun to provide insights into developing country violence and to offer more nuanced information on youth violence and the complex interaction of factors that influence its prevention, development, and reduction in the region. This has been an important step in expanding the research base beyond studies carried out in industrial nations, most notably, in U.S. settings. The impact of the national citizen security programs as a whole have not been adequately measured, because of numerous challenges in (1) the types of indicators to monitor and evaluate these complex operations, (2) the lack of reliable data sources, and (3) scarce references in the development literature and operational experience in the early years of their establishment. Micro evaluations, which determine whether beneficiaries of specific interventions (for example, an afterschool sports program) have lower levels of violent behavior than comparable nonbeneficiaries, have been carried out. These efforts, along with others in the region and globally, are adding to the available knowledge of good practice interventions.

Citizen security programs for at-risk youth largely focus on young people who engage in risky behavior but have not yet suffered severe negative consequences (for example, youth who are often absent from school but have not yet dropped out, youth who are involved in delinquency but have not yet been arrested). These programs also work with young people experiencing severe negative consequences as a result of risky behavior (for example, youth who have dropped out of school, youth who are in violent street groups or gangs, young people who are being released from correctional institutions back into their communities). The types of interventions include strengthening academic performance and skills training programs, providing incentives for youths at high risk for violence to complete secondary schooling, and offering accelerated training to reenter formal schooling. In addition, these programs provide vocational training for youths and young adults and income-generation programs to facilitate youth's entry into the labor market. School-based prevention activities to promote mediation skills and coexistence are offered in schools in Uruguay, Colombia, Honduras, Jamaica, and

Trinidad and Tobago. Afterschool and weekend programs have been included in all IADB operations to promote the constructive use of recreational and leisure time.

Although these programs show promise in reducing various forms of violence among youth and young adults, further evidence is needed to confirm their preventive effects on violence and aggressive behavior. The experiences with programming for at-risk youth suggest that many of the practice models need to be substantially augmented. Evaluations from the programs in Uruguay and Colombia suggest moderate success in interventions that place youth in the labor market, encourage youth to reenter school, and change aggressive attitudes. No data, however, are available on the effects of these interventions on reducing violent behavior. In Bogotá, Cali, and Medellín, Colombia, skills training interventions (including life and social skills) were provided to youth between the ages of 16 and 29. The evaluation of these programs showed that they had positive results; they were more accepted by the community and were statistically significant in positively changing youth attitudes and values related to perseverance and discipline (outcomes of personal efforts), improvement in self-esteem, peaceful resolution of conflicts, and against the use of force to settle disagreements. Job employment had a more limited success, however, because some of areas of training were not on demand by the local labor market (CISALVA 2005). In Uruguay's program, only 24 percent of the youth were able to enter the labor market immediately after completing the program and only 15 percent that received the training decided to go back to school (Bastón 2004).

A similar program to improve the employability of at-risk and marginalized young persons who are not engaged in the formal school system has been implemented in Jamaica (in 26 high-crime communities). The lessons learned during the implementation underscore the limitations of existing training programs, as a result of delays in matriculating young people, delays in the issuance of registration documents for undocumented youth without birth certificates, lack of training by vocational training staff in how to work with at-risk youth, and the high literacy and numeracy entrance requirements that prevented many prospective applicants from high-crime communities to apply. Additionally, and perhaps most important, the adverse economic conditions of persons interested in vocational-skills training programs resulted in them being unable to meet the associated costs, namely, transportation and lunch, to attend these institutions. Current citizen security efforts have incorporated a much more robust and long-term approach to working with youth, which include the following:

- An integrated approach that includes vocational-skills training, social-skills training (topics include personality and self-identity, self-esteem, values, conflict resolution, anger management, decision making, employability skills, team work, civic responsibility, and counseling services), remedial education, and mechanisms for engaging the parents of participants.
- Significant assistance to participants to allow them to access training programs.

- Practical training, job search assistance, and general social support for at-risk youth.
- Basic reading and numeracy, as many participants come into the program barely recognizing the letters of the alphabet.

All the vocational and occupational areas are sanctioned by the training agency and are deemed in demand by the labor market. Despite these efforts, the unavailability of placement opportunities has been a major issue. This issue is tied to the wider macroeconomic environment and will not be significantly affected without positive developments in that area.

Activities in the areas of sports and music have been implemented in Bogotá and Medellín, Colombia, and in Jamaica. Evaluations of afterschool and recreational activities in Bogotá appear to have had the largest impact. Youth that were part of these interventions expressed interest in creative and artistic activities as an alternative to training. The beneficiaries showed significant changes in the perception of violence and how to confront it, whereas the control group still believed that the only way to solve conflict was to carry a gun all the time without engaging in dialogue or any other means to avoid an escalation of the conflict (Muñoz 2005).

In addition, the beneficiaries perceived that their participation in the program also contributed to the reduction of crime and violence. Some of the reasons given by these young people were that these programs reinforced the development of values and promoted peaceful coexistence. In addition, they also perceived that these programs provided alternatives to occupy their free time and noted the development of their identities as social agents in their communities (CENDEX 2003).

Another youth-skills-training model was the creation of a rehabilitation center, with capacity for 300 male offenders ages 18 to 29. The purpose of the center was to provide these youth with comprehensive interventions, such as job-skills training, education, and skills for rejoining the family and community in a minimum-security setting. The aim of these comprehensive interventions was to reduce the rate of recidivism by 10 percent after five years of implementation. Because of delays in completing the building's renovation, the center began functioning in 2002 and was not able to house 300 inmates until 2004. At the end of the loan execution in 2004, only 101 young men had been admitted (Davreiux 2004).

A set of indicators was developed to monitor and evaluate the progress made by these young men and measure the effectiveness of the interventions. Unfortunately, because of the delay in constructing the building, the first full evaluation of the program was not available until 2006, after the inmates had completed 24 months of rehabilitation. Available data at the end of loan implementation show that 17 percent of the inmates enjoyed work furloughs; that beneficiary testing and family visits every six months improved family relationships; and that 15 percent of the inmates developed more advanced social and cognitive skills. Despite the above achievements, the effectiveness of this intervention appears to be quite low when its high cost (US$11.6 million) is taken into account.

The experiences cited above (skills training and school-based interventions in Uruguay and Colombia, and recreation and leisure activities in Colombia) illustrate that interventions with at-risk youth could reduce levels of violence by diminishing youth's idle time, increasing their human capital, and changing aggressive attitudes. At the same time, they also suggest that tertiary prevention activities, such as the rehabilitation center in Uruguay, can have low cost-effectiveness and take longer to yield significant results.

LESSONS LEARNED

A number of lessons can be learned from the violence prevention efforts implemented in the region, incuding the following:

1. Responding to the challenge of youth violence requires strong leadership, and policy approaches that can successfully integrate security, justice, and social development. Cities and nations need to provide leadership; developing individual programs is not sufficient. A sustained political commitment is required on the part of local, state, or national governments to the implementation of preventive social strategies, which may take a substantial time to mature and show an impact. Support from political leaders is not only necessary to ensure proper funding and effective legislation, but also to give prevention efforts increased legitimacy and a higher profile within the public consciousness. Commitment is as important at the municipal and provincial or state level where the day-to-day functioning of many interventions is controlled, as it is at the national level, where policy and legislative decisions are made. The programs need to be part of broader local and national government strategies and ensure the commitment of a wide range of partners—service providers, organizations, and individuals—to ensure that they are sustainable beyond the life of one government or the length of one mayor's or a minister's or president's term of office.

2. The appropriate public policy response is a combination of efforts that result in an immediate impact, with the incorporation of mid-term and long-term intervention strategies oriented to address the most modifiable risk factors that take longer to yield results. Given the gravity of the crime and violence situation in the region, public opinion puts pressure on national or local political leaders to show that they are dealing with the matter expeditiously. As a result, politicians tend to favor policies and interventions that offer short-term results. Certain factors—alcohol abuse is a prime example—can be addressed with interventions that are both inexpensive and deliver results in a short time frame. Also, situational violence prevention initiatives, oriented to making the physical spaces less conducive to crime, can provide high impact in a short time frame. Complementary social prevention actions still are needed to deal with more deep-rooted causes of crime and violence. Recognizing this, ten municipalities in Antioquia, Colombia, have banded together to advocate

and develop an integrated 20-year public policy agenda to prevent and control violence.

3. Efforts that see youth violence and victimization as a public, multisectoral problem, that are inclusive and participatory, and that use a strategic approach built on careful analysis and a balanced array of interventions are likely to be effective in the short and the long term. To improve criminal justice, social service delivery systems should be a part of the approach, and the underlying factors relating to the environment and social and economic opportunities available to young people must be addressed. Local responses require a careful analysis of local contexts, and they must be tailored and adapted to those contexts. This type of approach tends to address risk factors at all levels, if appropriately implemented. It targets youth and their families with much-needed basic services (social development, education, health, security) as well as positive alternatives to crime and violence (through second-chance programs, extra-curricular activities, and life-skills and occupational training). An impressive amount of experience is waiting to be translated into effective strategies to prevent and reduce youth violence and gang activity.

4. One lesson learned is that there is no ideal implementing agency, and regardless of where the coordination efforts are located, different institutional weaknesses need to be addressed. Depending on its target level, the framework can be undertaken at the country, regional, or city level. Given the multi-causality of youth violence, effective prevention requires cross-disciplinary interventions involving several public agencies, at whatever level efforts are undertaken. Such a framework also needs to effectively map the existing interventions, identify critical gaps, and prioritize limited resources in terms of filling essential omissions. The implementation unit should have the mandate and be attached to sufficiently high political level to achieve compliance from the different institutions. An appropriate oversight structure should be provided to facilitate coordination, collaboration, and communication among participating agencies, service delivery agents, and partner communities. When the various actors report to an executing agency to which they are ultimately responsible, commitment to the project's goals is more likely. Finally, the project coordinator must have the mandate, influence, and technical capacity to effectively move the project forward.

5. Avoid overambitious design and objectives. Many risk factors are associated with youth behavior, ranging from early exposure to domestic violence, and association with violent peers, among others. No violence reduction program should attempt to address all risk factors, because such a project would involve so many activities that it would be cumbersome to implement. Therefore, country-specific diagnostics should be developed to identify the profile and types of youth violence most prevalent in a country, region, or city, as well as to identify the most modifiable risk factors responsible for the violence and to set a priority on what issues to attend. The role of communities in the identification of problems and in the implementation of solutions is an important mechanism

to use for the proper development of crime and violence prevention programs. Also, avoid overstating what the project can achieve in a short period of time (four or five years) because prevention is a long-term proposition with time lags in results. The indicators chosen to measure impact should give preference to intermediate indicators that better reflect the program performance.

6. Emphasis has been insufficient on evaluation of interventions. This is an area that needs continued emphasis because, with a few notable exceptions, interventions have not been subject to careful evaluation. Most of the efforts have been concentrated in following budget allocation, resource expenditures, and monitoring beneficiaries. A more concerted effort needs to be introduced to support and carry out impact evaluations that measure the effect of the project on the outcome variables of interest and that inform future program design. As citizen security projects tend to be multifaceted, defining project indicators and designing a system of monitoring and evaluation are absolutely essential. Without a system in place as an integral part of the project, monitoring and evaluation become nearly impossible.

7. An evidence-based selection model is not commonly utilized to inform intervention and service delivery. A common mistake is to undertake interventions based on unfounded commonly held beliefs, or customary practices. There are examples from Colombia and Jamaica in which interventions were selected on the evidence of their results in industrial countries. These interventions were adapted to make them culturally appropriate and responsive to identified community needs and they have shown promising results in implementation. At a national level and municipal level, a number of countries have published authoritative reviews recommending the adoption of an evidence-based approach to crime and violence prevention. This convergence is in part due to explicit efforts at ensuring cross-fertilization between the different efforts, and in part to a broader shift in many fields toward the adoption of an evidence-based approach for development and social policy programming, internationally and nationally. In the area of youth violence, the evidence base for specific approaches, programs, and principles is extremely strong—and further programming should be strongly encouraged to identify proven approaches.

8. Expand programming for groups at high risk of victimization or perpetration that currently are addressed inadequately in programming. Programs related to the reintegration of youth in conflict with the law have been implemented in Colombia, Guatemala, El Salvador, and Mexico. In the case of Colombia, these programs also serve ex-combatant youth involved in the armed conflict that occurred in the country. While these are an emerging area in crime and violence prevention, the key aspect of these programs is that the integrated approaches consisted of not only vocational-skills training and employment placement, but also psychological counseling and mentoring. In the case of reintegration of ex-combatants, special attention needs to be given to the restorative process in communities that have suffered the armed conflict and now need to reintegrate the youth into their midst and make peace last.

CONCLUSION

Youth crime and violence continues as one of the principal problems that the LAC region faces. Recognizing the need to reduce the levels of violence and insecurity, governments have begun to implement preventive actions, but have largely fallen short. A focus on youth violence prevention and positive youth development is still the exception rather than the norm, and repressive responses still prevail. In the words of one of the citizen security program administrators,

> [T]hese initiatives have not been sufficient to stem the rise in youth crime and violence in my country. Family, school and social services are still failing to meet the demands and necessities of many youth. We need sweeping new policies beyond the usual repressive crackdowns, and corrective policies that address the injustices derived from the concentration of income, wealth and opportunities in the region that exclude so many youth. We must challenge a culture of violence. We have come a long way, but we still have a ways to go.

REFERENCES

Bastón, C. 2004. *Programa de Seguridad Ciudadana. Prevención de la Violencia en Uruguay*. Medellín, Colombia: Ministerio del Interior.

Buvinic, M., E. Alda, and J. Lamas. 2005. *The Inter-American Development Bank's Contribution to Reducing Violence in Latin America and the Caribbean*. Washington, DC: Inter-American Development Bank.

de Lima, R.S., S.P. Ferreira, E. Bordini, and V.C. Bessa. 2008 "Violent Crime and Murders in São Paulo: Underlying Factors and Recent Trends." Paper presented at workshop. in São Paulo, Brazil.

Gutierrez-Martinez, M.I., R. E. Del Villin, A. Fandiño, and R.L. Oliver. 2007. "The Evaluation of a Surveillance System for Violent and Non-Intentional Injury Mortality in Colombian Cities." *International Journal of Injury Control and Safety Promotion* 14 (2): 77–84.

CISALVA (Instituto de Investigación y Desarrollo en Prevención de Violencia y Promoción de la Convivencia Social de la Universidad del Valle). 2005. *Evaluación de Impactos Tempranos de Proyectos de Convivencia*. Cali, Colombia: Secretaría de Gobierno/ Alcaldía de Cali.

IADB (Inter-American Development Bank). 2002. *Technical Notes on Violence Prevention*. Washington, DC: Inter-American Development Bank, Sustainable Development Department, Social Development Division.

Davrieux, H. 2004. Program for Citizen Safety: Crime and Violence Prevention. Project Completion Report Memorandum. Uruguay. Unpublished manuscript, cited in Mayra.

Buvinić, E.A., and J. Lamas. The Inter-American Development Bank's Contribution to Reducing Violence in Latin America and the Caribbean. Washington, DC.

Londoño, J.L., and R. Guerrero. 2000. "Violencia en América Latina: Epidemiología y Costos." In *Asalto al Desarrollo. Violencia en América* Latina, ed. J. L. Londoño, A. Gaviria, and R. Guerrero. Washington, DC: Banco Interamericano de Desarrollo.

Muñoz, A.L. 2005 Interview Notes. Inter-American Development Bank. Bogotá, Colombia.

OCAVI (Observatorio Centroamericano sobre Violencia). 2009. "Mortalidad y Otros Presentación." http://www.ocavi.com/docs_files/file_661.pdf (accessed April 8, 2009).

OAS (Organization of American States). 2009. *Seguridad Pública y Privada en Venezuela y Bolivia.* Washington, DC: Organización de los Estados Americanos.

Trinidad and Tobago. 2008. "1994-2008 Crime Statistics - TTCrime.com." www.ttcrime.com/stats.php.

UNDP (United Nations Development Program). 2008. "El dilema estratégico de la seguridad ciudadana y el Estado Democrático de Derecho." Chap. 12, *Estado de la Región en Desarrollo Humano Sostenible.* www.estadonacion.or.cr.April 8,2009.

United Nations Office on Drugs and Crime. 2008. "Crime, Violence and Development: Trends, Costs, and Policy Options in the Caribbean." www.unodc.org/documents/data-and-analysis/Caribbean-study-en.pdf.April 8,2009

United Nations Office on Drugs and Crime. 2002. *Eighth United Nations Survey of Crime Trends and Operations of Criminal Justice Systems, Covering the Period 2001 – 2002.* New York: Division of Policy Analysis and Public Affairs.

Waiselfisz, J.J. 2008. *Mapa da Violência: Os Jovens da América Latina.* Brasilia, Brazil: Rede de Informacao Tecnologica Latino-Americana.

Preventing Youth Violence in a Community Mental Health Clinic Working with Child Welfare

Yoshiro Ono

THE NATURE AND SCOPE OF YOUTH VIOLENCE IN JAPAN

UNTIL RECENTLY, YOUTH violence in Japan was viewed as the domain of the juvenile justice system. Youth with violent behaviors usually have been treated as juvenile delinquents and placed under the guidance of the family court, or for more serious cases, placed in juvenile training schools for correctional education. Those "protective measures" by the juvenile justice system are not just punishment but also individual treatment for readaption.

Few public health or mental health services were available for these young people. Because of the priority Japanese culture places on educational attainment, the majority of social, public health, and mental health services have been directed toward children experiencing difficulty in school achievement. School refusal is common, as are anxiety disorders and depression. The one exception to this was violent behaviors that occurred in relation to school refusal. These children were viewed as suffering from a psychiatric disorder and in need of hospitalization.

Although delinquent youth frequently do not attend school, they are not viewed as school refusers but rather as children in need of greater discipline, and thus they are not referred for mental health services.

Although violent crimes by youths have declined in recent years (see figure 17.1) (National Police Agency 2009), the incidence of victimization through child abuse, neglect, and school bullying has been increasing, as has suicide. As a result, mental health professionals have become increasingly more involved in providing care and support for young victims of family and school violence. Victimization by any kind of violence has been shown to be a significant risk factor for later aggression and antisocial behaviors (Connor 2002). Mental health services are needed to address these connections and to provide effective interventions that can prevent problems later (Burns et al 2004). Japan has two primary systems for

Figure 17.1   Trend of the Numbers of Penal Code Offenders per 1000 Juveniles (14-19 year-olds)

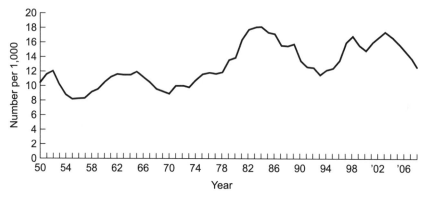

Note: There are four waves of juvenile crimes since 1950. Currently, the number of arrested juveniles has been decreasing since 2004, but still higher than that of 50 years ago.

delivering mental health services to children and adolescents: the specialty mental health services system and the child welfare system.

THE SPECIALTY MENTAL HEALTH SYSTEM

As conduct disorders have been recognized as a critical mental health issue related to a range of psychopathology in the last decade, a comprehensive research project funded by the Ministry of Health, Labor, and Welfare has been launched to investigate the epidemiology and to develop effective treatments. In 2005, the research team started a community mental health practice model in two areas, Ichikawa and Oita, which focuses on treatment of children and adolescents with multiple and complex mental health needs, including aggression and violence. This includes youths with behaviors that traditionally fell outside the mental health system, including those exhibiting antisocial and delinquent behaviors, conduct problems confined to the family context such as violence toward parents, and self-destructive behaviors such as deliberate self-harm. Both Ichikawa and Oita established a comprehensive system of care incorporating psychiatric hospitals, mental health centers, child welfare centers, the police and juvenile justice system, the board of education, and social service offices. When a referral is made to the system, case management meetings are held that include professionals from each member organization. Information is exchanged and a collaborative treatment plan is developed. Although it is a multidisciplinary process, youth and parents usually are not involved in the meeting because this model was a trial mostly focused on the interagency collaboration. Interventions then are implemented according to the individual care plan and monitored in follow-up case management meetings, again involving representatives from each of the collaborating service organizations.

A preliminary study of the initiative was conducted in 2008. Seventy-two cases were accepted from January 2005 to June 2008. The majority of these were adolescents who exhibited chronic social withdrawal without any aggression toward others or self (70 percent); only 30 percent of the cases involved youth with violent or antisocial behaviors (Usami 2009). This may reflect different base rates in the population of these mental health issues, or it may reflect the traditional ways of referring professionals in the community to see more children with internalizing problems than with aggression. It also may reflect the perception of professionals that aggression and antisocial behavior problems do not warrant mental health services, as described earlier. To make this system accessible for youths with aggressive and antisocial behaviors, the professional community and public need to be educated that violence and aggression are mental health issues, and not just a criminal justice concern.

THE CHILD WELFARE SYSTEM AND SERVICES FOR AGGRESSION AND VIOLENCE

The child welfare system of Japan is another resource for intervention services for aggressive and violent youths. Recent increases in reports of child abuse and neglect have brought attention to this sector and have led to the extension of mental health services to individuals victimized by child abuse and neglect. The Child Welfare Center (CWC) is a public child welfare agency responsible for supporting child rearing, providing services for children with physical or intellectual impairments, providing guidance for juvenile delinquents, and ensuring protection of vulnerable children. The 201 CWCs in the country have a range of professionals on staff that allow them to address a wide range of emotional and behavioral problems in children, including social workers, psychologists, and psychiatrists (Ono et al. 2004). Many of the CWCs also have temporary residential facilities where abused children or delinquent adolescents are protected and evaluated to create their care plans. Those protected in the temporary residential facilities are at particularly high risk for psychopathology and are evaluated by child psychiatrists as well as psychologists and social workers.

CREATION OF MENTAL HEALTH CLINICS WITHIN CHILD WELFARE CENTERS

A community mental health clinic (CMHC) was established in 2001 within the CWC in Miyagi Prefecture to provide mental health services to children and youth exposed to abuse and violence. The CWC refers children and adolescents under 16 years old who are suspected to have any psychopathology or developmental delay to the clinic. Similar to the U.S. Child Guidance Clinic of the 1920s (Jones 1999), the CMHC within the CWC accepts children and adolescents directly from families and schools, too. As most communities in Japan lack specialty mental health clinics for children and adolescents, the clinic in the CWC has been expected to complement the shortage of mental health resources in the community.

Since the Miyagi clinic was established, the model of a psychiatric clinic in the CWC has been adopted by several prefectures (that is, local governments). I have been involved in the development the CMHC in the CWC in Wakayama Prefecture since 2002. In the following section, I describe the clinical practice at the CWC clinic at Wakayama with attention to the prevention of violent and antisocial behaviors in children and adolescents.

Two hundred and fifty-nine children and adolescents (150 males and 109 females, ages 1 to 17 years old) were referred to the CHC between April 2003 and March 2006, including 78 maltreated youths and 68 juvenile delinquents. The predominant diagnostic category was conduct disorders (46 cases), followed by attention deficit/hyperactive disorders (23 cases), adjustment disorders (20 cases), and attachment disorders (19 cases). The majority of youth referred for conduct disorder were referred because of delinquent behavior. Seventy-six percent of youth referred for delinquency displayed evidence of mental disorders; 47 percent of maltreated children were identified as having a psychiatric problem. Among all youth referred to the clinic, 55 percent were diagnosed as having some sort of clinical psychiatric syndrome (Ono, 2006). These results indicate that children and adolescents involved in the child welfare services have substantial mental health needs.

In addition to evaluating children and adolescents placed in temporary residential facilities, the psychiatrists at the CWC at Wakayama provide services at the mental health clinic twice a week and accept referrals from the CWC, as well as parents and various agencies in the community. From April 2008 to March 2009, 93 children and adolescents were referred to the mental health clinic, and of these, 57 (61 percent) were internal referrals from the CWC. Twenty-seven (29 percent) had pervasive developmental disorders or mental retardation, and 52 (56 percent) were experiencing mental or emotional disturbance. Twenty-eight (29 percent) of the youth were referred for aggressive or antisocial behaviors. The majority (40 percent) of these referrals were made by the CWC. Only 11 percent of aggressive youths had been referred by outside agencies, suggesting a growing awareness and receptiveness within both the CWC system and the community to identify and refer aggressive and violent youth for mental health services.

In addition to delivering direct services, the CWCs are responsible for providing consultation and guidance concerning a range of problems from various child-serving agencies, such as schools, daycare centers, children's homes, police, and social service offices, as well as parents or caregivers. In general, children displaying aggressive behavior are more likely to be referred to a CHC than to private mental health services in Japan. For example, junior high school teachers are likely to refer their students with conduct problems to the CWCs. Thus, the CWCs are emerging as critical gateways for aggressive and violent children and adolescents and their families to access much-needed support services. The following case study describes how the CWC supported an adolescent displaying violent behavior in the home and the school.

CASE STUDY

Ken is a third-year junior high school student (15 years old) living with his parents and an elder brother. He had no birth complications or developmental delays. He had been hyperactive and sometime had physical fights with his peers during his elementary school years. Although he adapted well in junior high school, he became aggressive and emotionally unstable, behaving violently toward teachers and destroying school property in his final year. Also, he had various conduct problems in the community, such as shoplifting, staying late at night with bad companions, drinking alcohol, and smoking cigarettes. For the assessment and treatment of his emotional and behavior problems, he was referred to the CWC at Wakayama in December.

In the initial interview with the psychologist at the CWC, he said "I can't control my behavior once I've got[ten] irritable," "I am left behind academically," and "I am afraid that I could not go on to high school." As the psychologist suspected that Ken might have serious emotional disturbance, Ken was referred to the mental health clinic in the CWC for a psychiatric assessment. Ken was diagnosed as having attention deficit/hyperactivity disorder comorbid with conduct disorder, and pharmacotherapy as well as individual psychotherapy was prescribed. The psychotherapy was based on cognitive behavioral therapy focused on his irritability. Despite these interventions, his emotional and behavioral problems persisted for a few weeks, requiring temporary residential care.

Soon after placement in temporary residential care, Ken adapted well to the program. Care workers were supportive and encouraged him to keep adaptive behaviors, and psychologists continued cognitive behavior therapy. After intensive treatment for two weeks, he became rather stable and came back to his home in February. During Ken's stay at the temporary residential care facility, the social worker at the CWC had a case management meeting with school teachers and parents as well as the psychologist and psychiatrist, where care plans at home and school were discussed. By providing private space for Ken to calm down when he became irritable, he could safely return to school. Ken and his mother continued regular counseling at the CWC.

He continued medication and entered high school in April. He has not shown any violence and has remained in high school.

In the case of Ken, the CWC played the role of gateway for the treatment of emotional disturbance. Having a mental health clinic embedded in the CWC enabled provision of smooth and timely assessment and treatment for Ken. This case might suggest the efficacy of close cooperation between child welfare and mental health; however, it is not always this successful. Because many of youths referred to the CWC have serious adverse life experiences, including child abuse and neglect, more intensive support for the family is necessary in addition to mental health services for the child. For more effective intervention for youth violence, the CWC should enhance the case management function in the community mental health system of care.

CONCLUSION

Problems of aggression in teenagers usually are treated as maladaptive or delinquent behaviors, and youth with these symptoms typically receive guidance from teachers and social workers. Adolescents like Ken seldom are referred to mental health clinics, even if they seem to have serious emotional disturbances from the perspective of mental health. Thus, locating mental health clinics within the CWC appears to be a rather good way for children and adolescents with serious emotional disturbance to obtain access to appropriate mental health services.

Although mental health services for children and adolescents with violent behaviors have been underdeveloped in Japan, a few practice models are emerging. Of those models, the CWC-based system of care is considered to be the gateway of mental health services for those youths with serious emotional disturbances, and the approach is expected to develop further across the country. Moreover, it is important to have the public recognize that violence is a major public health issue and to develop and disseminate effective prevention and treatment systems nationwide.

REFERENCES

Burns, B.J., S.D. Phillips, H.R. Wagner, et al. 2004. "Mental Health Need and Access to Mental Health Services by Youth Involved with Child Welfare: A National Survey." *Journal of the American Academy of Child and Adolescent Psychiatry* 43: 960–970.

Connor, D.F. 2002. *Aggression and Antisocial Behaviors in Children and Adolescents: Research and Treatment*. New York: Guilford Press.

Jones, K.W. 1999. *Taming the Troublesome Child: American Families, Child Guidance, and the Limits of Psychiatric Authority*. Cambridge, MA: Harvard University Press.

National Police Agency. 2009. "Annual Report on Juvenile Delinquency 2008." http://www.npa.go.jp/safetylife/syonen38/syonenhikou_h20.pdf (accessed November 11, 2009).

Ono, Y. 2006. "Psychiatric Assessment of Children and Adolescents Referred to the Child Welfare Center." In *Child Welfare and Mental Health: Mental Health Practice within Child Welfare System*, ed. Y. Ono, 130–149. Tokyo: Akashi Shoten.

Ono, Y., and A.J.Pumariega. 2008. Violence in Youth. *International Review of Psychiatry* 20 (3): 305–316.

Ono, Y., Y. Ishida, H. Ide, M. Okamoto, J. Kataoka, S. Kameoka, H. Nakayama, A. Yamamoto, and H. Honma. 2004. "Psychiatric involvement in Child Welfare Centers in Japan." *Japanese Journal of Child and Adolescent Psychiatry*, 45 (Supplement): 35–50.

Usami, M. 2009. "Experience of Development and Operation of Community System of Care." In *Guide Book of Child and Adolescent Mental Health Practice*, ed. K. Saito, 283–290. Tokyo: Nakayama Shoten.

Reducing Youth Violence: Central American Coalition for the Prevention of Youth Violence

Lainie Reisman

INTRODUCTION

THIS CASE STUDY on Central America reviews the rise of criminal gangs, particularly in the Northern Triangle countries of Guatemala, El Salvador, and Honduras as well as the responses to the gangs, particularly the home-grown civil society response of the Coalición Centroamericana para la Prevención de Violencia Juvenil (CCPVJ, or in English, Central American Coalition for the Prevention of Youth Violence. Civil society groups, with diverse backgrounds, have a long history of working with the youth most at risk, whether on the streets, in juvenile detention centers, or within the community. Providing a variety of services and support, these organizations typically operate at the local level and historically have had little influence on broader policy-making processes. As more development actors, governments, donors, and civil society actors recognize the specific challenges and programmatic needs related to youth violence, there is a heightened interest in local experiences and an openness to engage multisectoral actors moving forward.

This particular case study is unusual as it tracks a local initiative that grew organically and is led by local actors, albeit with modest support from international donors. It highlights some of the major interventions as well as describes both the opportunities and challenges of an initiative of this nature.

CONTEXT

The issue of youth violence is not a new phenomenon in Central America. During the violent armed conflicts of the 1980s and 1990s, Guatemala, El Salvador, and Nicaragua were all embroiled in entrenched armed conflicts with high casualties (Correlates of War n.d.).[1] Guatemalan indigenous people suffered particularly with an estimated 200,000 killed and more than 1 million internally displaced persons. According to the Historical Clarification Commission Report, 93 percent of all killings were attributed to state security forces (Guatemala Memory of Silence n.d.). The impacts of the armed conflicts were felt in surrounding countries as refugees fled north (to Mexico and the United States) as well as south (to Costa Rica and Panama) in addition to fleeing to Honduras.

By the late 1990s, after the signings of the Peace Accords, the international community committed a tremendous amount of aid for peace building, reconciliation, reinsertion, and reconstruction, with hundreds of millions of dollars invested from major donors around the world. Key elements of this support were used for demobilization and reconciliation work, victim support, rebuilding of community infrastructure, creation of civilian security forces, and broader socioeconomic reforms. The United Nations established peace missions in Nicaragua, El Salvador, and Guatemala to coordinate assistance and verify compliance with peace agreements. A large emphasis was placed on constructing efficient civilian security forces, notably with the creation of the Policía Nacional Civil (PNC or in English National Civilian Police) in both Guatemala and El Salvador.

The creation of the civilian policing systems has been documented in numerous accounts (MINGUA/ONUSAL 2009; WOLA 2009) and has been fraught with both anticipated and unanticipated challenges. During this same period of time in which the security system was converted from a military to civilian structure, organized crime emerged. It was during this critical postconflict period, while struggling to transform its security forces from a military to a civilian command, that the security realm was quickly overtaken by sophisticated organized criminal structures. The most publicly visible face of organized crime was the criminal gangs that began to take hold in communities throughout the region.

There is no clear, simple explanation for the rise of the Central American gangs. Important to note is that the two most notorious gangs, *Mara Salvatrucha* (MS13) and *Calle Dieciocho* (18th Street) were founded in the immigrant neighborhoods in Los Angeles in the 1970s, before becoming entrenched in Central America in the 1990s and then proliferating throughout Latino communities in the United States in the early part of the millennium. The rise of Central American youth gangs has been attributed to a multitude of factors, including but not limited to poverty, exclusion, access to weapons, U.S. deportation policies, a culture of violence, and limited employment opportunities. Grounded studies indicate that all of these factors have likely contributed to the rise of gangs, but the crucial

---

[1] Casualties are estimated at 200,000 in Guatemala, 60,000 in Nicaragua, and 75,000 in El Salvador.

determinate factors relate to community structures, or lack of structures, in which gangs have flourished (Cruz 2007).

By the mid-1990s, crime rates began to increase alarmingly in Guatemala, Honduras, and El Salvador and by the turn of the century homicide rates were at an all-time high. It is particularly disturbingly that homicide rates have been consistently higher in both Guatemala and El Salvador than during the armed conflict (UNODC 2007). Taking El Salvador as an example, but noting the regional trends, the high levels of murder are clearly linked to the widespread availability of firearms as at least 70 percent of homicides in El Salvador are caused by firearms. Many experts argue that homicide rates in both Honduras and El Salvado are among the highest in the world, with official rates reaching 56 deaths per 100,000 inhabitants (UNODC 2007).

In response to the high rates of crime and violence, the governments of Central America launched an offensive against the most visible perpetrators: the gangs. At the time, gangs were easy to identify through their tattoos, clothing, hand signals, and weapons. The gangs became the prime targets of politicians as well as the newly created, but heavily militarized, police structures and in fact the populace as a whole. Guatemala, El Salvador, and Honduras enacted new legislation, policies, and operations that targeted the alleged perpetrators of the crimes and focused on repressive policing, arrests, and extended detentions. There was a corresponding rise in extrajudicial killings, referred to by many civil society groups as "social cleansing" as documented by civil society groups such as Casa Alianza in Honduras (Casa Alianza 2009).[2]

Of major dispute is the extent to which the gangs are youth gangs, or whether the majority of members are in fact adults.[3] Although the youth were unequivocally the target of policing interventions under the *mano dura* (iron fist) policies, studies have indicated that few of the most violent gang members are actually youth (IUPOP/UCA n.d.). Given the fact that less than 5 percent of all homicide investigations result in sentencing, the data are indicative, rather than conclusive, on this point.

Known as *mano dura* and *super mano dura* (super iron fist) policies, this repressive law enforcement approach was favored by governments to provide quick results and appease the growing frustration of the citizenry in the early 2000s. However, it quickly became evident that instead of helping to reduce crime, these policies actually contributed to a worsening of the situation. Data from El Salvador collected by the National Police showed marked increases in homicide and other crime rates after *mano dura* and *super mano dura* policies were implemented, respectively.

---

[2] Since 1998, 5,164 arbitrary executions or violent murders of young people under the age of 23 have been recorded.

[3] See the OECD Armed Violence Reduction Guide at http://www.genevadeclaration.org/fileadmin/docs/OECD-Armed-Violence-Reduction.PDF for a discussion regarding the complexities of defining youth.

According to the Washington Office on Latin America (WOLA) and several scholars,

> These *mano dura* policies have pushed the gangs underground and, as a result, they have become more organized. Many gang members have lowered their public profile. They are no longer tattooing themselves or wearing identifiable clothing nor are they congregating publicly; but they are continuing to meet, and to carry out gang activities. Meanwhile, the prisons have provided an ideal location for the gangs to become more cohesive. In addition to contributing to the mutation of gangs, repressive policies have done nothing to alleviate the rising level of violence and number of homicides in Guatemala, Honduras, and El Salvador. (WOLA 2006)

By the mid-2000s, the Central American gangs had consolidated control in the region and also notably began to gain strongholds throughout the United States. MS13 and 18th Street became more visible in cities with large Central American populations. When the gruesome Brenda Paz murder case became headline news in Washington, D.C., in 2003, the issue of Central American gangs took on a more transnational tone, with the U.S. public and lawmakers becoming more informed and demanding responses. Recognition was growing that something needed to be done to reduce gang violence.

Repressive state-sponsored law enforcement approaches had not been effective and attention was turned to the possibilities of focusing on the prevention of youth violence and rehabilitation of youth gang members. The rhetoric changed significantly, now emphasizing comprehensive responses focusing on the local community level. It is in this overall context that in 2005 the CCPVJ was founded by four key prevention specialists from the region. Groups like the Inter-American Coalition for the Prevention of Violence (IACPV), WOLA, and others advocated for the CCPVJ and provided initial technical support. These international organizations would later become key partners as the CCPVJ's work expanded beyond Central America to working at the international level to effect changes. The CCPVJ would evolve into the leading civil society voice pushing for a change in tactics favoring community-based responses that take into account the full range of prevention, intervention, and suppression responses.

CCPVJ (THE COALITION)

The CCPVJ was formed in 2005 by a small group of nongovernmental organizations (NGOs), along with the Nicaraguan police, during one of the first conferences held on the issues of Central American youth gang violence in Washington, D.C. The objectives of the CCPVJ are to promote prevention programs and policies to address youth violence, to coordinate efforts of government and nongovernmental entities, and to develop and support integrated and inclusive public strategies for youth violence prevention that also respect human rights throughout the region. The founding members include *Jóvenes Hondureños Adelante–Juntos Avancemos* (JHA-JA, Honduras),

*el Instituto Universitario de Opinión Publica de la Universidad Centroamericana
José Simeón Canas* (IUDOP/UCA, El Salvador), *la Asociación para la Prevención
Del Delito* (APREDE, Guatemala), and the National Police of Nicaragua.

After some time, the CCPVJ morphed into an inclusive space for civil
society groups working on issues related to youth violence, largely service providers
but also including academic and research institutions. It currently has 20 members
from Guatemala, El Salvador, Honduras, and Nicaragua and coordinates closely
with counterparts in Panama, Costa Rica, and Mexico. Its members share a
common vision of the region (Central America) in which the violence that affects
young people, and in particular gang violence, is reduced. Its objective is to
promote social and institutional changes that lead to a more comprehensive and
integrated response to youth violence in the region. It is not focused explicitly on
maras or pandillas (gangs), although given the circumstances, much of its work
has focused on this phenomena.

The founding of the CCPVJ was organic and not driven by a particular donor or
country. No significant studies or assessments were undertaken before its establishment other than the work done by its members, notably the research undertaken by
IUDOP Director Jose Miguel Cruz. Since its inception, however, the CCPVJ and
its members have been involved in the multitude of international studies, conferences, and workshops held on the issues of youth violence. In essence, the CCPVJ,
or its members, became a key entry point for almost all donors and programs,
including but not limited to the United States Agency for International Development (USAID), the Pan-American Health Organization (PAHO), the World Bank
(WB), the Inter-American Development Bank (IADB), UN-Habitat, the European
Union, *la Agencia Española de Cooperación Internacional para el Desarrollo*
(AECID), and a host of others. Its research and that of its members has influenced
countless assessments of youth violence in the region.

Since its inception, the CCPVJ has been a local initiative, led by recognized
leaders and NGOs from each country. While it has received support, both financial
and technical, from partners such as WOLA, the Kellogg Foundation, and the Ford
Foundation, the strength of the Coalition is its members and their commitment to prevention as a critical component of any strategy addressing youth violence. Perhaps
most relevant, the work of the Coalition is regional, thus drawing on experiences
throughout Central America and creating a support structure for local groups that
previously operated independently and often in conflict with the state. The structure
of the CCPVJ is decentralized, and a national committee exists in each of the four
countries; however, the CCPVJ uses a common voice to address issues regionwide.

Key Strategic Elements

Following are the CCPVJ's key strategic elements:

1. Civil society membership with strong relationships with other sectors: The
   CCPVJ is a group of civil society organizations that has the experience,

independence, and flexibility to work collaboratively and engage in collective analysis. This is not to say that the CCPVJ does not work with other actors, as it has a Consultative Committee consisting of both government and academic institutions (without decision-making authority). The CCPVJ also has a group of key allies, including international agencies and programs that inform its work and also open spaces for direct and indirect advocacy.

2. Regional orientation: The structure of the CCPVJ is in line with the regional approach to Central America as highlighted by the Central American Integration System (SICA). This enables members to benefit from experiences across borders and share important information. This is particularly important in addressing issues of gang violence, as the gangs have proven to be quite fluid and able to move across borders. The work of the CCPVJ is also complemented by an information system known as the *Observatorio Centroamericano Sobre Violencia* (OCAVI), which serves as a virtual library for studies and statistics related to violence.

3. Advocacy focus based on direct intervention experience: One of the strengths of the Coalition is the ability of its members, and its secretariat, to undertake high-level advocacy with public officials while speaking with direct on-the-ground experience. Member organizations bring in youth members to ensure that the youth voice is clearly articulated. This has proven to be powerful and effective, both with governments of the region and the U.S. government, as the CCPVJ has been actively involved in the Merida Initiative, the security cooperation agreement between the United States and the government of Mexico and the countries of Central America. In Central America, the CCPVJ has contributed to ensuring significant resources were allocated to prevention initiatives.

CCPVJ Activities

The CCPVJ, recognizing the grassroots work of its member organizations, does not engage in direct service delivery. Rather, the CCPVJ prioritizes a series of activities drawing on the strength and knowledge of its members and contributing to the Coalition's overall objectives. Its lines of action include the following:

1. Advocacy: Since its inception, the CCPVJ has been a recognized voice advocating for prevention alternatives for youth violence and a human rights approach to dealing with violent youth. This initially took the form of showcasing successful alternatives to *mano dura*—showing that they exist and are effective. The CCPVJ has held meetings with local elected officials, national government representatives, regional bodies (like SICA), and international donors and agencies, and has had a direct line of work related to the U.S. Merida Initiative, in which Coalition members visited with congressional leaders as well as

executive agencies such as the State Department and USAID to make the case for prevention.

2. Research and investigation: The Coalition, working through its members as well as outside consultancies, has published a variety of studies related to youth violence as well as supported members in their own publications. Given the relative paucity of any grounded scientific investigation of issues related to youth violence and gangs, the CCPVJ has become a hub for up-to-date information. By drawing on its direct contact with youth, the research is more solidly evidence based than on pure speculation.

3. Awareness raising: The CCPVJ has become a regular participant in the multitudes of conferences, workshops, and meetings held regarding youth violence in Central America. Whether taking the form of addressing congressional leaders in Holland, working with the town council of Barcelona, or participating in U.N.-sponsored events, the CCPVJ and its members have acquired a reputation as being critical participants in any event discussing youth violence and gangs. This also has enabled critical partnerships to be formed with other government organizations and NGOs.

4. Technical training for members: Recognizing the need to strengthen the capacities of individual members, the CCPVJ has hosted workshops for members on topics ranging from advocacy to incorporating youth voices.

5. Dissemination of knowledge: In addition to presenting its experiences in varied venues, the CCPVJ publishes and circulates a quarterly bulletin and conducts regular press activities, including paid campaigns, editorials, and submissions for media coverage.

6. Youth development: Not losing sight of its core beneficiaries, the CCPVJ has a specific line of work supporting youth development and youth leadership. Prime examples of this include the incorporation of a delegation of CCPVJ youth to the Inter-American Forum on Youth (2008) and participation in the Central American Parliament.

These activities are undertaken by the CCPVJ secretariat along with the support of the member organizations, based on their own interests and priorities, which are extremely diverse. A sampling of some of the CCPVJ members, and their key programmatic approaches, provides an indication of the diversity of experiences of CCPVJ member organizations (see table 18.1).

Success Story: Merida Initiative

The CCPVJ points to its involvement in the design and implementation of the U.S. government's Merida Initiative as one of its most successful interventions and as indicative of the potential of the Coalition. The Merida Initiative is a security cooperation plan between the United States and Mexico and Central America aimed at combating drug trafficking, transnational crime, and money laundering. While

Table 18.1   Sample of CCPVJ members and key approaches

CCPVJ Member	Key approaches
Instituto Universitario de Opinión Publica (IUDOP/UCA) El Salvador	Academic research on gang issues. IUDOP began researching gangs in the 1990s and has provided the most solid and evidece-based research on gang issues over the past 15 years.
Asociación para la Prevención del Delito Guatemala	Human rights approach to work on crime prevention by working with youth at risk of joining gangs as well as gang rehabilitation focusing on training and social development work to improve self-esteem.
Jóvenes Hondureños Adelante—Juntos Avancemos (JHA-JA) Honduras	Therapeutic psycho-social interventions for youth at risk and reforming gang members. Solid support for youth mobilization and leadership.
Equipo Nahual El Salvador	Focus on young people's need for identity and belonging. Build on principles of self realization and cultivation of personal identity through individual and group therapy with gang members.
Centro de Prevención de la Violencia (CEPREV) Nicaragua	Overall focus on a culture of peace, working with diverse family members and emphasizing gender issues.
Paz y Justicia (Mennonite Church) Honduras	Spiritual elements and focus on role of family members, HIV/AIDS prevention, tattoo removal, and gang member rehabilitation.
Grupo Ceiba Guatemala	Initiated work with drug rehabilitation and gangs and expanded emphasis to youth at risk. Activities emphasize youth participation, peer to peer street outreach, and alternative education.

the majority of resources in Mexico are oriented toward drugs, the case is quite different in Central America, in part due to the efforts of the CCPVJ. Working in collaboration with WOLA, the U.S.-based human rights organization, the CCPVJ made numerous trips to Washington, D.C., to meet with lawmakers and their staff to present the case for resources to be oriented toward prevention activities. The CCPVJ also held workshops with civil society organizations in each of its countries as well as press activities to create a more solid base of support to pressure the national governments, as well as SICA, to include prevention on the agenda. The results of this work were clear, as close to 25 percent of the overall Merida package was oriented toward prevention activities in Central America, compared with little to no support whatsoever in Mexico, where a similar advocacy process did not take place.

KEY CHALLENGES AND LESSONS LEARNED

The CCPVJ is a relatively new entity, brought into existence in 2005 by a group of committed and long-term youth violence practitioners. It was founded at a time when the issues of *pandillas* (youth gangs) were of high visibility, crime rates were skyrocketing, and government institutions were responding with heavy-handed repression approaches. Many of the member organizations, which had been working with youth-at-risk for years, were deflated as they watched their participants being drawn into more violent crime and many being killed. According to the Director of the Centro de Formación y Orientación "Rafaél Palacios" (CEFO – a CCPVJ member institution based in El Salvador) Father Antonio Rodriguez, he had been to hundreds of funerals for youth in his town of Mejicanos in El Salvador and felt compelled to seek solutions at a higher level.

The group developed its institutional structure while simultaneously undertaking the substantial work of the CCPVJ. Its development, while organic, was also awkward and fraught with many challenges and lessons learned. Many of these are yet to be fully resolved.

1. Membership: The CCPVJ institutional structure has changed over time. It was initially a loose collaboration of interested organizations, representing both civil society and government institutions. The membership of the Nicaraguan Police was critical in 2005 as the Nicaraguan police were unique in that the overall policing philosophy in regard to youth violence was preventative rather than repressive. Many experts in fact identify this as one of the main reasons gangs have flourished in El Salvador, Honduras, and Guatemala and not Nicaragua. Regardless, the police and more specifically the Child and Adolescent Unit were key allies at the time and the impact of a uniformed policeman promoting prevention and respect for human rights was tremendous. However, over time, it became apparent that the commitment was personal, rather than institutional in nature. In 2006, at its first formal strategic planning session, the founders of the CCPVJ opted for membership to be limited to civil society organizations. The intent was to enable the CCPVJ to act independently and not be subjected to political oversight or decision making. While strategically important, this also led to some association of the CCPVJ as an opposition group, which complicated relationships with certain government officials.

2. Human resources: The members of the CCPVJ are all civil society organizations with great commitment but often limited capacity and resources. Almost all depend on external financing to carry out their activities and staffing and resources are tight. Thus, any work for the CCPVJ had to be assumed on top of existing responsibilities. While initially opting for a rotating presidency, the CCPVJ quickly realized a small dedicated staffing structure was required. At first manned by volunteers, the position of the CCPVJ director later would become a professional staff position once resources were secured.

Similarly, the CCPVJ did not establish itself in any one country as an independent NGO or body; since 2006, however, it has been hosted by IUDOP/UCA, which serves as the conduit for all organizational issues such as hiring and fundraising.

3. Capacity and knowledge base: The capacity of local groups working on youth violence is limited, both in terms of technical and institutional capacity. Because these groups tend to be community based and working on some of the most challenging and entrenched issues, they often do not have exposure to trainings, workshops, studies, best practices, and exchanges that might enable them to improve their work.

4. Security: Security is a major challenge for the members of the CCPVJ and indeed any organization working seriously on issues relating to youth gangs. Member institutions cite numerous examples of their beneficiaries, and even their staff, being killed or threatened. Rehabilitated gang members are often most at risk of retaliation from their own gang or rival gangs; however, their role as peer mentors and outreach workers is a critical component of most programming. Local organizations also report being threatened by security forces and vigilante groups that want to take matters into their own hands.

5. Financial and external support: Although operating at a modest budget (around $150,000 per year), the CCPVJ does require external funding to support its secretariat, enable its members to travel to CCPVJ activities, publish timely updates and information, and participate in conferences and workshops in addition to providing support for its members. This support has been provided in the past by progressive foundations that believe in the work of the CCPVJ and its members. It often is these very funders that support the members themselves, and with the global economic downturn and overall decline in funding levels, medium- to long-term support is uncertain. Finally, as donors struggle to find a sector in which to place armed youth violence programming, little support is provided directly in this area.

6. Oversight: Although the CCPVJ attempted to set up a Consultative Committee and an Experts Committee, for the most part, its work is independent and there is little overall guidance or oversight regarding its actions. This lack of a board of directors–type structure has hampered the CCPVJ's efforts to undertake medium- and long-term strategic planning processes as well as its fundraising capacity.

7. Prioritization: The CCPVJ, its secretariat, and its members are committed individuals who want to participate in all relevant activities. Straddling the worlds of youth development, security sector reform, informal education, and civil society networking, the CCPVJ has an almost limitless range of possible engagements. This also means that at times the organization has had a hard time prioritizing activities and has been distracted from its core mission and activities.

8. Monitoring and evaluation: An external evaluation of the CCPVJ has never been undertaken and a monitoring and evaluation plan was never put into place. Unfortunately, this means that while the CCPVJ can draw on anecdotal and output information, it cannot detail the impact that it has had.
9. Effective strategies to engage the public sector: As mentioned above, the CCPVJ has struggled with strategies to engage the public sector at all levels, relying more on personal contacts and relationships than institutional arrangements. Viewed by some politicians as being soft on crime or as playing an adversarial role, the CCPVJ is sometimes identified as being critical rather than proactive in its relationship with the public sector.
10. Sustainability: The CCPVJ does not have a clear sustainability plan. Its continuing existence will largely be influenced by the availability of external funding and commitment of member institutions. In theory, the CCPVJ secretariat will rotate in 2010, but it is unclear whether any other institution has the capacity to management such an endeavor.

CONCLUSION

Youth violence in Central America is largely associated with *pandilla* (gang) activity, although this is but one of a host of types of youth violence evidenced in the region. Over time, most governments of Central America have shifted away from treating gang violence as purely a security threat to be dealt with by the police, to placing more emphasis (in rhetoric, if not actual resources) into a more holistic approach recognizing the social, political, economic, and cultural factors that fuel violence. The CCPVJ, a locally led community-based affiliation of civil society organizations, has become a leading voice on youth violence promoting holistic approaches that respect human rights. Drawing on the experiences of its members, the CCPVJ has played an important role in raising awareness on the issues of youth violence in Central America, ensuring that support is provided to prevention and intervention activities, and maintaining the involvement of youth in youth issues. Without an unbiased external evaluation, it is unclear to what extent the CCPVJ has had an impact on actually reducing youth violence; however, further study of the initiative is strongly recommended.

REFERENCES

Casa Alianza. 2009. *Análisis de las Ejecuciones*. (Noviembre–Diciembre).

"Correlates of War." n.d. www.correlatesofwar.org/ or http://users.erols.com/mwhite28/warstat4.htm.Janury 2010.

Cruz, J.M. 2007. *Street Gangs in Central America*. San Salvador, El Salvador: Universidad Centroamericana.

Guatemala Memory of Silence. n.d. "Table of Contents." http://shr.aaas.org/guatemala/
    ceh/report/english/toc.html.January 2010.

IUPOP/UCA (Instituto de Opinión Publica de la Universidad Centroamericana). n.d.

MINGUA/ONUSAL (United Nations Verification Mission in Guatemala, and United
    Nations Observer Mission in El Salvador).

Protect and Serve. Washington, DC: Washington Office on Latin America.

UNODC (United Nations Office on Drugs and Crime). 2007. *Crime and Development
    in Central America: Caught in the Crossfire*. New York: United Nations Office on
    Drugs and Crime.

WOLA (Washington Office on Latin America). 2006. *Youth Gangs in Central America.*
    Washington, DC: Washington Office on Latin America.

PART IV

Conclusion

Putting Violence Prevention Efforts in Perspective

In earlier sections of this book, we provided a framework for understanding the nature and scope of the problems of youth violence as well as the various approaches for addressing this critical issue. Epidemiological research and the examples of violence prevention described in this book confirm that violence among young people is a significant and pervasive problem. Although the extent to which youth violence occurs varies among countries, even in cultures generally perceived to have low levels of aggression, such as Singapore, Japan, and Canada, we see growing concern about rising levels of violence among young people.

In the following sections, we will review the case examples presented earlier to identify similarities and differences and attempt to understand factors that account for these patterns. We will examine these prevention efforts in relation to the taxonomy of youth violence policy and intervention approaches described in chapter 3 to assess the usefulness of this framework as well as to explore why cultures might select a particular strategy for addressing youth violence. We attempt to glean salient factors, issues, and themes that may contribute to our understanding of the core components of effective violence prevention approach. We then ask how this information can be used to develop successful strategies for reducing and preventing violence in the United States as well as other countries. Finally, we offer recommendations for future development of policies and practices for promoting alternatives to violence.

WHAT CAN WE LEARN FROM THESE CASE STUDIES?

In chapter 2, Bronfenbrenner's human ecology model was introduced as a tool for understanding the multiple levels in which young people function. His model helps us understand that all of these subsystems, including family and other social relationships, community, and the broader society, can significantly affect the development of young people. Recognizing that all levels of the ecosystem play an important role in positive youth development in violence prevention, we proposed that prevention efforts can focus on each or all of these levels and offered examples of the types of strategies that might be applied at each stratum of the ecosystem. A core assumption of this model is that intervening at multiple levels is more likely to produce greater benefit than simply targeting a single level within the system.

COMPLEX PROBLEMS REQUIRE COMPLEX SOLUTIONS

This multilevel approach is clearly illustrated in the description of the Viva Rio initiative in Haiti, in which attention was focused at national and local levels to engage multiple government and community entities in a comprehensive violence prevention campaign. Participating agencies and organizations encouraged and supported competence development for individual youth. They also worked at the community level to foster nonviolent approaches to conflict resolution and improve collaboration among government and local groups, including the police and military. Viva Rio is focused on enhancing basic infrastructure, such as the provision of clean water. By employing these various strategies, the leaders of the Haitian effort were able to mobilize a comprehensive, multilevel campaign to addressing youth violence.

The extent to which one or more ecological levels are targeted by an initiative is influenced by broader factors within the municipality or country, including social, political, cultural, and economic forces. For instance, the programs in Japan and Singapore focused on assisting at-risk youth in dealing with mental health challenges, which made them potentially more vulnerable to episodes of aggressive behavior. These countries are characterized by having highly structured, stable governments and strong nuclear families. Within these countries, it may be culturally more acceptable to ascribe aggressive behavior to factors that reside within the individual rather than attribute these problems to societal shortcomings.

Like most social phenomena, simple explanations do not suffice. Although aggressive behavior is viewed as socially unacceptable in Asian countries, considerable stigma is still attached to mental illness in these cultures. Societies in general and families in particular are often reluctant to acknowledge that mental illness exists because this may reflect poorly on the family of the person with a psychiatric disorder. By selecting a mental health service approach oriented to at-risk youth, these countries, at some level, have chosen the least aversive of several socially undesirable alternatives.

Conversely, countries that have been battered by government and economic instability as well as pervasive violence such as Haiti, Guatemala, El Salvador, and Honduras, have turned to strategies that emphasize empowerment of local communities and strengthening social and economic infrastructure. In Northern Ireland and Israel, where strong government structures exist but where regional armed conflict has been pervasive over a long period of time, comprehensive approaches also were put into place. These efforts, however, were more circumscribed, focusing on restorative justice programs and employing systematic planning processes driven by a rich database to develop individually tailored responses to concerns about school safety.

Viewing the case studies through a lens that focuses on the complexity of violence prevention produces a somewhat counterintuitive finding. One would expect that highly developed, resource-rich nations would tend to develop more sophisticated and comprehensive approaches to this issue. Yet, paradoxically, many of the poorer, less developed nations actually generated strategies that are more compatible with the multilevel human ecology model. We can conjecture about whether the launching of these comprehensive approaches by developing nations was inspired by the recognition that anything less than a bold and ambitious initiative would have little chance of making a significant impact, or whether they evolved from a shared cultural concern about the well-being of the whole community and an awareness that all members of the community needed to assume responsibility for contributing to the positive development of youth.

Although we do not have sufficient data upon which to draw a definitive conclusion on this matter, it is evident that many of the countries that had scant resources ascribed to the philosophy that "it takes a village to raise a child."

A DEVELOPMENTAL APPROACH

Prevention efforts occur at different points along the developmental cycle. Primary prevention efforts are directed at situations in which no violent behavior has yet been manifested. Secondary prevention interventions target individuals who display early indications of problem behavior and tertiary prevention focuses on reducing the likelihood that individuals who already act aggressively will do so in the future. Some programs, such as YouthBuild, which offers a wide array of individual and community development opportunities, may operate at all three levels. The program guides youth who are at risk of becoming involved in antisocial activities onto more positive pathways. YouthBuild redirects young people who are already engaged in aggressive behavior into more pro-social activities.

Working with young people in communities to ensure that they have appropriate skills and opportunities before they become involved in antisocial activities is clearly the preferred option. Limitations in resource availability and the inability to identify with precision who may be at risk impede communities and nations from implementing comprehensive primary prevention programs. The sheer magnitude of personal and community challenges as well as other impeding factors makes it unlikely that sufficient primary prevention efforts can be put into place. Therefore, it is important that targeted secondary and tertiary prevention efforts be employed to supplement primary prevention initiatives.

Strategies primarily focused at the secondary or tertiary level may also produce broader primary prevention benefits. If the reconciliation strategies utilized in Northern Ireland are generalized to other settings, it may be possible to assist individuals not already involved in conflict to develop pro-social alternatives that will enable them to avoid getting into a situation in which forgiveness may be required.

COMMON ELEMENTS OF SUCCESS

Although the initiatives described in this volume address a wide array of issues, employ a range of strategies, and operate within diverse environments and contexts, common themes may be found. The authors of these case studies have identified several core guiding principles and strategies that appear to have contributed to the effectiveness of their programs. The major lessons learned about developing successful programs include the following:

- One size does not fit all.

    Effective prevention efforts must take into account local contextual factors. Political and cultural considerations influenced how each prevention strategy was designed and implemented. Even within each case study, consideration was given to differences within the geographic area. In Israel, interventions were tailored to the specific patterns of aggression and local conditions for each school. The Central American armed violence initiative adjusted its approach to be responsive to the specific conditions and dynamics of each locality as well as the broader regions. Canada also encouraged each region to adapt the overall program approach to the specific conditions of each locality.

    Tailoring programs to specific local needs requires more than just an accounting of characteristics of the local community. Successful adaptation requires that leaders of the program empower localities to play an active role in understanding how the strategies can be molded to work well in their local environment.
- Suppression alone does not work.

    In Canada, the government previously had mobilized a comprehensive campaign to punish offenders and otherwise discourage individuals from exhibiting violent behavior. Similar to the experience of Project Exile in the United States, the Canadians found that, at best, this approach had only temporary effects on reducing violent behavior. This awareness led to the development of a more comprehensive approach that addressed individual and community root causes of violence. In all instances, leadership did not ignore the importance of ensuring public safety. Instead, they complemented these efforts with a fuller array of strategies to enhance personal functioning and environmental supports.

    In most of these countries, engagement of the police and military sectors was redefined, giving members of these organizations a more constructive role in relating to youth and participating in community development initiatives. By reframing the participation of police and military in Central America, community leaders were able to reduce tensions between young people and

authorities, while also enhancing their ability to actualize projects that would improve quality of life in those communities.
• Doing more with less.

After successfully demonstrating the impact of the YouthBuild's comprehensive approach in the United States, the developers of this program began working with other countries. In exporting this approach to areas outside of the United States, YouthBuild's leadership discovered that they needed to significantly modify the program to meet the unique conditions of each site. In some countries, economic and community development focused more on self employment, which is more feasible in developing nations. The creation of community assets has expanded beyond housing to include schools, orphanages, playgrounds, and sustainable "green" infrastructures. Some programs have focused exclusively on women, who face daunting cultural challenges in many parts of the world. Also, as might be expected, many of these countries have fewer resources and less ability to allow young people to spend several years in this type of program. In these instances, YouthBuild had to adapt the length of the program and the cost per young participant.

The availability of fiscal resources influences violence prevention efforts in other ways. In well-developed nations such as Canada, Japan, and Singapore, there is a greater reliance on formal societal structures (that is, the government) to organize and implement prevention programs. In less developed nations, which have fewer financial resources, responsibility for developing and managing prevention initiatives often falls to indigenous groups of individuals, including de facto community leadership groups and local societies.These less formally structured entities typically have a smaller pool of material resources on which to draw.

Indigenous, grassroots efforts seem to have advantages over their more developed, formally structured counterparts. The passion and dedication of the participants, combined with their knowledge of the local community, yield positive results that may surpass those found in more formal systems where tension exists between groups that control resource allocation and citizens of the community. In the CeaseFire program in Iraq, which was adapted from a successful model employed in Chicago, the project's leadership was pleasantly surprised by the extent to which the local community wanted to be actively engaged in their violence prevention initiative.

Some of the most striking examples of municipal or statewide reduction in violence have occurred in areas with sparse fiscal resources. The successful efforts to reduce violent deaths in Bogotá, Medellín, and Cali in Colombia and São Paolo, Brazil, illustrate how well-designed, comprehensive campaigns conducted by multistakeholder collaboratives can produce positive results in spite of fiscal limitations. Bogotá is one of the only cities in the Western Hemisphere to maintain a declining pattern of homicides over an extended period of time.

It may be argued that having minimal expectations about what kind of outside help will be provided may motivate participants to accept ownership and work harder to succeed.

• Strategies for redirecting intergroup tensions are critical for success.

Tension between groups is almost always at the root of youth violence. Whether these tensions emanate from a tradition of armed conflict between cultures or territorial rivalries among gangs, widespread violence almost always is associated with intergroup conflict. Many of the strategies for violence prevention are based on a program philosophy that encourages providing more constructive conflict resolution alternatives or realigning incentives to reduce violent behavior. The strategies employed in Haiti include encouraging youth to participate in hip hop competitions among communities, offering incentives for individuals to further their education and awarding prizes when the community sustained a period of time without homicides or confrontations involving weapons. The leaders of these rival groups participated in sessions that facilitated the use of mediation rather than violence to deal with intergroup concerns.

In Canada, which has relatively low levels of violence, considerable effort was focused on working with Aboriginal youth who are disadvantaged and disenfranchised, and who tend to be over-represented in youth gangs. Multistakeholder collaborations were formed to address the unique needs of this population by improving community conditions, including poverty, housing, education employment, mental health, and racism, as well as providing alternative pro-social opportunities for youth engaged in gang activity.

The Homeboy Industries (HBI) program in Los Angeles uses the slogan "nothing stops a bullet like a job" to underscore the importance of offering constructive alternatives to young people in order to redirect them from gang membership and participation in violent behavior.

• Culture counts.

In addition to the obvious ways in which local culture affects the perception of and response to violence, the examples described in this book elicit questions about more subtle influences of local beliefs and customs on issues of violent behavior. For instance, are particular approaches to reducing or preventing violence more acceptable and effective because they are compatible with the cultural norms of a country or region? Did the reconciliation-based strategy used in Northern Ireland work so well, in part, because the principle of making amends is consistent with the doctrines of the Catholic religion?

The violence prevention initiative in Australia was designed to address the relationship between alcohol consumption and violent behavior among college-age youth. Understanding the cultural norms underlying excessive drinking in this environment was critical to identifying relevant and appropriate policies and interventions.

• Youth violence does not exist in a vacuum.

Many of the case studies were conducted in settings in which the problems of violent behavior among youth reflected a broader history and culture of violence. Armed conflicts in Latin America, Northern Ireland, and Israel provided fertile ground for cultivating aggressive behavior as a preferred strategy for venting frustrations and dealing with conflicts and other differences. It would have been futile to attempt to address the problems of violence among youth without first dealing with the broader issues of violence that pervaded the culture.

In some instances, the youth initiatives flowed directly from the work conducted to achieve peaceful resolution of these larger armed conflicts. Coalitions of diverse stakeholders, including military personnel and community leaders, were instrumental in creating youth and community development programs and encouraging mediation among rival youth groups using the core principles of collaborative problem solving. Virtually all of the case studies share basic tenets of how to address complex social phenomenon in an effective manner. The core components necessary to achieve success with these endeavors include the following:

1. Bring together all of the stakeholders, including those directly affected by the problem, that is, youth and residents of the community.
2. Develop a shared vision and common set of goals that participants in the coalition agree to support and work toward.
3. Ensure that the recipients of the program have a strong voice in identifying concerns and solutions and feel that they are empowered participants at all stages of the process.
4. Develop a targeted but multistrategy plan that acknowledges the complex nature of violence prevention, that is, deterrence, suppression, and positive youth and community development, and establishes feasible short- and long-term objectives.
5. Take into account and incorporate the unique cultural, social, political, and economic conditions of the area in which the prevention initiatives are being developed.

SCIENCE AND PRACTICE

Given the current emphasis on evidence-based practice, it is tempting to prescribe that all youth violence programs must be based on sound empirical evidence. In some instances, particularly those situations in which interventions are directed at specific behaviors of individual youth, this may be possible. We should acknowledge, however, that science has not yet matured to a level at which it can adequately address complex, multilevel approaches that must be adapted to geographic areas with vastly different political, social, cultural, and economic conditions. Even if sufficient resources miraculously became available, it still would be difficult to develop a research methodology that would allow investigators to control for all relevant variables and identify viable outcome measures that could be directly tied to a specific intervention strategy. Many highly successful programs like YouthBuild acknowledge that they utilize certain core guiding principles and components but must adapt their approach to be compatible to the unique conditions of each site.

This caveat is not intended to suggest that those engaged in developing violence prevention programs should ignore the research literature or sound program development methodology. Much can be learned examining the prevention efforts of others. All prevention initiatives should attempt to clearly identify specific objectives and measurable outcomes. This degree of precision and transparency is needed to ensure that those engaged in implementing and promoting violence prevention efforts are delivering what they promised. Monitoring programs and measuring outcomes is essential if we are to learn from efforts to grapple with youth violence and enhance our ability and capacity to prevent these destructive behaviors.

FINAL THOUGHTS

What conclusions can be drawn from the diverse array of efforts to confront youth violence described in this book? That each city or country needs to shape its interventions to accommodate local customs and cultural norms is obvious. We also would be on safe ground to infer that in designing interventions it is important to take into account other contextual factors, such as local, state, and national economic and political dynamics. Recognizing that political will and community support are essential ingredients for mobilizing successful violence prevention efforts, attention must be paid to educating and engaging community leaders at all levels.

One sobering lesson that can be drawn from these examples is that effective violence prevention is difficult. Those expecting quick results certainly will be disappointed. Conducting successful campaigns requires passion and endurance. Establishing long-term and interim goals may be useful for maintaining the positive energy needed to sustain the involvement of those developing and implementing the interventions.

It is apparent that working in the complex and challenging field of violence prevention requires a high tolerance for ambiguity and uncertainty as well as personal commitment and stamina. There is one unequivocal conclusion that emerges from the multiple examples from various regions of our globe: simple, unidimensional approaches, especially those that rely primarily on suppressing violent behavior through tough enforcement of laws, are unlikely to succeed. Youth violence is a complex phenomenon that requires comprehensive, holistic approaches that build on the strengths of the individual youth, their families, and the communities in which they live as well as targeting the destructive behaviors of young people.

Index

About the Editors and Contributors

EDITORS

JOAN SERRA HOFFMAN, PhD, is a consultant to international organizations, including the Inter-American Bank, the World Bank, the Organization of American States, and the U.S. Agency on International Development. Her published works include *Youth Violence, Resilience and Rehabilitation*. Hoffman was the founding co-director of the Inter-American Coalition for the Prevention of Violence and was the recipient of the Rockefeller Foundation Next Generation Leadership Fellowship.

LYNDEE KNOX, PhD, is chief executive officer of LA Net, a community-based organization that supports nonprofit groups working in low-income communities. She serves as co-director of the Southern California Academic Center of Excellence on Youth Violence Prevention. Her published works include *Connecting the Dots to Prevent Youth Violence: A Training and Outreach Guide for Health Care Professions* and she is editor of *Youth Violence Prevention and the Health Professions: Core Competencies for Effective Practice*.

ROBERT COHEN, PhD, is professor and vice chair in the department of psychiatry at Virginia Commonwealth University (VCU) in Richmond, Virginia. His published works include *Chiseled in Sand: Perspectives on Change in Human Services Organizations* and *Hammond's Choice: A Marty Fenton Mystery Novel*, a mystery novel focused on the child mental health system. Cohen was the principal investigator of the VCU Center for the Study and Prevention of Youth Violence.

CONTRIBUTORS

ELA ALGERSY, MA, is the National Supervisor in the Counseling Department Counseling and Psychological Services (SHEFFY) in the Ministry of Education in Israel.

REBECCA P. ANG, PhD, is Associate Professor with the Division of Psychology, School of Humanities and Social Sciences, Nanyang Technological University, Singapore. She obtained her PhD in School Psychology, with an emphasis in Clinical Child Psychology, from Texas A&M University. She is a Nationally Certified School Psychologist in the United States and a Registered Psychologist in Singapore. Her research interests include general developmental child psychopathology, and in particular, antisocial and aggressive behavior, as well as related prevention and intervention work. Her research has been recognized internationally, and she was awarded the International Council of Psychologists Seisoh Sukemune/Bruce Bain Early Career Research Award in 2006.

RON AVI ASTOR, PhD, is the Thor Professor in Urban Social Development at the University of Southern California. He holds joint appointments in the School of Social Work and School of Education. His body of work examines the role of the physical, social-organizational, and cultural contexts in schools related to different kinds of school violence (e.g., sexual harassment, bullying, school fights, emotional abuse, weapon use, teacher/child violence) in different cultures across the globe. He is currently working on a large-scale project that aims to build academic and social supports for military connected schools. Findings from his studies have been published in more than 100 scholarly manuscripts across diverse fields. His research has won multiple awards from the American Psychological Association and the American Educational Research Association, including an AERA Best Book Award, Palmer O. Johnson Award, and two Distinguished Research awards (Human Development and Counseling) from AERA. He has been a Fulbright Senior Scholar, an H. F. Guggenheim Dissertation Fellow, and a National Academy of Education Fellow. His work has been funded by the Department of Defense Educational Authority, National Institutes of Mental Health, William T. Grant Foundation, Israeli Ministry of Education, Spencer Foundation, and the W. K. Kellogg Foundation.

DANIELA BERCOVITCH is Deputy Director in Haiti for Viva Rio. She has been with the organization since April 2007. Viva Rio is a non-governmental organization, headquartered in Rio de Janeiro. Its main goal is to promote a culture of peace and social development through fieldwork, research, and formulation of public policies.

RAMI BENBENISHTY, PhD, is a Professor, Louis and Gabi Weisfeld School of Social Work, Bar Ilan University, Israel. He is studying school climate and safety, child welfare, and child abuse and neglect. With Ron Astor, he won a number of national awards, among them the Outstanding Book Award, American Educational Research Association, 2007.

SUSANA BONIS, EdD, was Director of Development and Communications at Families in Schools, a nongovernment organization in Los Angeles. She has worked as a management/program analyst at high levels of the U. S. Department of Education, on issues ranging from strategic planning to preparing tomorrow's teachers to use technology. She was a Fulbright teaching assistant at Eotvos Loran University in Budapest. She received her MAT from American University and her BA *summa cum laude* with a double major in English and history, from George Washington University.

PATRICK BURTON, MA, is Executive Director of the Centre for Justice and Crime Prevention, a Cape Town-based nongovernment organization engaged in the field of social justice and crime prevention, with a particular focus on children and youth. He holds a Master of Science degree from the University of Kwa-Zulu Natal in Durban and has published, among other topics, on victimization of adults and youths, youth resilience, school violence, and cyber-bullying.

CHRISTINA A. CHRISTIE, PhD, is Associate Professor, Department of Education, Graduate School of Education and Information Studies, University of California, Los Angeles. She is the editor of two recently published books, *Exemplars of Evaluation Practice* (with Fitzpatrick & Mark; Sage, 2008) and *What Counts as Credible Evidence in Evaluation and Evidence-based Practice?* (with Donaldson & Mark; Sage, 2008).

TIM CROSS is President of YouthBuild International. Previously, he led the national field operation at YouthBuild USA. YouthBuild is being adapted for implementation by local partners in 13 countries and at 237 locations in the United States. Mr. Cross has been a community based youth worker and helped to lead citywide, regional, national, and international efforts to build organizations that support the full development of all young people as engaged leaders, life-long learners, productive workers, and entrepreneurs.

KRIS DE PEDRO, MA, is a PhD student at the Rossier School of Education, University of Southern California. His research interests include school and classroom climate, military students, and African-American students.

R. BRENT DECKER, MPH/MSW is the International Program Coordinator for CeaseFire, a national public health strategy based in the School of Public Health at the University of Illinois at Chicago, which has been scientifically proven to reduce shootings and killings. He developed the cultural adaptation process for application of the program in Basra, Iraq, and was part of a team who provided the training for

Iraq-based conflict mediators and staff. Additional responsibilities include providing technical assistance and training to national and Illinois partners.

LAURA DUNBAR, Research Assistant, Institute for the Prevention of Crime, University of Ottawa. Ms. Dunbar obtained a Master of Arts degree in Criminology from the University of Ottawa in the Fall of 2010. During her graduate studies, she worked as a Research Assistant for the Institute for the Prevention of Crime at the University of Ottawa. Among other projects, she assisted in the production and dissemination of "Making Cities Safer: Action Briefs for Municipal Stakeholders," and conducted a review of Canadian research on criminal youth gangs from 2000–2010 to develop a comprehensive inventory on the topic.

TODD M. FRANKE, PhD, MSW, is Associate Professor of Social Welfare in the School of Public Affairs at UCLA. Dr. Franke, an educational psychologist by training, has been involved with agencies that serve thousands of families representing unique geographic and cultural communities, particularly southern California counties. He has numerous years of experience conducting cross-sectional and longitudinal research in the fields of education (e.g., LAUSD— School Mental Health), child welfare (Los Angeles Department of Children and Family Services), and adolescent violence, particularly for gang-involved youth.

DANIEL SHUEN-SHENG FUNG, has been the Vice Chairman Medical Board (Clinical Quality) at the Institute of Mental Health, Singapore, since 2009. He has been a Senior Consultant and Chief of the Department of Child and Adolescent Psychiatry since 2006. He is an Adjunct Associate Professor with the Duke-NUS Graduate Medical School and the Division of Psychology, School of Humanities and Social Sciences, Nanyang Technological University. He has received several awards including the PS21 Star Service Award in 2009, National Council for Social Services long service award in 2008, and the Singapore Children's Society Silver Service Award in 2007. He has published more than 50 journal articles, book chapters, and books.

JULIE MEEKS GARDNER is Head of the Caribbean Child Development Centre of the University of the West Indies, Open Campus. Her work has focused on child development and child rights issues in Jamaica and the Caribbean, with lessons that have been useful across the developing world. She is author or editor of a number of monographs, including the Caribbean Report to the UN Secretary General on Violence Against Children

JOSH GRYNIEWICZ handles communications and development responsibilities for CeaseFire, a national public health strategy based in the School of Public Health at the University of Illinois at Chicago. The CeaseFire program has been scientifically proven to reduce shootings and killings. Mr. Gryniewicz assisted in authoring CeaseFire's cultural adaptation process and is helping to develop their international expansion plan. He has worked with displaced and vulnerable populations for more than a decade, supporting programs that address human trafficking, medical and psychosocial care for conflict survivors, and protections for immigrants, refugees, and asylum seekers.

KATE GUNN is Interim Executive Director with REACH Edmonton Council for Safe Communities in Edmonton, Canada. Ms. Gunn supported the work of Edmonton's Taskforce on Community Safety in 2009 to produce the groundbreaking "REACH Report: Building a Culture of Community Safety in One Generation" in 2009 (www.reachreport.ca). REACH Edmonton is a new center of excellence, launched in 2010, that emerged from the REACH Report and that inspires citizen engagement and leads coordinated agency action around the prevention of crime and violence.

NANCY G. GUERRA, PhD, is Professor of Psychology at the University of California at Riverside and Director of the Academic Center of Excellence on Youth Violence Prevention. She is an outgoing Associate Editor of the journal, *Child Development,* and current editor of *Journal of Research on Adolescence.* Her work emphasizes the understanding and prevention of aggression and violence in children and youth. She has published numerous research articles examining predictors of aggression and has developed and evaluated several preventive interventions. These interventions include the *Metropolitan Area Child Study* multi-component, school-based program, *Viewpoints* cognitive behavioral program for juvenile offenders, a program based on core competencies for risk prevention and positive youth development, *Positive Life Changes,* and a new home visitation program for parents of children and teenagers, *Child Development Parent Training.* She has coedited several related books, including *Preventing Youth Violence in a Multicultural Society* (APA Books, 2005), *Treating the Juvenile Offender* (Guilford Press, 2008), and *Core Competencies to Prevent Problem Behaviors and Promote Positive Youth Development* (Jossey-Bass, 2008). She has also served on numerous study groups, panels, and advisory committees including the *President's Council on Juvenile Justice and Delinquency Prevention.*

ROSS HOMEL, PhD, is Foundation Professor of Criminology and Criminal Justice at Griffith University in Brisbane, Australia, and Director of the Griffith Institute for Social and Behavioural Research. He has published nine books on crime and violence, as well as more than 100 peer-reviewed papers and numerous high impact government reports. He is an Officer in the Order of Australia "for service to education, particularly in the field of criminology, through research into the causes of crime, early intervention and prevention methods," and has been recognized as a "Queensland Great." In 2009, he was short-listed for Australian of the Year.

NEIL JARMAN, PhD, is Director of the Institute for Conflict Research, an independent, not-for-profit, policy-orientated research unit based in Belfast, Northern

Ireland. He earned his degree in anthropology from University College London and has written extensively on issues associated with the political transition in Northern Ireland. His study of the visual politics of Northern Ireland *Material Conflicts* (Berg 1997) won the Folklore Society's Katherine Briggs Award.

JORJEC. LAMAS has more than 20 years experience in social and economic development with a particular emphasis in the Americas, especially Central America; for the last eight years, he has led pioneering citizen security and violence prevention efforts at municipal, national, and regional levels. He led the Inter-American Development Bank's (IADB) interdisciplinary teams in the elaboration of investment and technical assistance operations regarding citizen security in Argentina, Bolivia, Jamaica, Trinidad and Tobago, Guyana, and Perú and has served as a technical expert in the design and implementation of crime and violence prevention projects in Central America. He has also participated as Team Leader in the preparation of diagnostic citizen security studies in the Bahamas, Barbados, and Surinam, and in projects that stimulated investment and policy reforms that promoted the development of human capital in vulnerable groups in different countries of the Latin American and Caribbean Region. Under his leadership, the IADB organized the first Inter-American Seminar on the Reintegration of Youth at Risk on research and practice in the reintegration and resocialization of gang, excombatant, and serious youth offenders. In addition, he directed the IADB's operation to develop a crime and violence indicator standardization project for the entire Latin American Region.

JORJA LEAP, PhD, has been Adjunct Professor of Social Welfare at the UCLA School of Public Affairs since 1992 and has served as a lecturer, researcher, and consultant in both the private and public sectors. She has worked nationally and internationally in violent and postwar settings, and her current research interests focus on gangs and youth violence. As part of these efforts, Dr. Leap is currently the senior policy advisor on Gangs and Youth Violence for Los Angeles County Sheriff Lee Baca, and she is an expert reviewer on gangs for the National Institute of Justice, testifying at the local, state, and federal level. Dr. Leap has completed numerous evaluations of anti-gang programs and is currently conducting a five-year longitudinal evaluation of Homeboy Industries, the largest gang intervention and re-entry program in the United States. Dr. Leap is the author of numerous evaluation reports, articles, and the book, *No One Knows Their Names*. She is now completing *Home Front: Living with the Gangs of Los Angeles,* on her 30 years of work, to be published by Beacon Press in 2011.

YOSHIRO ONO, MD, PhD, is Director of Wakayama Prefecture Mental Health & Welfare Center. He is a child psychiatrist and has published more than 70 scientific articles and 13 books on child and adolescent psychiatry. He is an officer of the International Association for Child and Adolescent Psychiatry and Allied Professions and Vice President of the Asian Association of Child and Adolescent Psychiatry and Allied Profession.

YOON PHAIK OOI, PhD, is a Research Fellow at Child Guidance Clinic, Department of Child and Adolescent Psychiatry, Institute of Mental Health, Singapore. She holds a PhD in Education (Counselling Psychology) from Nanyang Technological University, Singapore. Her clinical and research interests focus on autism and disruptive behavior disorders, specifically in diagnostic assessment and effectiveness of intervention. To date, she has published in numerous books and international peer-reviewed journals.

LAINIE REISMAN is Senior Youth Technical Advisor for the Education Development Center, based in Nairobi, Kenya, working on youth programs in Somalia and Kenya. Prior to her relocation to East Africa, Lainie spent more than ten years working on Central American issues, focusing on youth gang violence prevention. She has published numerous articles, as well as reports for multiple agencies, including USAID and the World Bank, as well as testifying before the United States Congress.

DAVID RATNER, MA, is in The National Authority for Measurement and Evaluation in Education at the Ministry of Education in Israel.

TAL RAZ, PhD, works with The National Authority for Measurement and Evaluation in Education (RAMA) in the Ministry of Education in Israel.

HANA SHADMY, MA, is the Director of Counseling and Psychological Services (SHEFFY) for the Ministry of Education in Israel.

GARY SLUTKIN, MD, is an infectious disease physician, trained at University of Chicago, University of California San Francisco, and the World Health Organization. He is founder and Executive Director of CeaseFire. After leading efforts to reverse epidemics including tuberculosis, cholera, and AIDS in the United States, Somalia, Uganda, and other counties, he worked with leaders in Chicago, Illinois, to design a public health-based approach to stop violence. This new strategy, CeaseFire, uses behavior changes and epidemic control methods and has successfully reduced shootings and killings in more than 16 communities. CeaseFire, proven scientifically effective in a sudy commissioned by the U.S. Department of Justice, has won many awards and is being adapted in several U.S. cities and other countries.

ZAINAB AL-SUWAIJ is cofounder and Executive Director of the American Islamic Congress, a civil rights organization promoting tolerance and the exchange of ideas among Muslims and other peoples. Prior to founding the AIC in 2001, Ms. Al-Suwaij worked as a refugee case manager in New Haven, Connecticut, for Interfaith Refugee Ministry. Among her most special cases were working with the Lost Boys of Sudan, young African Christian victims of persecution at the hands of Sudan's National Islamic Front. Ms. Al-Suwaij is a member of the Connecticut

Attorney General's Hate Crimes Advisory Board and sits on the Boards of Religions for Peace (New York) and the Center for World Religions, Diplomacy and Conflict Resolution (George Mason University). Her writing has appeared in the *Wall Street Journal*, the *New Republic*, *USA Today*, the *Boston Globe*, the *Houston Chronicle,* and the *Hartford Courant*. She has been interviewed on National Public Radio, CNN, CBS News, Fox News, and MSNBC's *Hardball with Chris Matthews*.

KAREN VOLKER is the Director of the Middle East Partnership Initiative (MEPI). MEPI provides assistance to civic activists in the Middle East and North Africa. MEPI has a 35-person office in Washington and two regional offices in the region (in Tunis and Abu Dhabi).

IAN WALKER is Lead Economist in the World Bank's Social Protection unit for the Latin America and Caribbean Region. He has worked extensively on social protection and human development issues worldwide, most recently as coauthor of the study "Achieving Effective Social Protection for All in Latin America and the Caribbean—From Right to Reality." Before joining the World Bank in 2005, Mr. Walker was chief economic advisor to the government of Honduras and Director of ESA Consultores in Honduras.

IRVIN WALLER, PhD, Full Professor at University of Ottawa, uses evidence and international success to change crime policy. His influential book *Less Law, More Order* is already in five languages. His sequel, *Rights for Victims of Crime: Rebalancing Justice,* is coming out in English and Spanish. His prize-winning career work includes leading organizations devoted to change in government, with governments, and outside governments.

KIRK R. WILLIAMS received his PhD from the University of Arizona and was a post-doctoral fellow at Yale University. He has held faculty appointments at the University of Memphis and at the University of New Hampshire, where he maintained an affiliation with the Family Research Laboratory. He also was a professor at the University of Colorado at Boulder, where he was the founding Associate Director of the Center for the Study and Prevention of Violence. Dr. Williams is currently a professor of Sociology, Co-Director of the Robert Presley Center for Crime and Justice Studies, and Co-Principal Investigator for the Southern California Center of Academic Excellence in Youth Violence Prevention at the University of California Riverside. He has published widely on the causes and prevention of violence, particularly involving youth or adult intimate partners, with the most recent publications addressing bullying, juvenile offending, and domestic violence risk assessment. He has received numerous grants from federal and state funding sources, in addition to private foundations to support his research. His most recent federal grant is from the National Institute of Justice, supporting a study of youth homicide in the nation's 100 largest cities from 1984 to 2006. He also has worked extensively with community-based groups, schools, and agencies in violence prevention planning, implementation, and evaluation.

MICHAEL ZEHARIA, MA, is the National Supervisor for violence prevention and life skills in the Counseling and Psychological Services (SHEFFY) at the Ministry of Education in Israel.